Is There an American in the House?

THE MACMILLAN COMPANY
NEW YORK · CHICAGO
DALLAS · ATLANTA · SAN FRANCISCO
LONDON · MANILA
IN CANADA
BRETT-MACMILLAN LTD.
GALT, ONTARIO

Is There an American in the House?

by DAVID CORT

New York - The Macmillan Company - 1960

For the late
Thomas W. Chrystie
Ambrose and Lydia Cort
James E. Hart

Author's Note

Permission to reprint most of the following pieces has been handsomely granted by *Commonweal, The Nation, Harper's Magazine, Western World, Freedom and Union*—magazines for whose continued existence I naturally pray, in this world of mass consumption and indiscrimination. The only escape is into reality, which remains original, various, fascinating, and nonindustrialized.

This collection naturally reflects the major drives of the American people I know: to play the devil, to communicate, to progress, to build empires, to be American, to higher-communicate, and to be reassured. This is a wholly American book; the writer has nowhere he can go back to, even if you disagree with him. If you have a place you can go back to, to get away from all this, better go back.

DAVID CORT

Contents

I

The Devil

The Fix
(1952)

The first three days of October, 1951, brought out the best and the worst in large numbers of the American people. Events, as if written by a master of melodrama, had laid it on the line. Either a man had the fortitude to go on hoping, or he hadn't. The bars were filled with people for whom the suspense had been drawn to too fine a point. Not for a long time will the issue again be put quite so sharply.

During those three days I spent some time in front of a television store where the set in the window was tuned to the play-off games between the Dodgers and Giants in the National League. By the third and last day, the hard core of regulars was pretty well known to one another.

After a while you knew who were the Giant fans and who the Dodger fans, but nobody made an issue of it. Everybody was polite and wonderfully patient. When a little girl ducked up front and blotted out the screen, nobody complained until she had got bored and gone away.

A tall thin Yankee fan with a querulous voice and a permanent crick in his neck had established himself as the arbiter and premier authority in our group. But on that last day of the play-offs he was challenged by a newcomer. This was a handsome, middle-aged man with an incisive executive manner but a surprisingly imperfect command of English grammar. He had a considerate, persuasive way of making his points that suggested that he might have been a salesman.

The stranger moved in quietly, asking for the score, about the fourth inning, when the Dodgers had a one-run lead they had squeezed out of Maglie in the first inning. With Newcombe blowing down the Giant batting order, it looked as if that one run would be ample. "One-nothing Dodgers," the Yankee fan said impartially. At this intelligence, the stranger just looked wise and tolerant, giving away nothing, and settled in to watch the play.

For an inning or two he made various knowledgeable comments on the players' records and known abilities.

In the sixth inning the Yankee fan said: "Wait till the seventh. That's when the Giants begin hitting."

The stranger said in a pleasant, conversational voice, without taking his eyes off the screen, "They get people all excited about this thing, but you know and I know it's fixed," and then he turned and looked pleasantly at the Yankee fan. "It's crazy to get excited. They're laughing at we customers, and them knowing how it's fixed to come out."

The Yankee fan returned the look warily. You could see he was thrown off stride. Superior cynicism about both Giants and Dodgers had been his specialty until then. He may have been impressed by the salesman's superior knowledge and perhaps he wished he had thought of the deflationary idea that the whole play-off had been prestaged.

However, taken by surprise, he mumbled indifferently, "I wouldn't know about that."

"Look at it this way," the salesman said reasonably. "The receipts on these three games goes to the owners. So the Dodgers had to drop that 13½-game lead. Now they want three games, not just two, so yesterday the Giants pitch Jones. Brooklyn can do anything they want with Jones. See what I mean? Now the board of strategy figure a Dodger-Yankee World Series has a bigger gate, so the Dodgers take the play-off. It's simple as that. You know it."

"That don't sound right," the Yankee fan replied. "The Polo Grounds is a bigger park than Ebbets Field. How's it smart to fix it for the smaller park?"

"Let's look at this thing," the salesman said. "You don't think they just let the best team win, not with all that dough kicking around. I don't mean paid admissions either. I mean betting money.

That's the big money. Why, there's millions riding on this, with all the suckers all hotted up."

"It ain't necessary," the Yankee fan complained. "They don't have to fix nothing. Why, the Giants don't even rate being out on the same field with the Dodgers. Look at Robinson, look at Cox, look at Reese. The Giants don't have a ballplayer fit to carry their bats."

The stranger looked thoughtful but did not comment on this, still not revealing where his sympathies lay. Instead he replied persuasively: "I don't say the teams are in on the fix. It ain't safe to let five, six guys in on a fix. This kind of thing, it's done from the top. Like pitching Jones yesterday. Why, they knew Maglie would be a little wild today and give up a run or two. They know more than we do, out here. They know; we don't. That's why we jump out of our skin, hoping for a run or a hit when it's already settled behind closed doors."

The Yankee fan's objections were weakening. "Maybe so, but I won't believe it till I see it. I don't say you're wrong, but I got no proof."

"Come, man," said the salesman with a smile. "You know the saying, 'A man's only as good as he has to be and a woman's as bad as she dares.'"

This got a brief chuckle from the group in front of the television store.

"It's the way the world runs," the salesman went on, gratified. "Who do you think actually owns all these teams? Frank Costello, that's who. And Costello don't like to gamble, when he don't have to. No use our kidding ourselves."

"He don't own the Yankees," said the Yankee fan.

The salesman gave him an indulgent look and returned his gaze to the television screen, where the little figures in Giant uniforms were putting together a couple of hits and a long fly ball to push a run across and tie the score.

With that run, the Giant fans grew quiet and tense, again concentrating on the incredible vision of victory that had so often just failed to fade out forever. Again it had just not died; and now it grew very bright.

Even the Yankee fan was emboldened to tell the salesman, "That fix is looking kind of funny right now. Didn't you tell us this was in the bag for the Dodgers?"

"Pay no attention," the salesman advised. "They gotta make it look close, don't they? No use getting worked up, though."

This lofty cynicism was not in the least compromised by the events that immediately ensued, as Maglie gave up hits to Reese, Snider, Pafko, and Cox and a walk to Robinson. Three of these Dodgers crossed home plate with runs, making the score 4–1 for the Dodgers, as Frank Costello had assertedly decreed.

The salesman leaned back judicially, watching the screen and pushing out his lower lip. He didn't say anything but he didn't have to. I still couldn't figure whether he was a Dodger fan or just pleased with his own analysis of events.

The Giant fans there in the eighth inning were feeling terrible. It seemed then as if it had all been in vain: the interminable pursuit, the incredible percentage of .830 since mid-August, the stubborn faith of the whole Giant team that they could yet do it. The record books, unsympathetic toward failure, would note only that the second-place team for 1951 in the National League had been New York. Like men who die on the slopes of Mount Everest a few hundred feet short of the summit, the Giants would be mourned by comrades and relatives but unknown to fame.

In front of the television store the Giant fans never took their eyes off the screen, but their feet were moving, shuffling, teetering, scuffing the pavement.

To the Giant fans, judging by myself, the salesman's talk of a fix was meaningless; it had nothing to do with this affair on the screen. If the game had been fixed for the Giants to win, it had reached a pass where only a superhuman effort could win it, even with the full cooperation of a large part of the Dodger team. If it had been fixed for the Giants to lose, there was no trouble.

Just three outs were left in the 1951 National League baseball season, three Giant outs against Newcombe with his jutting farmer's jaw and the sinewy arm that was blasting the ball past the Giants.

Not much was asked of the next three Giants—only that they bounce a white ball out of reach of a scattering of men in a child's game. But that little thing was something they had not, when they were minutes and hours younger and more sanguine, been able to do much of.

The wrappings of eight innings of failure constricted their arms and legs, smothered their spirits, made it hard to see the white ball when it loomed suddenly out of the fog of failure. It was still a small thing to do, but they were stalled in a routine of being unable to do it. If they did it now, they had to do it standing in a hole eight innings deep.

The first Giant batter was Dark. He kept spoiling the strikes with foul balls and ran Newcombe to the full count. It seemed as if the big, high-shouldered pitcher might just possibly be tiring. And then Dark did it. He hit the little ball out of reach of the first line of men in the field.

All year Giant fans had grown accustomed to building dreams on far less than a hit. Anything was suddenly possible again. But it was still actually a good way from probable.

It was infectious. Mueller got a hit. Newcombe had ceased to be invulnerable. The possible looked more possible. Monte Irvin, who could not fail, popped up, and the possible looked only possible. Then Lockman tore a steaming double off Newcombe. A run came in with Dark. It was 4–2, with Giants on second and third, and two outs to go. Any decent hit would bring them both in and tie the score.

Mueller had sprained his ankle, changing his mind about sliding into third. Two separate knots of players gathered around Mueller and Newcombe. Mueller's disability was easy to diagnose; Newcombe's was more subtle and required more consultation among men standing with bowed heads, avoiding one another's eyes, around the pitcher's mound.

But to the salesman it was still quite clear. "They're making it look close all right. Now watch. See if Bobby Thomson don't line into a double play. That wraps it up, nice and neat. But first they gotta give you heart failure. That's smart business, that's all. Smart business."

Mueller was taken off in a stretcher and replaced by a pinch-runner. Newcombe was allowed to walk off the field.

The replacement for Newcombe in the pitcher's box was Fearless Ralph Branca, whose first chore was to pitch to Bobby Thomson.

After Branca had had his fill of warm-up pitches, Bobby stepped into the batter's box and took a loose, crouching stance. Without any more ado, Ralph fearlessly whipped a strike past him.

"Here we go," said the salesman. "This is it."

Precisely how that next ball approached the plate may be debated for years. Thomson, however, was of the opinion that it was trying to get past him high and inside, a bad ball for him. Not liking the ball very much, he nevertheless swung at it. . . .

On television it wasn't much to see. It just seemed as if, for no good reason, everyone had gone crazy.

The camera tried to follow the ball into the left-field stands, and then it showed grown men leaping and cavorting on and off the base paths. There on the sidewalk in front of the television store the Giant fans were screaming and hitting one another on the back, and passersby were gathering at the back of the knot around the window. Somebody, possibly the Yankee fan, was howling, "No! No! No! Whaddya know!"

The salesman, I noticed at last, was not among the jubilant. He hadn't moved or said a word. He stood staring at the screen with his jaw pushed out for half a minute, and then he turned and walked off slowly, not looking where he was going, stumbling a step or two before he got his bearings.

I stopped to wonder why none of the Giant fans with their absolute faith had punched him in the nose for his story of a "fix," or even contradicted him.

But of course the salesman had known what he was doing. The belief in heroism, in purity of motive and character, was all but dead. The contrary or "only human" theory of human conduct dominated America from bottom to top. The salesman was vending safe and sound clichés. The Giant fans, on the other hand, were harboring a wild and eccentric faith.

Bobby Thomson's home run was a triumph for faith and heroism. Certainly, like any home run, it was an accident. Possibly Bobby was not quite the peer of Don John of Austria, though no Giant fan would be so objective. But in its context the event described a pattern in the heroic tradition, so unusual that the sportswriters fell back on the lingo of melodrama to describe it for their jaded and cynical readers. It was so untypical and even improper that everybody set about forgetting it as quickly as possible. Life, it was said, is not like that.

Perhaps the salesman had not had the stamina to go on hoping in the void of destiny. Perhaps he had needed a sure thing, a "fixed" thing. And so his natural instinct had been to besoil the intolerable suspense with the "only human" version of human behavior.

That at least is one theory about the salesman. But I prefer another. The handsome man smiling at the television screen with his superior knowledge, dropping his plausible and debilitating cynicisms, filling the air with the faint, sharp smell of sulphur, may have been our old friend the Devil.

The Faces of Treason
(1952)

Things are getting more and more mixed up on the subject of traitors. Where they are not at all mixed up, as in spy melodramas, they seem much too simple.

Toward getting this subject back to some certifiable reality, I can offer the one actual, convicted American traitor I think I ever knew, insofar as I know what I knew.

I found Robert in Vienna in the sensitive year 1937.

My expertness on even this one traitor has only the tired credential: "I ought to know. I was there." And yet I can see that "there" was not an especially good vantage point. How can anyone take the proper notes on the middle of a story unless he already knows how the story will end or indeed what story is being unreeled? My recollection of Vienna and Robert in 1937 may be impaired by the facts that I did not actually *know* that night would fall on Vienna with Hitler's *Anschluss* in 1938 or on western Europe in 1940 or in fact that Robert was actually what he was.

This was bad enough, but I was also wearing a special set of mental spectacles that may have blurred my vision. I was approaching Europe in the lofty and dilettante mood of "a foreign news expert" who already "knew" that Europe was going over the waterfalls in a barrel. In the current mood of American detachment, I had advanced to the point where I did not plan to meet a head of state to listen to those wonderful 1937 hypocrisies faithfully reported in the American press. I had another idea.

It was to focus my attention on the night life of the capitals from London to Budapest. This policy would certainly have been useful in 1815 or even 1914; and it still had some merit in 1937 in those countries where the country was still run by a few families whose more unstable members were found at least half the nights in any week in one of three or four night clubs.

Commercial night life is a universal medium in which unusual local differences are more likely to be apparent to a stranger. The attitude toward foreigners, the incidence of bar brawls, the complacency of the female entertainers toward the men, the comparative intensities of the lust for money, the degree of tolerated drunkenness, the respect given to and earned by local personages, even the service, were still clues to the *Zeitgeist* which the stranger could not avoid noticing.

Perhaps one can determine in advance on such data whether a nation will stand or fall. But at least in collecting such data one will not be bored.

Robert's assigned role in this was that he was then the Vienna correspondent for a great American news service and, more or less on the side, for the smaller news organization in which I had lately been made a medium-sized wheel. It was only office routine to notify Robert that if I reached Vienna, he would have to minister to another foreign editor.

He did not, as I remember, meet me at the train. But I was of course met by that imperial city which is always described as "on the Danube," though it is deliberately two miles off the Danube, with a perversity that is typically Viennese.

Vienna is a character in this episode, fully as important as Robert. To an American, it seems only a barrack-like mass of brownstone buildings, classical, baroque, and Renaissance, built over a few medieval stones that might once have been interesting to the tourist. But in 1937, though beheaded from its former empire, it was still the terminus for secret aqueducts of news reaching into the Balkans as far as Istanbul. The nourishment of Vienna was rumors, even before hot chocolate. The really starved were the naive and uninformed, but anyone who had heard the latest rumor had an air of frantic health.

However, a Viennese rumor never had a simple and obvious value. As M. W. Fodor, the dean of Viennese journalists, always tried to explain to visiting journalists, nothing in Vienna could be understood without reading a hundred pages of history. Rumors were for experts, and every Viennese was an expert. Current events were written on the margins and between the lines of old history books.

Regarding the problem of *Anschluss,* Fodor's admirable book published that year ends on two predictions covering this question: "The danger or the probability of the *Anschluss* is not imminent" and ". . . the most probable solutions in Central Europe will be the *Anschluss* . . . or Danubia. . . ." This diagnosis of Vienna's destiny still seems to me, after fifteen years, practically perfect.

Only a fool will have to be reminded that at the time the ultimate answers were not available on anything or anyone.

So I looked up Robert. I wanted only to know where to go.

Robert was no beauty. He was fleshy, rumpled, and dilapidated and he somehow reminded me of the strange characters who haunt American public libraries. (Oddly enough, this description exactly fits another traitor I knew at the time—Whittaker Chambers; but I do not see how a generalization can be drawn from this.) I soon noticed that he was guilty of small crudities of manner, an uncoordinated brusqueness, but these lost their offense by the curious and friendly gleam in his eye. (Chambers to the life, again.) However, Robert awoke my sympathy because he seemed awed and rattled by something, whether by his job or by Vienna I did not know.

I saw at once, of course, that he would not be a social asset to me, but he might know at least where to go.

I still have, scribbled on the back of a map of Vienna, Robert's catalogue of what to expect in the various coffeehouses. This list told me to look for chess and Trotskyites at the Central, musicians at the Museum, the Imperial Guard at the Goethe, the "Hapsburg colors" at the Dehmel, racing enthusiasts and prostitutes at the

Imperial and only the latter at the Europa and Feustergucker, aristocrats' ladies at the Sacher, journalists at the Rebhuhn, and stamp collectors and journalists at the Louvre. (What violence fifteen years must have done to this stratification!)

Robert's headquarters was a table at the Louvre.

As I watched him there and drank the hot chocolate, we were interrupted by a succession of human oddities. These, he told me at last, were some of his informers, indispensable to Viennese journalism.

I had just surveyed a neat housewife type and a pimpled youth. "What in the world could they find out? Who would tell them anything? I certainly wouldn't."

"That boy is one of the best in Vienna," Robert told me with sudden heat.

I realized that he might think my criticism was meant in an official capacity, and so I added: "Believe me, I don't care how you run your business. It was just an impression. If they're good enough for you, that suits me."

At this moment, a sort of slattern slum product shambled up to the table, with hair in her eyes. I turned away to hide my laughter, and Robert cut short his conversation with her.

Actually Robert's coffeehouses and informers left me cold. I had no great taste for chocolate and spoke no German. The night clubs or cabarets, of which my list notes two, the Femina and Broadway, were more suitable to my line of investigation.

That night Robert led me to the door of one and there left me. He firmly refused to come in, even at my expense.

The international manners of waiters and captains of waiters soon made me comfortable. Looking about me guardedly, I first discovered the two eternal types of Viennese beauties, described locally as "the fat ones" and "the thin ones."

The "thin ones" in circulation that summer included three or four of the most distinguished-looking beautiful women I have ever seen. Their skin was invariably perfect, their bone structure exquisite, and they had the eyes of angels, limpid and compassionate. The plump ones were less interesting to me. Later I was to notice that they all had a curiously gentle and motherly manner, especially surprising to

an American, toward the men of Vienna, who had recently been
through some bad times.

I remember that when I got to know them, every one of them told
me the same story of being the illegitimate daughter of a working
woman by a rich manufacturer. The third time I heard this story,
from a blond and clear-eyed beauty who had obviously never had
a care in her life, I told her that an American always saw his lady
to the door of her home. (I need not explain that her English was
as good as mine.) She agreed but at the last minute demanded that
I let her out of the taxi half a block from her door. A minute later
I drove past the building she had entered, on whose ground floor
a cabinetmaker's shop displayed the same last name she had given
me. This was her guilty secret, that she was the perfectly legitimate
daughter of a respectable artisan family.

This transparent lying seemed to me typical of the supposed
sophistication of Vienna in 1937. ("Janus-faced Vienna," says
Fodor.) It is given here not in scorn, or even mirth or pity, but as
the innocent foil for two other kinds of deception.

Robert's kind lay in a candor that was startling and even embarrassing.

One would suppose a traitor would also be a natural liar.

Not at all. Robert was perfectly frank about his Fascism, except
that he chose Mussolini's "corporative state" instead of Hitler's
version.

Simply as an idea, the corporative state struck me then, as it
strikes me now, as a fairly ingenious answer to mankind's problems.
In defending it, as I recollect, Robert used more Labor words than
Capital words, for at that period the Fascist argument was trying
to get as far to the Left as it could. My rejection of it was no proof
of mystical virtue. I merely sensed that Robert's whole argument
depended on an assumption that no people can have the unorganized
good sense and good will to do themselves good, without direction
from somebody like Robert.

If one accepts that premise, anything goes. Fascism or Communism.

I did not hate Robert for his erroneous opinion. Nor do I now.
His talk fitted naturally into the Labor-versus-Capital hoo-rah then

going on in the United States. Robert simply had the answer to all the questions, if you accepted his premise. I rejected his premise, his answer, and even his questions, but perhaps only to be contentious.

I remember that we were both standing in the Mariahilferstrasse bus, yelling jaw to jaw about the corporative state, while the Viennese, always discreet toward other people's emotions, avoided looking at the indiscreet Americans.

In Robert's favor is the fact that he told me that Austria was at least one-third Nazi in 1937 and, believing him, I wrote a story to that effect. The story notably failed to deflect the march of Nazi destiny or even the fixed idea of the American press that there were very few, if any, Nazis in Austria before the *Anschluss*.

The best way to invite confidences is to give complete and embarrassing candor about one's own personal life; and here Robert outdid himself. He had gone to the same university as I, and during summer vacations had worked as a conductor on the New York Central Railroad, usually on the night run to and from Buffalo.

He remembered the New York Central, if not our university, with nostalgia, because of an experience that might interest a psychiatrist and certainly fascinated me. The most interesting part of it was his telling of it at all. It seems that a very beautiful female passenger had retired early with a heavy dose of sleeping medicine. When Robert came to collect her ticket, he found her drawing-room door unlocked and her asleep on top of the bedclothes without a nightgown.

Robert's response to this situation was, after he had completed his ticket collection, to spend the night alone in the drawing room with the naked passenger. He just sat there and looked at her the whole night, as he told it, but probably for at least four hours. I would suppose that any adult man with the reckless impudence to have stayed at all would have begun to feel frightened or idiotic after ten minutes. But Robert thought that his marathon adoration of the unknown nudity proved some unique virtue in him. He felt chivalrous toward her still, as if she had been the Cynara of the poem.

It did not occur to me that Robert was inviting confidences on my part, and I gave him only the usual small talk about women. I thought instead that he was trying to impress me with the fact that he was an original personality.

And in fact he had done so. I remember adding it up. As far as I could discover, he had never been part of any group whatever, anywhere. He never spoke of friends or relatives in America. He knew nobody at the university we had both gone to. He had no connections in Vienna, apart from the informers, visible to me. (I am speaking only of what I know.) He had evidently struggled hard for everything he had ever got, and he had not thought much of it after he had got it. I had begun to see him as the boy with his nose flattened against the windowpane of the pastry shop, reveling in a gluttony that is never satiated, so long as one stays outside.

Vienna was human in drowning its real anxieties in rumors and hot chocolate, lies and hopes. Robert seemed to me to have passed on beyond hope, into a room that had a hollow echo and only Robert.

The climax of the story of Vienna, Robert, and me was brought on by a girl. In one of the cabarets I had found a very pretty girl with the identical childish, empty face of an American chorus girl. It is not until one has left America that one discovers this to be quite a rare human type. I gravitated toward this one as toward a talisman. She was everything I had hoped, even to her bored and prissy good manners. She was not Austrian, but German, and not especially popular with either Austrian or German men, who prefer very different types. She was the breath of Broadway to me, a racial sport growing far from her natural habitat, a real collector's item.

I saw her as often as I could, coping with her complete lack of English, my lack of German, and her intermittent attempts, with this imperfect communication, to induce me to buy her something very expensive. I did actually buy her one bathing suit at a drygoods store, on our way to the public baths, the Diana Bad, where it developed that she could not swim.

The next day she failed to keep a lunch date.

That afternoon I found Robert at the Louvre coffeehouse, his head lowered over one of the marble-topped tables, listening to the pimpled boy who was his informer.

I sat down wearily. The boy rattled a few last words and hurriedly left the table and the coffeehouse.

Robert turned to me. "How are you doing with the girls of Vienna?"

"Not very well," I replied. "One of them just stood me up for lunch."

"Would that be a little German girl who looks like an American?" he asked.

I stared at him in amazement, not untouched by anger. "How the hell do you know?"

"Look, I don't mind an argument, you know that, but not here. Too many people listening. Why shouldn't I know? Vienna's a small place, really, and it's known you're my protégé—"

"I'm your protégé!"

"They don't understand here. They just see you with me. Let me ask you a question. Are you going to see that girl again, after she stood you up?"

"I know only one man whose business that is, and that's me. To tell the truth, at the moment I don't know. She doesn't speak any English and it's a little difficult—"

"She doesn't speak English!" Robert exploded, and his face turned ruddy. "That's the last straw. I forbid you to see her again."

"Why, you impertinent jackass—" I began, and then I had another thought. "Skip that. If you know her, why were you surprised when I said she doesn't speak English?"

I need not add that it had occurred to me before that the girl might be a Nazi agent in Austria. Central Europe was crawling with agents in those days, but I naïvely supposed they would not be interested in an American subeditor of a magazine that had difficulty reminding its readers that Europe still existed.

At any rate, an expression of fear swept over Robert's face. I interpreted this as sheer concern for me in the hands of a Nazi agent, and I was touched. "Do you mean she really knows English?" I asked.

"No, no," he stammered, and then appeared to collect himself. "She's making a fool of you in front of all Vienna. Perhaps you don't care, but it makes all Americans look ridiculous. Think of me. I have to live here."

"You'll have to get used to it," I said coldly. "And Vienna might as well learn that there is a wide variety of Americans. You're one kind. I'm another."

A habit of reticence had so far prevented me from telling Robert, or the German girl either, that I was leaving Vienna the next day to go on to Budapest. Any discussion of my relationships in Vienna was therefore fairly pointless. However, I was enjoying it too much to give Robert this terminal information now.

"I'm your friend," Robert was telling me, on a new approach, and I was inclined to believe him. "I know that girl is out to make you dance to her tune. Will you promise me, just between us, that you won't see her again?"

Only a firing squad could have kept me from her now, but I promised Robert in some disingenuous phrase that I would not betray the American cause in Vienna by letting the German girl make a fool of me.

If the German girl were actually an agent, her procedure had been interestingly peculiar. Either she did not like me, and was disgusted with the assignment, or she had already realized that nothing of value was to be got out of my type, whatever she had conceived that to be. Or, finally, she was playing a long-range game with me, over-estimating the length of my stay in Vienna. In this last case, her pretense of not knowing English could only become useful if I talked to another American (whom but Robert?) or even (presumptuous thought) talked in my sleep.

Meanwhile I diagnosed Robert's resentment of her not only as concern for me but also as the jealousy of the boy outside the pastry shop, still separated from the sweetmeats by the wall of glass or the rules of the New York Central.

Since I had no such inhibitions, I improved my last night in Vienna by looking once more into that lovely empty face and trying to surprise what childish game it was playing with me, for it was for this that I had come to Europe.

That night she was very sure of herself, encased in her shell of newly ripened perfection and my forgiveness of her for breaking our date. She smiled on me, in a new and promising way that would have told me, in other circumstances, that she thought I was cute. Once she laid her hand on my knee, as she pointed to the word in the German-English dictionary I carried that meant "necklace." She had already shown me the word for "gift."

As the evening developed, aided by the metallic-tasting German champagne, I opened to the word for "beautiful" and taught her to point at herself and say "Janus-faced tomato."

She did so, at first apprehensively and then, as I smiled with enraptured approval, confidently, lifting her hand to her throat with an exquisitely feminine self-consciousness.

While we were engaged in this, I glanced at the plate-glass front of the cabaret and saw, above the half-curtain, the face of the pimpled youth who was Robert's informer, staring in at us. I stared back with some irritation, when the German agent laid her hand on my knee for the second—and, sad to say, last—time. To distract me from the window, she gravely pronounced, again, "Janus-faced tomato," and then, as she pointed at herself, gave a throaty, altogether charming, giggle.

Next day I departed Vienna.

I did not see Robert's name again until the war was ended and he was caught, tried, convicted, and sent to prison for having broadcast for the Nazis after America entered World War II.

Trying to remember him, I saw him as being, in prison, still behind the plate glass, separated from the real world, as he had been on the New York Central, in the Nazi underground, and finally in Hitler's Festung Europa.

Trying to remember him, one small loser in a world-wide civil war of humanity, I found I did not hate him at all.

And then I thought of writing him a letter in prison, perhaps to prove that hatred was not an American habit.

But what should I say? I might remind him whimsically of Mussolini's ingenious idea of the corporative state, which had led to so much humiliation, enmity, pain, and death. It did not seem very whimsical. I thought of reminiscing about Janus-faced Vienna. But this subject too was covered with blood.

And then I remembered the German girl.

Trying to remember, I saw that I had been honored by the attentions of two agents, the girl and Robert. Remembering Robert's anger and fear when he learned that the girl was pretending to know no English, I saw now what he had seen then. Her job was solely to eavesdrop on my conversation with Robert, should I ever bring them together. She was not espionage, but counterespionage. And the Nazis did not trust Robert. When he had cried, "That's the last straw," it had been the last protest of a free man's self-respect, faced with that distrust.

Small wonder that it had been followed by the look of fear. Even that protest might open the trap of the pit beneath him. I might betray him or the Nazis might betray him to me. When his superiors thought about the meaning of "Janus-faced tomato," the choice of guilt had to fall between Robert and the girl. Robert must have learned that as a traitor he was still behind the plate-glass window that shut out mercy, trust, and hope.

I began to see difficulties in finding an approach to a man who has spent the intermission with Hitler. One cannot pick up the conversation as if one had merely left to telephone. On the way back, one looks for the comforting words that will put Dr. Jekyll at ease, and then sits down to console—Hyde!

But in sober fact the greater probability is that as one braces oneself to face the horrible Hyde, whom should one find but that sterling fellow Dr. Jekyll?

For Robert's treason was that he agreed with Hitler that the No. 1 enemy was Communism. This was his defense at his trial. Still thinking that his choice of Hitler as mankind's savior was a little hasty, the court gave him life imprisonment. A few years later, with the same story, Whittaker Chambers became a best seller.

Whether this is ironic, pitiful, funny, or meaningless I do not really know.

But I believe that Robert's error was not so much that he had the right answer a little too soon, as that he was too certain that he had the answer at all, based on doubt of the free peoples' good sense and good will to make their own fate for themselves.

Probably it was that doubt that made his answer the wrong answer in any year. Indeed, I would not have any great confidence, given that doubt, that Robert's presence in prison would make that prison any safer against Communism.

Sex Scares the Professor
(1957)

The more naïve newspapers had galvanizing news in January: "Americans are becoming victims of a sex mania as malign as cancer . . . in the same manner that marked the downfall of . . . Rome and Greece. . . . Sex bribery and blackmail . . . are now as prevalent as monetary corruption. . . . Sexually infamous persons or their protégés" occupy high office. "Among our public officials, there is a vast legion of profligates, both heterosexual and homosexual."

Hot diggety! The source of these eschatological doom sayings is *The American Sex Revolution* by Pitirim Sorokin, head of the Harvard Research Center in Creative Altruism. A number of clergymen, pundits, and Senator Flanders of Vermont promptly swallowed the bait and tore off in various directions.

The last charge, against people in government, can be examined first, as the most local and easily checked. Reporters are agreed that a brothel is now hard to find in Washington, D.C. The few operators permitted to exist cater chiefly to lobbyists. Professional vice is undercut by the great mass of female government employees, but they have to go to work in the morning. The massage parlors that flourished during the war have long since flown. Across the line, in Virginia and especially Maryland, some small-time vice may occasionally have a big night. But in general Washington is no Sodom.

That leaves the more important sex life of 120,000,000 more or less adult Americans. Before we examine the professor's scandalous accusations, it must be noted that Sorokin is an original and independent thinker. He has a very poor opinion of his fellow sociologists and anthropologists. Originally a Finno-Ugrian in Czarist Russia, he was an illiterate orphan at ten, imprisoned at seventeen in 1906, and a Kerensky man in the Revolution. The Communists employed, imprisoned, released, condemned, and finally exiled him. He invented Harvard's Department of Creative Altruism, which must have something to do with magnanimity. He has had only one wife, a Russian, and seems to be regarded at Harvard as a nice old gentleman who garde.1s. With his thirtieth book, he confirms an old pattern of rushing into print on the subject of sex.

The professor's intensely personal insult to every American is entitled to a fair hearing. If he is right, we are in serious trouble and had better overlook the insult. The reference of sex mores to national history may not be a popular specialty, but it is certainly a valid one. If there is a relationship, we want to know it.

However, Professor Sorokin's use of history to support his case that "sexual anarchy" and national decadence coincide is such as to strengthen anybody's suspicion that anthropology is not a science, but rather an amateur sport that any number can play. His proofs must therefore be briefly reviewed here.

For example, in trying to connect sexual austerity with an advancing culture, he says that the introduction of Christian chastity brought culture to the Teutonic tribes. But the barbaric Teutons were chaste; Christian culture coincided with the debauchery of the Frankish Merovingian and Carolingian courts.

Sorokin lists the twelfth to sixteenth centuries as the most disorderly until modern times. But these had the most rigid code of chivalry, and the two omitted, the seventeenth and eighteenth, were far more disorderly, both sexually and politically. Indeed, the professor's most horrible examples are then drawn from these latter, which also produced some of the greatest ornaments of our culture.

As "proof" that sexual indulgence shortens life, he shows that 332 monarchs died on the average earlier than 3,090 Christian saints (of a total of about 20,000). This is such a rank example of comparing pigs and pitchforks that one begins to wonder. A king becomes a king at any age simply by the death of his predecessor; a saint must have lived long enough to prove himself a saint even to get into the records. A king is usually a product of inbreeding and intense family supervision; a saint is generally a vigorous specimen from the mass of people. A great many kings were severely repressed; a great many saints started as spectacular rakehells; namely, St. Augustine, St. Ignatius Loyola, St. Francis of Assisi, *et al.* A king is not conditioned to be what a saint is, especially long-lived; or what a plumber or high hurdler is.

"Most European countries," Sorokin says, "are barely maintaining their populations." Flatly untrue. Population increases between the thirties and the latest census run from 10 to 20 per cent in England and Wales, Italy, Denmark, Yugoslavia, and Sweden, in that ascending order. Even France shows a small increase.

Sorokin refers loosely to "excessive sexual activity" as if "normal" were exactly the same for everybody, including the professor, who is now sixty-eight. The late Kinsey pointed out sadly that the wide differences of opinion held by educators on sex instruction were contested by people who might have had only one or two sexual experiences a year as against others with ten or twenty a week, and that neither of these groups could ever understand what the other was talking about. Kinsey certainly proved, and observation confirms, an enormous variation in performance. Taking his median frequency for married men's heterosexual intercourse, the United States figures for successive five-year periods from ages twenty-one to sixty were 634, 561, 491, 447, 379, 288, 244 and 205, or a virtual life total of 3,249. To begrudge the "median" man any of this is not nice, especially since a few men do as well in two years, according to Kinsey. With only two at-bats a week in his best years, this "median" American seems all too immune to sex mania, sex anarchy, or the professor's bad dream.

The professor cites juvenile delinquency as one proof of the general demoralization of our society. Yet the New York City Health Board has found that 75 per cent of the delinquents come from the same 1 per cent of the city's families—those characterized by alcoholism, drugs, mental illness, disability, desertion, violence and/or sexual immorality. This 1 per cent must compare very favorably with serf life in feudal times or even Dickens' Victorian London. I cannot compare it with a century certified as virtuous by Sorokin, for he names none.

He makes much of the appearances, plain to everybody, in the present American moment. The police courts, jails, insane asylums, psychiatrists, divorce courts, are indeed all busy; adultery is a commonplace in all dramatic media; the provocative picture of the female is indeed seen everywhere; a show of leg and bosom is obligatory for news photographers at air terminals. But whether these phenomena are all related is unknown to Sorokin or me. He gives other data: a quarter of America's forty-five million children do not live with both parents (maybe they're away at school or orphans);

every twenty-fifth wife has been deserted (was it ever better?); abortions are between "330,000 and 1,000,000 annually" (which is it?); illegitimate births were thirty-eight of every thousand in 1947 (what happened afterward?).

The professor has named the crucial sickness "sex addiction," which must be something like "food addiction" or "air addiction." His gift for overstatement leads to such remarkable understatements as, "Sex is often the main reason for many a Cinderella becoming the wife of a millionaire." (He means only one, not many, to each millionaire; but he thinks even that is horrible.)

Some more recognizable picture of American sex mores is required, if only to comfort the professor. He has overlooked a few small points.

The first is that society is divided into men and women. The men may be open to sexual debauchery, but ordinarily they must deal with women. Modern women, however, have almost complete control of their own decisions; and their decision is nearly always against an orgy: they prefer something quieter. The profligacy of ancient Greece and Rome and of the ninth century (the professor admires its nice religious art) was real; it dealt in women who could be bought, controlled, and raped. Today only a few Victorian relics are so afraid for their reputations that they can be raped—singly or en masse—without their yelling bloody murder.

The bull market in sex was in the twenties. People growing up then had a frantic view of it that has quite died. People born then, and now around thirty, have had love and sex thoroughly oversold and deflated. Even in twenty-year-olds there is no automatic enflaming at the sight of a haunch of the opposite sex. These latter groups seem appallingly unromantic to their elders.

Adultery is a commonplace only in certain suburbs and among the inhabitants of bars and grills. Yet a woman who has got out of control is exceedingly rare; the men haven't enough energy for a big romance; and even delivery boys grow up.

Visual eroticism is largely bludgeon-selling. It goes to new extremes because it fails to sell competitively, and the vendors get desperate. A provocative picture of a woman does not give any useful information about any woman: it can't talk, it doesn't move, it can't have babies. Most men sense this. The only sort of harm the Marilyn Monroes could possibly do would be to persuade all the men to wait for an equivalent; but to believe this possible is to understand nothing.

In a world of visual and imaginative sexuality there may be a good deal of vicarious licentiousness; but I believe that this is largely purgative. Its effects vanish when confronted with real charms. Furthermore, I believe that Americans are increasingly disinclined to leap into an imaginative or transient embrace that offers no hope of a many-sided relationship. A stupid or boring man or woman has a sharply limited choice, no matter what his or her physical beauty.

The professor discredits Freud and the pleasure principle. Yet I believe the psycho-social sciences have tried, and successfully, to recruit the pleasure principle as a booster charge for work; that is, people are encouraged to choose work they like. The professor obviously has chosen work he likes; his little book uses enough passion to charge a year in a brothel. And if all his readers could find work they like, I don't believe they'd demoralize society.

The final clue to the professor's view of virtue comes late in the book where he explains that sexual anarchy follows when "wives and children [are] emancipated from the absolute power of the *pater familias.*" The professor's counterrevolution goes back to J. D. Unwin's *Sex and Culture* (1934) and on back of that. At bottom, when all the nonsense about the necessary "desexualization of our culture" for salvation has been cleared away, Sorokin and Unwin are only echoing the cry of Gregory of Tours, "No one fears his king, no one fears his duke." Sorokin invites us back to a new feudalism where the authoritative *pater familias* can bang an iron fist into a dead silence, as all the delinquent, lascivious eyes are cast down.

Is There an American in the House?
(1954)

There was a day—one need not go far into history—when an American could not be frightened politically. In that golden age an American entertained absolutely any thought or dogma or iconoclasm that happened to enter his mind, and some of them were very wild. An American knew that all other Americans found their convictions in the American air. An American defied anybody on earth to invade his mind, and did not presume to invade the mind of his neighbor.

That day passed and the Roman degeneration of the republic was confirmed when an honorable magazine said editorially: "Because ideas can lead to betrayal, the impulse toward orthodoxy in a period like ours becomes almost compulsive. Conformity, sameness, and agreement tend to replace originality, diversity, and the free play of opinion as national ideals." For these lines describe an atmosphere that no American could, or would, breathe. They declare the repeal of the perpetual democratic revolution. And they seem to guarantee that there are no Americans left in America.

If there had been a few Americans present at the McCarthy committee hearings of recent years, it is irresistible to speculate on how one of them would have responded. The following dialogue is certainly not definitive. It is simply a sentimental exploration of what might have happened had this vanished American found himself in the witness chair.

McCarthy: Gliaou wham gringle pistlewait fursun ettike olem mommy nissy you wabbit (*and so on, for ten minutes. McCarthy pauses, as if expecting an answer.*)

The American: Could you boil that down a little?

McCarthy: It makes me mad deep down may I say when a simple answer to a simple question to expedite this investigation to save this land from Communist subversives I don't know where I find the strength to go on (*and so on, for three minutes.*) I want an answer: yes or no.

The American: As soon as I hear a question, I'll give an answer, if I know one. Are you gargling, sir?

McCarthy: If the witness finds these proceedings funny, I'd like to know it. What are you—an intellectual?

The American: Don't be deceived because I speak better English and have better manners than you, sir. I'm just as common as you. Maybe commoner.

McCarthy: I see. You want the protection of the Fifth Amendment to keep you from incriminating or degrading yourself.

The American: I'm not afraid of self-incrimination. But degradation—that's different. I don't propose to testify in any way that would degrade me in the eyes of my friends.

McCarthy: Well, we'll give you a chance to use the Fifth Amendment. Are you a Communist?

The American: I am not now, never have been, and never will be in any foreseeable future a member, associate, affiliate, co-traveler, puppet, stooge or whatever, of the Anarchist, Syndicalist, Trotskyite, Lovestoneite, Communist, Fascist, or National Socialist parties of this or any other country. Does that cover it?

McCarthy: I didn't ask you about those last two parties. Let them be stricken from the record.

The American: I flatly forbid that. To do so would degrade me by putting me in a class with the chairman of this committee.

McCarthy: Who does this witness think he is, giving orders to the committee stenographer?

The American: I'll tell you. I'm a member of the sovereign power under this form of government. I considerably outrank you. The sovereign power occasionally delegates, but never alienates, certain rights. A long time ago we gave fairly broad privileges to the members of the United States Senate. We reserve—and have always reserved—the option of canceling those broad privileges if they become a matter of sinister abuse, tending to endanger the whole operation of our government and the dignities of the sovereign power.

McCarthy: Gliaou wham gringle pistlewait fursun ettike (*and so on . . .*)

The American: This is one proposition you will have to meet head-on. Acting like a greased pig or a gopher or a schizophrenic paranoid will get you nowhere. I repeat, I am a member of the sovereign power. Hear that, and remember that.

McCarthy: Gliaou wham gringle pistlewait . . . Are you or are you not an anti-anti-Communist?

The American: That's not a simple question but I'll give you a simple answer. In some cases and some circumstances, I have been an anti-anti-Communist just as in certain circumstances I have been an anti-anti-Fascist, and during Prohibition in this country I was anti-anti-alcoholic. The circumstances are determined somewhat by the nature of the Communist, Fascist, or alcoholic whom the antis are anti. Sometimes the antis are fakes, and their victims have not been Communists, Fascists or alcoholics at all. In those cases, I have automatically been anti-anti.

McCarthy: You're anti-McCarthy. And I think it's fairly well-known that I'm an anti-Communist.

The American: On the contrary. A genuine anti-Communist would have asked the help and advice of most of the people you have persecuted. Some of them would actually know a Communist when they saw one, as you have not yet proved you do. To call twenty years of Democratic administration twenty years of Communism *is* obviously subversive. You are clearly a subversive, though not of the Kremlin variety.

McCarthy: Name calling will get you nowhere. You have admitted to being an anti-anti-Communist. I want that on the record for action by the Attorney General.

The American: So do I. America has been anti-anti from the beginning. Abraham Lincoln was anti-anti-Negro but that didn't mean, as his enemies said, that he was hankering to run after young Negresses. Washington and Jefferson were anti-anti-people and fought a Revolution to prove it. In 1917 we were anti-anti-Belgians and Czechs and Serbs and Rumanians but we didn't expect them, automatically and forever, to be perfect democrats just by saying the words "self-determination of peoples" over them. In 1931 and 1941 we were anti-anti-Chinese. As far as Hitler went, we were anti-anti-people, but you can even be that today without thinking that all the people in the world are still wonderful after the age of five. America today is anti-anti-peace, anti-anti-freedom, and anti-anti-American. The anti-antis are generally for people.

McCarthy: These Communist subversives we're ferreting out are people. Are you for them? That's what I'm trying to find out.

The American: As people, I am for them, as people. Especially these college boys who decide they're Communists for a year or two and then decide they can make some better sense out of their lives.

McCarthy: So now you want to subvert our precious American youth.

The American: We put a boy in college to try to get him to think. The best way he knows to think is generally to disagree with all the adults. I'm for him, no matter what idiotic thought he thinks he thought for a couple of years there. And I'm certainly against anybody who's against him, either then or ten or twenty years later.

McCarthy: This is open and shameless treason.

The American (laughing): I thought it would sound peculiar to you. That's not treason; it's ancient Americanism. Probably sounds just like treason to you.

McCarthy: I know just as much about Americanism as you do, and probably a little more.

The American: Well, perhaps. America is so magnanimous it accepts even second-class citizens such as yourself.

McCarthy: So you're bringing in race prejudice?

The American: No, prejudice prejudice. First-class citizenship is open to anybody of any race, creed, or color or parentage or place of birth who roughly understands and accepts the American system, the American dream, and the American constitution. You have deliberately and consciously opted for second-class citizenship—and that is your right under a democracy. You do not believe that the citizen is sovereign over the state. Get back in the second-class coaches, boy.

McCarthy: I'll get you if it's the last thing I do.

The American: My last word to you about America is this. Americanism is not afraid. It is not afraid of Communism or Fascism. It will eat Communism and you, possibly both together, possibly one at a time.

McCarthy: Gliaou wham gringle pistlewait fursun ettike olem memmy nissy you wabbit . . . (*The American closes his eyes and dreams and presently fades away into a shadow, which faintly darkens the witness chair and then is gone, nobody knows whither.*)

American Knight and Serf
(1959)

It will be generally agreed that the foremost enemy of Man is himself. But here I should like to isolate this strange schizophrenia in a single area. Two small examples:

On a quiet Saturday afternoon, a distinguished and well-loved lawyer and his wife were walking across an avenue, *at the intersection and with the green light,* when a neighbor lady, driving across in the opposite direction in some haste, fearing that the light would soon turn red, made a left turn directly into the faces of these two pedestrians. They were unrecognizable and dead. In the newspaper stories, there being at that time in New York City a campaign against "jaywalking," the dead couple were naturally described as "jaywalkers"—because they were dead.

On another evening a delivery driver for the New York *Daily News* ran directly across the path of an oncoming, screaming fire engine and didn't quite, qui-i-i-te, make it. Two firemen were badly hurt, one nearly lost his sight, the truck driver was slightly jarred. The driver had a record of countless traffic violations *and five convictions*. This incident was absolutely ignored, not only by the *News* but by every other New York City newspaper. Why? Because this union, which has lately gone further and shut down the whole New York press for nineteen days, wouldn't have liked it. But its brutality, corruption, and power were already visible then, in this small incident.

The news driver and the lady were not going anywhere very urgent; indeed, in their whole lives, it may be doubted whether they are going anywhere much. They were sorry to have hurt anybody, though they may have hurt others. Both were far less important to the whole society than the people they maimed or killed. Better to have maimed or killed *them* than their victims. And both are still busily on the business of maiming and killing, always with the tears streaming, and the remorse, which little by little diminishes.

A sort of concern, very largely ineffectual or hypocritical, over this slaughter is a condition of the present American society. We shall now briefly review, while we still have our hats off in respect for the lawyer and his wife and the two firemen, some of these rich and powerful expressions of concern.

1. *Fortune,* September, 1958, "The Nonsense About Safe Driving," by John D. Williams, head of the Math division of the Rand Corporation (which had earlier recommended to the Air Force that there was no earthly point in trying to defend American cities against Russian H-bomb attack): "I am sure that there is, in effect, a desirable level of automobile accidents—desirable, that is, from a broad point of view; in the sense that it is a necessary concomitant of

things of greater value to society." Mr. Williams' greater value is buying automobiles; his lesser value is killing people. These values can be respectfully noted, with due respect to the Rand Corporation.

2. National Safety Council estimate of people injured by motor vehicles in 1957: 1,400,000.

3. Insurance companies' estimate: 2,500,000.

4. U.S. Public Health Service estimate: 4,500,000.

5. Guy E. Mann, vice president of Aetna Casualty and Surety Company, addressing the International Association of Chiefs of Police, Miami Beach, October 28, 1958: "It takes a few minutes for the significance of those discrepancies to penetrate human understanding, it is so shocking." (The reference is to the discrepancies shown above.) ". . . Approximately 12,000,000 motor vehicle accidents in the country each year . . . the figure keeps going up and up and up . . . economic loss from $5,200,000,000 to $7,250,000,000 per year. . . . The only thing we are sure of is that the figures we possess are pure minima, including deaths. . . . At heart, the people of this country want traffic safety. Every opinion poll ever taken proves that beyond question. But the same polls show that nine out of ten Americans believe they are above-average drivers. And, curiously enough, *all* of those with a record of traffic violations rated themselves above average."

6. Several universities, including Cornell and California, are doing crash-injury research. Cornell has produced an exhibition car which can withstand a head-on collision at fifty miles an hour without injuring the people inside, in contrast to the superb killing and maiming characteristics of the cars on sale. Harvard is beginning a five-year study of accidents with a team that will get to the scene immediately after the accident (but not, unfortunately, before).

7. And then, of course, there is Governor Ribicoff of Connecticut, who means business. In 1956 he took the hair-raising political risk of ordering that the licenses of all convicted speeders, *without exception*, be revoked for thirty days, those of second offenders for sixty days, third offenders indefinitely and, later, fourth offenders (without a license) be fined $500 and/or jailed six months. Ribicoff had to refuse to intervene in the license-suspensions of friends and big politicians. One man wrote to him, "Is it your policy to make bums out of solid citizens?" But the deaths dropped by thirty-eight that

year and have kept on dropping. And Ribicoff was handsomely re-
elected. A poll showed that Ribicoff's program was favored by 60 per
cent of the people, but overwhelmingly opposed by drivers who had
ever been stopped for speeding.

But even Ribicoff's program is far from enough. All thinking about
traffic accidents is crippled by two ineradicable difficulties. First, it is
impossible, in nonmathematical terms, to describe an accident, which
is a continually changing, but mutually influenced, set of relationships in space and time. Witnesses never see it all, or see it the same
way. Even a movie would not adequately show all the elements in an
accident.

The critical elements are in the brains of the various drivers and
pedestrians. And this is a subject far trickier than nuclear physics,
and will remain so.

As a human being slides behind the wheel of a car, he actually
begins to feel brave. At the wheel, a man is reminded of his man-
hood, a woman of her virtue and rightness. The custom is to smile
gently at such vanity and folly. Stop smiling. That folly is a killer.

A sensible young lady was actually heard to say on a Monday,
while driving rather aggressively, "I'm sick and tired of these pedestrians," and on the following Friday, while walking rather recklessly,
"I'm sick and tired of these drivers."

This schizophrenia is, however, universally shared, and the second,
pedestrian half of it is dominant when we are walking in the areas
near our home or working-place—the areas where we feel safe and
authoritative and where most pedestrians are hit.

The driver, intent on his superior and momentous business, feels
toward a pedestrian a good deal like a soldier in combat toward a
civilian native who gets into the line of fire. A feudal mounted knight
may have felt so toward a heavy-footed serf. But in the modern case,
knight and serf are the *same person at different times*. But generally
he prefers to forget the serf-time and to think of himself in his
knight-time.

Two real solutions are available for the traffic slaughter. The first
is inevitable; the second volitional.

First, the automobile has flooded the courts with 75 per cent of the
cases now on the calendar—personal-injury cases. A few records have

been compiled for the years between 1940–1941 and 1956–1957. Between those years, in the Supreme Court of New York's Brooklyn and Staten Island, the average jury award in personal-injury cases rose from $3,740 to $16,957. In the Bronx and Manhattan, it went from $6,518 to $20,499. In the five counties just north of New York City, it went from $2,876 to $16,808. For the Supreme Courts of all the counties of the state, it rose from $3,490 to $11,188, up 321 per cent.

These astonishing figures naturally made the Association of Casualty and Surety Companies, whose members had paid most of these bills, turn a deathly green.

And so they tried two more counties, Cook in Illinois and Creek in Oklahoma. In Circuit Court of Cook County, the average jury award in personal-injury cases, between 1947 and 1957, ballooned from $7,690.06 to $31,397.19. In Superior Court, it went from $9,566.11 to $21,010.70. But Creek County, Oklahoma, was the bonanza of them all. Average jury awards rocketed up, between 1947 and 1957, 3,500 per cent. In the latter year, there was one jumbo verdict of $650,000. Eliminating that (but why?) and modifying the low 1947 figure with another, bloodier year, the rise was still 573 per cent.

Pleased for the plaintiffs as one must feel, that is not quite the whole of the matter. Insurance companies do not let themselves be plundered. In this same period auto-insurance rates have also been rising. In Connecticut the companies have just filed for a new increase averaging 19.3 per cent for the state and up to 34.7 per cent in Hartford. In Missouri the companies have been granted a new 10 per cent increase, piled on earlier raises of 63 per cent and up. The St. Louis *Post-Dispatch* commented editorially to the effect that the higher rates are required by a combination of independent evils: drivers are incorrigibly feckless; garages, doctors, and hospitals are incorrigibly greedy; and manufacturers are incorrigibly irresponsible in making new cars ten times as expensive to repair. A crumpled fender which one could once hammer out oneself now calls for half a new side assembly; the expensive wrap-around windshield is impossible to repair, and so on.

The groups mentioned by the *Post-Dispatch* are not in conspiracy to raise insurance rates, but they might as well be. The safest possible prediction is that the rates will go up and up and up. In that case, prediction becomes still safer and easier. Only the rich will be able to afford auto insurance. The unpropertied and young will drive without it, and when their small wages are attached for damages, will simply move away to become an itinerant labor population. The propertied laboring and middle classes, who cannot meet insurance payments but can be bankrupted by damage claims, will either have to do without cars or be pauperized.

This is the solution to traffic promised earlier. It involves a strictly up-to-date, 100 per cent American version of the decline and fall of ancient Rome. I hope there is *somebody* who will make a profit out of it but I can't see who, unless he would be the Gibbon of a succeeding civilization.

To get to the second possible solution, let us look at an example of the reality: an intersection I know, a northbound one-way avenue crossed by a westbound one-way street which serves as an exit from a throughway. The lights on the avenue are staggered. Say the lights on the avenue turn red. What happens? The first row of cars and trucks goes through the red light. The second row reflects, "Why not me too?" and goes through. One or two of the third row follow along, naturally at increased speeds. The pedestrians meanwhile are inching out, and the cars on the side street are pushing forward, blowing their horns, because the cars behind them are blowing theirs.

Now the first side-street car comes sweeping in a sharp right turn into the avenue, blowing the pedestrians back. One man makes a dash across its front and is stopped by the second car making a wide right turn. The later cars put on speed to stay right on the tails of the cars ahead. Finally the pedestrians—all "natives" of this intersection: a mother with baby carriage, a crippled old man, a young man with a heel blister—manage to get into the middle of the avenue. Whereupon the lights, naturally, change. This is the open hunting season on people. They can now be legally killed, though not legally taken home. The immediate danger, however, is from the last side-street cars speeding through the light at up to forty miles an hour, and from the cars moving up from a block south on the avenue, also roaring at speed through the breaks in the line ahead of them.

This is the scene *at the intersection with the lights.*

Dreadful as it is in fact, in operation, hour after hour, day after day, every step is perfectly human and understandable. One step leads to another; and the last step is 38,000 quick deaths a year, at least that many slow deaths, hundreds of thousands of cripples—and higher insurance rates.

The original, causative guilt in any accident is almost impossible to find, retroactively, but to the bystander the dangerous, unconsciously wicked driver is all too obvious. The first car that caused the second car to do the killing is a block away by the time of the accident, and nobody even remembers it. The only conceivable answer in this dilemma is that the guilt for every accident lies on all the drivers of all the cars on all the streets and roads. This is the truth that is totally unacceptable, the confession that can never be made, the little margin of folly and evil that resides even in saints. For of the saint in an automobile, one must demand not even a dozen saintly acts a day, but an unbroken continuum, without exception, year after year. Since this is far too much to ask, we must fall back on other measures.

"Good" people try to find others who are demonstrably worse than themselves, such as drunken boys. "Efficient" people blame pedestrians for getting killed. Such a crusade is now under way in New York City, against "jaywalkers." Pedestrians are given tickets for jaywalking and, as a modest rider to the ordinance, drivers are directed to give pedestrians the right of way at the intersection with the lights. The rider turns out to be the key part of the campaign, at least at the heavily populated, policed intersections. The drivers, to their amazement, have to slow down and even stop before making a turn. A humorous columnist headlined his column: "Drivers Must Yield (Hey, Wanna Bet?)"

After a little of this, a perpetually virile tabloid, the New York *Daily Mirror*, editorialized: "The anti-jaywalking picture is not so rosy. Traffic has been decidedly slowed. Pedestrians get the green light first, ahead of motorists making turns, and the result has been pileups and spillovers and *agonizing* delays." (Italics mine.) "Agonizing" is normally the suitable word for death and maiming and grief and life-long loneliness, but to the *Daily Mirror* it is just the right word for being held up ten seconds on one's obsessive rounds. The *Daily Mirror* may feel manly, but it needs a long, long rest in a good sanitarium, with plenty of hot baths.

Traffic safety requires a very different tone of voice, that of good manners and human respect. The opposite (un-American?) attitude is to be seen in its finest flower on the streets of Moscow. A year ago, Moscow removed all speed limits and replaced the regulation that only four lanes of traffic could move abreast. Now the law of the jungle obtains. Cars rush at full speed at groups of pedestrians caught between curbs. Right turns are permitted on red lights. The only pedestrians able to cross the very wide downtown intersections, before the light changes, are those in perfect physical condition.

Here the voice of the pedestrian is not heard at all. Our second solution, therefore, is aimed at giving the pedestrian a greater voice.

The American citizen, as pedestrian, lives in a climate of half-conscious fear, impotence, and frustration, as if he were a subject race. This is reflected in his general manners and morals, and, in turn, his own tyrannous conduct when he becomes a motorist. The American, as motorist, is having his moral sense atrophied. After he has killed or maimed a fellow citizen, he should self-impose his own penance and self-revoke his own license. But he never will.

The driver who will ultimately maim or kill is driving now in a way predictably calculated to do so, or to force someone else to do so. A hundred times a day he betrays himself to any observer, and leaves a wake of infuriated people behind him (or her). But no laws and no police force can stop this driver until he (she) has finally committed his (her) dreadful crime.

The solution is to enlist the American citizen, as pedestrian, to detect himself, as motorist.

Technically, it is easily done. The newspapers would announce a central office in any community where the citizen, as pedestrian, could send the noted license number of a car driven by the citizen, as motorist, that had moved in a menacing, reckless, and ominous manner. This postcard (only postcards accepted) would have to give the writer's name, address, and telephone number, the car's or truck's license number, and the time and place of the performance. Anonymous cards would be thrown out.

Perhaps two file clerks and a good filing system would be required. This file would be reviewed at stated periods, and anyone complained of by more than a determined number of pedestrians would be notified, or get a physical and psychiatric examination, or simply have his license revoked, or be given an unusually careful driver's test.

Both as pedestrian and as motorist, with such an arrangement, the American would be happier, calmer, better adjusted, and live longer.

A last word can be borrowed from Governor Ribicoff's Connecticut: no exceptions. And those two file clerks had better be unapproachable. Are there two such Americans left today? I believe there are at least three.

Prometheus on the Fire Escape
(1952)

Every newspaper ran courtroom photographs of the principals in the affair. There was one of a handsome, smug, even self-righteous, boulevardier, who might have becomingly sat "ringside" at the gaudier East Side night clubs. This was the bookmaker who was testifying that he had bribed the police officers. The other faces had searching eyes and ruthless mouths, but one could see that these were the good fellows; the bookie was the snob. These were the police officers, a former commissioner and a brace of inspectors, who were accused of taking the little snob's bribes.

The bookie was inscrutable, a self-made personality, *sui generis*, but the others were perfectly recognizable members of society. They had the faces of those who accept the world as it runs. For them, a thing could not be a corruption if it had ever been accepted by a man they knew as brave and good, a friend. They lived in the world, girt in values that had continuity. In the mornings, as they pulled on their pants heavy with the money, and looked at the morning sun, the hillside was no less dew-pearl'd, nothing less right with the world.

I showed the newspaper at lunch to my old friend in the night-club business for whom it was breakfast.

"Just looking at the pictures, I'd say any one of those faces would take a bribe," he said. "If I were doing business with them."

I said something indignant.

His surprise seemed genuine. "You mean this kind of thing is news to you?"

When I said that I still had a reasonable doubt, he went on a little about the twilight world of a big city. He mentioned a former police officer who was known by tens, hundreds, perhaps thousands, of night-working citizens to have been part owner, while he held office, of a string of night clubs that pandered to the most degraded elements of the city. He told of a world-famous "clean" night club openly owned by a pathological criminal and secretly owned by one of the most powerful racketeers in America.

I had heard all three names and knew one of the men personally, but recently I had read most often of their charitable works. I had supposed they were all beyond ambition or avarice, having been translated to that rarer air of philanthropy which is the latter state of great wealth or great virtue. I don't mean that any of them had become elder statesmen, but I would not have imagined that any of them wanted anything bad enough to have crossed the street against the lights.

"If that is true, or any of it, somebody would certainly have done something about it before now," I said, not troubling to hide my disbelief.

"It just isn't done," my friend said. "Look. There used to be a captain in my precinct who broke every law on the books. Sure, he was crooked and maybe he was crazy. He ran a reign of terror. It got so bad the department had to investigate him. He committed suicide. Nobody had testified against him; nobody was going to. But it was so bad that if you dug the rest of your life, you would never find anybody to say a word against him. In fact, I'll bet the records showed he died a natural death. That man threatened to kill me. Told me so. But what was worse he said he'd have my children killed. A whole year there, I couldn't sleep at night on account of him."

"And you didn't do anything about him?" I said.

"You don't understand," he told me. "You've got to show you can take it. Sometimes it's part of the deal. I just had to take it."

"Not like that," I protested. "That doesn't have to be part of the deal."

"You don't understand."

"I understand that if you take that, you're not against it, you're not against anything. And if you're not against anything, how can you ever be for anything?"

Even to myself, I sounded pompous just then, pompous and safe. And my friend had not been exactly safe, and was not being pompous.

The thought angered me and I got stubborn. "I still say it's wrong. I don't care how I sound."

"Sure, sure," he said. "Look at it. I'm not against a guy with an organization that can make me disappear off the face of the earth and no questions asked. A guy who feels like doing it, or even just tells me he feels like doing it. So maybe he can't do it, so what? Am I the guy that's got to prove it?"

"You're not yellow," I said, for indeed I knew he was not.

"No, I don't think I am," he agreed gracefully. "It isn't that at all. If I had gone up against that captain, or any of the others, I'd think I'd blown my lid. And so would everybody else. I know my friends would have begun to avoid me. My help would have quit. My credit would have been shut off." He smiled. "I'm pretty sure my kitchen would have been officially declared a health hazard, my exits a fire hazard, and maybe the insurance company would have raised my premiums."

"It would have been interesting to find out," I said, from the side lines.

I looked again at the photographs in the newspapers.

The really big one had a thin upper lip and pale guarded eyes that suggested a certain limited kind of working sense of humor. One side of his face was lined smoothly; the other was sweetly dimpled with the corrugated scars of hypocrisy. Almost all the others (one was cranky) were similarly loaded with this same unamusing sense of humor.

As I drank my coffee, I glanced from the paper to the face of my friend.

He was a humorous man himself, but with a difference from these others. His face had the ordinary citizen's overlay of politeness, of the absence of power, of tolerant allowance for the continued existence of other kinds of people.

Somehow it occurred to me that he was the kind who would walk quickly past the cages of the big cats in the zoo and feel a trace of guilt because he was free and the lions and tigers and panthers were behind the bars. But he had just described to me a world where the polite and tolerant Homo sapiens was the one in the cage, while the lions and tigers and panthers with the murderous sense of humor prowled freely past outside and stared contemptuously in.

As soon as I had the thought, I dismissed it. It seemed to me that it was a purely literary, or poetic, thought.

However, I remembered that I knew about the symbolic lions and tigers elsewhere, which were amused by watching me inside the cages they had made. I knew about the waterfront where the "shape-up" system had evolved into a situation where a single Communist boss could pick a crew that would sabotage outgoing war matériel and unload a Communist atom bomb or several or thousands. I knew, on the more ordinary level, about the real horrors of the famous food market in an unfrequented corner of the city where the people's vegetables were daily manhandled so as to acquire an outrageous addition in cost to the housewife and a layer of unnoticed but unspeakable filth.

I had not acted on either of these actionable knowledges. I was not "yellow" either, but I suddenly desisted from any further criticism of my friend.

"I wish you hadn't told me that stuff," I said.

"It's in the papers," he replied patiently, for he had had more practice than I.

He suddenly seemed devoid of a sense of humor. The lions and tigers, I thought, the ones looking in at us, were the only good fellows left. It must be wonderful to be a member of that fellowship, where everybody knew the appropriate joke for every occasion, even for the Flood, the Apocalypse, and Armageddon.

Somehow I wanted to get away from my friend. So I stood up. He said patiently, "Don't worry about the world now."

"Not till they pay me for worrying," I said. "I'm walking up to the zoo."

It was a quiet Saturday afternoon in the city. As I walked along a crosstown street, I was thinking how irritating an idea like that— Homo sapiens in the cage—can become. I wished I hadn't thought of the good-fellow lions and tigers walking the streets, for of course the picture was absurd. Ordinary people were passing me. And indeed the ordinary scene soon exercised its power to disperse such precious fancies.

A block later, I sniffed and identified the odor of smoke.

I stiffened at once, for though the smell of wood smoke is comforting to a countryman, it is unnatural and calamitous to a city man. I looked up and saw the visible curl of it bending over a renovated brownstone house ahead of me, on the opposite side of the street. Even before I had come level with the house, the fire engines were banging up behind me.

The house was evidently one of several that had been renovated as one, with a common entrance. From a third-floor window of one of the others, the heads of two women projected, their necks lengthened by their present self-appointed function.

The younger called authoritatively to the firemen, "On the top floor in the rear." Several helmeted firemen stopped and craned their necks. "Top floor, rear," she repeated. The firemen all started for the door at a trot, a hustling team taking the field, and the two heads were pulled inside.

A hose truck had moved down to the corner, near the closest hydrant. The hose had crawled into the doorway of the house. A fireman had returned to yell back, "More hose!" Other men, running, but without waste of energy, pulled out the folded corners of the hose along its whole length on the street. "Nothing coming yet," one said, and ran back to the engine. Another cry, "More pressure!" was passed down the line. At least a dozen men, fastening coats and carrying axes, had disappeared inside.

For all this, the smoke had grown thicker. For the first time I noticed that the top-floor windows in front were wide open and that two thin streams of smoke were issuing from them.

A moderate crowd of perhaps fifty citizens had assembled on the pavement and stoops opposite the calamitous house. A band of eight-year-olds had taken charge of the commentary. "Another false alarm," yelled one, noting the absence of the passionate, flickering red of fire hunger. "The water's in the hose," another reported.

The adult audience had so far reserved judgment. The professionals of the fire department had the business in hand. Nor was it yet clear whether this incident would dwindle away, or enlarge to the dimensions which might put it into the unspeakable terms of a story in tomorrow's newspapers.

Neutral, we waited. There was nothing to be seen except the wisps of smoke emerging from the two windows of the top floor, front.

And here at last there was a very small thing to see.

Somebody was behind the window opening on the iron fire escape. A glimmer of white moved behind the curtains. A little later it came right up to the window and took form as a man in a white shirt, leaning against the frame of the window. Whoever it was, he was standing in a river of smoke. Yet even from the street, one could sense an unnatural air of negligence. For fully five minutes, the figure hardly moved. And then it disappeared.

A minute later, with a coat and pullover sweater, it reappeared and emerged through the window onto the fire escape. It was a man in his early thirties, of a superior white-collar type, with a brachy-cephalic head and all his hair. He was wearing dark gray slacks and a tweed jacket of a good-enough cut. He looked as if he might read a good deal and smoke a pipe. I had the social impression, I do not know why, that he had come to New York from the West or South five or ten years before.

However, his appearance greatly relieved the growing boredom of the eight-year-olds, as once the first scrawny martyr brought from the mob in the Colosseum the roar of their deepest hunger.

"Hey, look, he's gonna jump!" yelled one.

A thrill of excitement entered all the voices as they took it up. "Jump! Jump!"

This was not, however, the scenario as written. The man was examining the fire escape as if he had never really noticed a fire escape before. After a prolonged inspection and consideration, he climbed down the first flight of stairs, holding the railing and walking sideways with his face to the wall of the building.

This adventure brought him to the window on the third-floor, front, and I supposed that there he would rap on the window and ask his neighbor for permission to walk through the house to the stairway. However, he kept on going down the next flight of steps, to the second-floor landing of the fire escape. Perhaps he was friendlier with the people on the second floor and planned to visit with them, on the natural excuse of this community commotion.

But he had stopped on the landing, as if he had no intention of rapping on the window.

If he had hoped to get to the street level, he had to go to work on an iron ladder which was in the customary, raised position. He gave this one look and turned his back on it. I suppose that it was unfamiliar to him, that he suspected it might jam, that he was reluctant to risk frustration in front of an audience, and that he felt that the second-floor landing was as far as he wanted to run from the smoke.

This was all understandable. But it left him isolated on the fire escape with fifty people looking at him. They had watched his descent with absorption, examining him closely and forming their several tentative opinions of him.

His manner had continued negligent, as if this excursion down the fire escape had been a free choice, a whim he permitted himself. But now he made one small admission of the compulsive nature of his present position. Under a pretense of blowing his nose, he took out a handkerchief and quickly wiped his eyes, which must have been streaming from the smoke in the room. This finished, he turned and looked up and down the street with assurance, but not at the audience opposite.

There was one inevitable and available support he had not yet called on. A minute later, he remembered it and lit a cigarette. He took a deep puff and then removed the cigarette from his mouth, holding it at the base of his fingers instead of with the tips, his hand half-closed in a fist. His negligence became at once more convincing. He even glanced at the crowd. Then, as if to make himself one with the crowd, he did what they were doing: he bent his head back and stared at the trickle of smoke coming from his own windows.

The cigarette used up ten minutes. But at the end of that time the smoke was undiminished, the crowd still waited and the man was still suspended in the barred iron cage of the fire escape, increasingly ill at ease, but conveying a resolution to hold his ground until he could climb back in his own window and disappear once again into his own private world, now probably somewhat smoke-damaged.

Certainly he had done nothing wrong or unnatural.

It was what he had not done. He had not been able, or not chosen, to knock on the windows of his own neighbors. To avoid asking them the small favor of letting him walk through their apartments from the window to the door, he had unhesitatingly preferred the pillory of the fire escape.

To flinch from so ordinary an act, to prefer discomfort, embarrassment, and even danger, a man must be guarding some powerful and indispensable illusion. Such a choice gives away the heart's deepest secrets.

The man on the fire escape could only be saying that, even in the shadow of calamity, he was not part of anything. His inappropriate cigarette was a defiance of life as convincing as if he had shaken his fist at the heavens and screamed. All honor and dignity had been frozen into a paralysis that was his sole remaining response to any challenge. He had locked himself in the cage and given over the streets to the lions and tigers. The mischief had all its own way, while Prometheus lay chained to the cliff.

Suddenly I could not bear to go on watching this frozen and solitary honor. I walked away, and so for all I know he is still there, between heaven and earth, in his iron cage, smoking another cigarette.

II

The Tin Ear: Communications

Nobody Reads Any More
(1957)

The publishers' complaint, "Nobody reads," is not meant literally. It describes instead a generally recognized mood of nonexcitement about the printed word, of diminished hope of reading anything unforgettable, and of resignation to that minimum of reading which is essential just to "keep informed."

Most people "read" perhaps two newspapers a day; if they are commuters they certainly do. They glance at the current crisis headlines and skip down the story; they read all about several local human tragedies; they pick what they want out of the sports section or business section and may read all of a favorite column. Housewives get the primary news, incredibly condensed, on TV and radio all day; the husbands get a little at night. The later-evening interview programs also reflect the news world enough to give the listener the sense of being still in touch with world events.

Toward the end of the week, the family will look at *Life, Look*, the *Saturday Evening Post, Time* or *Newsweek*, to confirm the fact that they exist in the world of the moment. But all they have read that week will have disappeared from their minds two weeks later: they cannot even be sure whether that was the week the little boy fell down the well, or the week the doctor presented his $1,500 bill.

In the sense that Dickens' early serialization stories were the life of England and the Continent, today: nothing.

The blame for the current impotence of the printed word is generally laid on the writer (all right, where's Dickens?) by such editors as those of *Life*, or on the reader (we give the people what they want). Oddly, these two answers by editors demolish one another.

Both answers are, in my opinion, wickedly wrong. Readers and also writers, are above criticism; their qualities and interests are subject to examination but not to blame.

The thing that has been added, most outrageously in this country, is the corporate-publishing operation, whose crux is the editor or board of editors. If the passionate reader is dead in America, these are the people who have killed him. In their hands the printed word has slowly, imperceptibly, approached the state of being a lifeless, mechanical tool, instead of an unexpected window in a closed room.

It will be instructive to examine how the printed word was killed in American journalism. And this leads us to the "rules" of mass-magazine editing, given below in my own order—not that of a journalism school:

1. Fewer words in bigger type on a page, so that a *Life* or *Post* page looks more and more like a display advertisement, and says less and less.

2. The naïve faith that a story is "headed up" by including in the first paragraph the latest possible "news," no matter how anti-climactic, irrelevant, and unnewsworthy it is. The unimportance of news can be demonstrated by reading a ten-year-old *Life*, *Post*, or *Reader's Digest*. The issue will be exactly as interesting, or un-interesting, as this week's; and reading it has the advantage of showing how silly editors were ten years ago.

3. Topicality, or the abuse of presold themes. In the May 25th *Saturday Evening Post* there were three separate wars with Bol-shevik Russia: (1) H-bomb attack; (2) Russian capture of an American atomic submarine; (3) Russia's race to educate more scientists than we. There were also articles about a millionaire, a crook, a neurotic, a new governor, and Groucho Marx. How safe can you play it?

4. Look as if you're saving America. The press has put us in just the right mood fo fight Russia about fifty times. If the fifty-first time should turn out to be the all-out necessity, this propaganda may have stopped working. I accept the uses of propaganda; but this isn't well-planned propaganda. In fact, it was planned only to sell copies, not to save America. Who cares about saving America if he can scare it?

5. Everything in each magazine is written in the same style. This sounds impossible; it is certainly not easy; but the editors manage it.

6. The use of superlatives, as that the United States has the world's biggest steel production, Pakistan all the world's jute, the Dutch use the most fertilizer per acre, Indian politicians do the most talking, and so on. All the foregoing can be checked, but that does not make them less deadening. This fashion must be laid to Time Inc. The laugh about superlatives is that everybody and everything is in some way most, least, best, worst, first and last. (I, too, have sinned in this department.)

7. The positive search for material that will not irritate Protestants, Catholics, or Jews; men or women or children; whites, Negroes, or mongoloids; elderly, middle-aged, or young; any ethnic group; dogs, cats, parakeets, or goldfish; hunters or fishermen; farmers or trade-unionists; and so on, and so on—and the prompt abdication to any letter-writing group of complaining lunatics.

8. All material must seem to help, or at least not hinder, parents bringing up children. (But the other half of the magazines on the newsstands are aimed at debauching children. These are the ones the children buy.)

9. All public figures are nice people. The reader knows the world assays fairly high on sons of bitches, but evidently the percentage drops precipitately in the seats of the mighty.

10. The smell of public-relations work gradually fills the nose of the faithful reader. By what magic is Bernard Baruch at the right hand of God, Walter O'Malley a father of his people, Robert Moses the Ajax of the American way of life, Thomas Watson's whole family supermen, any president of General Motors a barefoot boy, Eisenhower a military genius (no point giving the title to Bradley, who deserves it), Thomas Edison the greatest American, Joe Consolidated the next greatest, and so on? Nobody really believes any of this rot, but nobody exactly disbelieves it either. Everybody slowly stops believing in anything.

11. Superficially exciting themes completely crowd out less dramatic statements of significant survival truths. A rare example of the latter was a small, unattractive picture story in *Life* around 1938, pointing out the weapons lessons of the Spanish War; namely, the victory of the big-gunned tank over the German little, fast tank.

These lessons were a safe bet to dominate the upcoming war. But this sort of undramatic service is almost never given the reader. Insofar as it isn't, I suggest that the whole press is very largely a waste of wood pulp.

12. Each publication's insane pretense that it is the only one in existence. No hurrahs for stories in other publications are ever published, with the sole regular exception, so far as I remember, of Walter Winchell's column. (Naturally, reviews of books, plays, movies, and so on, are quite another matter.) Credit to other publications for information, far less for ideas, is never given, except by the most intellectual magazines. This fashion, too, can be traced to Time Inc.

13. As a corollary or result of this, enthusiasm and wonder are taboo to the printed word. Anybody except a sportswriter is forbidden to let go. The general impression created by the word is that there is nothing and nobody worth believing in. The enthusiasms that are acceptable are for *South Pacific*, not *Carousel*, for Mary Martin's Peter Pan, not for Cyril Ritchard's Captain Hook. Such is not the sort of spiritual climate where anything very good gets done. The only honest voice possible is one of dissent. Perhaps that is why so much high-minded, if perhaps overgenerous, sympathy has gone to the American Communists who are believed, incorrectly, to have the talent of dissent.

14. Overediting, on the frayed excuse, "Any piece of writing can be improved by editing." The writer's all too human personality can indeed be combed out of the words by editing; in this sense, the perfect piece would be a blank page. The editing is in the direction of broad and corny signals to the reader, and away from what the individual writer wanted to convey.

15. The coterie of pet writers who monopolize any given magazine. Editors are averse to another magazine's pet, and completely cold to strange new voices.

16. An inane contempt and hostility by most editors toward most writers, except ex-fellow-editors. The writer is not a member of the editors' club; he is a sort of screwball. Thus, writers try to get into editing, and after some of that into public relations. A countermovement is detectable, from editing and advertising into writing, but I have no faith in it.

17. The resultant level of American writing is such that large numbers of nonwriters can meet it. The Gypsy Rose Lees and Diana Barrymores are entitled to their hearing. But the dull boys and girls who "learn" to write in schools, and the college instructors who are subsidized to earn their next promotion by writing articles, are largely dead weight. There is even a kind of "fine writing," for which Flaubert must take responsibility, that can be quite adequately taught to any fool. You just keep trying out different words in each spot. The ancient truth that good writing is only good thinking and good feeling is stone dead. The perennial crop of new writers who are too busy inventing their own techniques to go to school are evidently drowned at birth now.

18. I would certainly include in this list the big publishers' failure to try to improve the independent writer's income-tax position. A writer's one good year after ten years of famine, all equally hard work, will usually ruin him, because it will heighten both his creditors' and his own appetites. A writer has to remain outside the whole American system of time-credit on the security of corporate wages or property. If he is, after the inventor-discoverers, the most important person in the culture, he ought to be encouraged by the government to stay in business.

The reader suffers by the mutilation of the writer, just as the writer suffers by the gradual mutilation of the reader's mind. Enough has been given to show that both these processes have been going on in America, and both at the hands of the corporate editors.

Is all this just diaphanous nonsense?

Well, let us look at the results of feeding the American people, for thirty years, with topical information about the rest of the world. Looking back, the information was little better than a cloud bank to hide the chasm ahead.

We were carefully conditioned to separate Fascism and Communism, and then in 1939 they became allied.

We were ready to love dear old China, but now it hates us.

The Arab world was an archaic delight until Egypt tried to cut off the oil.

We were prepared to applaud India's emancipation, but suddenly it was the persecutor of Pakistan.

The one sure thing was that Japan was wrong in attacking Pearl

Harbor, and now even that, in an astounding counterpropaganda in *The New Yorker* magazine, has been taken away from us.

Today, partly through our efforts, our late-defeated enemies, Germany, Italy, and Japan, are the liveliest and most prosperous nations in the world. With the same help, our late ally, Soviet Russia, is the only menace to us.

Were the people given the wrong information? I should think so. But more than that, American public opinion, informed or uninformed, has very little bearing on the decisive forces that control events. The only opinion of any importance is a personal, penetrating, sympathetic opinion based on a lot more than a reading of current journalism. (For example, talking a foreign language badly will get you swindled far worse than stubbornly talking your own language. In your own language, you can command a little respect because the translator speaks it worse than you do.) There is no cheap, easy way to having a valid opinion; you won't even know whom to believe.

The press has two approaches. One, the easier and commoner, is by way of the Leader, and his problems—exports, wages, inflation, deflation, steel production, oil, the military budget, a corridor to the sea. The other approach is large generalization about the people, illustrated with anecdote. The first of these has very little connection, in most countries, with the second. A valid general opinion about people as Japanese, French, or Egyptian is almost impossible to arrive at; and even if you find it, it is demonstrably irrelevant to what is going to happen.

Because the Leader approach is much easier and more readable, most of the American press is positively grateful to any country that has a strong Leader, and will forgive him much.

People make the press uncomfortable. Its solution is to treat people as lovable idiots. Rack your brains as you will, you cannot remember reading of a distinguished, slam-bang, stand-up individual in the recent press. This fashion of patronizing people has even entered slick magazine fiction: the characters are essentially a joke and their problems are solved with almost ribald contempt.

In any real sense, the editors have abolished the memory of all the dead people, that is, the past.

Subtract people and the past: what is left is the peopleless future—science-fantasy fiction, space travel, a moment when we shall all be turned instantly into a putrid gas, and then the leisurely inspection of the ruins by unidentified antenna men.

If one looks for some germ of rationality in this, it must consist of the concept, dear to current editors, that the future will be totally unlike the past. The concept takes its substance from obviously great changes in techniques, in the organization of the world, and a threat of annihilation of the centers of civilization, but not of the backward areas. In such a climate, what else are people, just people, to do but suspend thought and feeling? There is no apparent hope, they have understood, in a reading of the past. What is to be will be totally different from what has been. Beneath the ordinary chatter of living, you sense the two and a half billion people listening, waiting. In such a mood, how can anybody read?

And yet the past can tell us everything the future will tell. "The end of the world" is a recurrent event in the history of the world; in the year 999 nobody in Western Europe saved any food for the year 1000 because the world was coming to an end that New Year's Eve. There was hard going that next year but we're here, so somebody must have managed.

There is a hard basis of continuing truth. The past tells us what manner of men have always ruled in Moscow or Cairo or Peking or Washington, and what massive traditional and popular forces bear on them and re-form them in the shape of the past. For example, basic Russian foreign policy has hardly changed in four hundred years.

The past tells us of the marvelous new hope of a new generation who have the courage to start from the beginning and even prefer to make a new world, though it will not be as nice as they think.

People and the past, truth and salvation, despair and glory, these are the province of the printed word. But certainly not the province of the limp symbols that the editors manicure in the current American press.

Still, as surely as the word has died, the word will be reborn.

Sophistication in America
(1957)

Sophistication is one of the most embarrassing words in the language because one can hardly tell whether it is being used in a complimentary or derogatory sense. It may refer to a person with a lack of taboos, an experience of wines and women, mere unshockability, a fatigue of life, an affected manner, three university degrees, or true wisdom, whatever that is. Originally, according to Merriam-Webster, it meant altered or adulterated.

Nevertheless, when I speak of sophisticated magazines, everyone knows I don't mean *McCall's* or the *Reader's Digest*. Indeed, the sophisticated magazines are for the people who are presumably tired of these others.

The incredible news is that sophistication, or a reasonable facsimile, has quietly become the most profitable line, dollar for dollar, in the magazine business. The highest rates for an advertising page per thousand of circulation have long been charged by the sophisticated magazines (and five business magazines). The 1956 figures (in dollars), omitting the business magazines, are: *Town and Country*, 22.16; *The Bride's Magazine*, 18.58; *Gourmet*, 9.96; *Harper's Bazaar*, 9.19; *Vogue*, 9.12; *Saturday Review*, 7.27; *Esquire*, 7.20; *Theatre Arts*, 7.10; and *The New Yorker*, 6.62. In the first six months of 1956 nearly all these showed good gains in circulation, while some of the mass magazines were floundering. Furthermore, they were selling lots of advertising.

A grateful nod is indicated toward our first sophisticated magazine, *Vanity Fair*, and its creator, Frank Crowninshield, the last great American gentleman. *Vanity Fair* reflected the real sophistications of moribund Vienna and the Parisian painters, as well as the manners of the English upper class decimated by World War I. With the Depression, it came under the influence of lady assistants headed by Clare Boothe, and it expired in February, 1936, after the advertisers discovered it was also read by ladies instead of just gentlemen. In the last issue the nightlife column was headed "The doe at eve," and the sex was a picture of Josephine Baker.

The loss was not considered serious at first because, besides the Depression, there was also *The New Yorker,* whose 1933 circulation of 114,000 has moved today to 415,000. The magazine has given much pleasure and instruction and is still regarded as the arbiter of big-city sophistication. Yet today most sophisticated people who see it at all, often look only at the cover and the cartoons. Its curious prestige has escaped serious examination, perhaps because the jokes are surprising and the formula is at once disarming and iron-bound.

The New Yorker has in fact a peculiarly fixed attitude, which comes in several sections. The early hands were debonair: Phil Wylie, Herman Mankiewicz, Peter Arno, Lois Long. But their boss, the late Harold Ross, met their high spirits with the manner of an unreconstructed hick or bashful farm hand at a barn dance. He doggedly stuck to this wooden pose in New York, perhaps to emphasize his differences from Crowninshield and Woollcott. The effect on a new arrival from *Fortune, Newsweek,* the *New York Times, Partisan Review,* and so on, was inevitably as if the newcomer had been plunged into a fit of the sulks. A pretense of defeatism and callousness soon enclosed him. He looked hangdog. He learned better than ever, ever to be the life of the party. I have sat at lunches with four of them where nobody spoke for five minutes. In this form of yoga, each tries to be more of an outsider than all the others. The winner is the real insider.

This is *la haute manière;* defeatism and callousness are the culture in the laboratory bottle. The people there are no longer to blame for it; the culture has a rampant life of its own.

The defeatism and callousness—or call them impotence and cruelty—are most easily read in the cartoons. (Incidentally, a great virtue is that the magazine can be read in one minute—just the cartoons; five minutes—cartoons and Talk of the Town; fifteen minutes—add the play reviews; several hours—throw in the rest.) Others may not see these qualities in the jokes I shall give, but I am more often saddened than exhilarated by *New Yorker* jokes unless they are Arno's.

Thus in a barroom fight: "Go pick on someone your own size. I'm wearing elevator shoes." Or a sign painter indoors finishes an "Exit" sign that happens to be pointing toward the window, puts on his hat and walks through the window. Or a wife snarls at her sick, bedded husband: "You called, Master?" Or a suburbanite, glancing at a melting snowman on his lawn, notices a human hand emerging. Or a cruise tourist worried about the pay-later plan joins the native boys to dive for pennies thrown by the other tourists. Or a broadcaster, just fired by his sponsor, tells the TV audience ". . . typical of the Strobolene approach. . . . And heaven knows what harm their cheap lubricant does to your car." Or an executive says to a man peeking over the edge of the desk, "Bascomb, why don't you come back when you have more courage?" Or a sultan, surveying an empty harem, says, "One day they all up and left me. The whole kit and caboodle."

Most comedy anywhere is based on the fat man falling down, but *The New Yorker* makes him unnaturally impotent first and then trips him up when he feels perfectly safe or superbly angry or sedately amorous or already flat on his face. The comedy is more or less existentialist: defeat is the only destiny; man is a cockroach with false teeth and a truss. The fiendishness is repeated in some of the stories and gets a college try from Wolcott Gibbs' play reviews which suffer from a do-it-yourself understatement and owe the word "captious" a long rest in Nassau.

The fiendishness is offset by the very gentle Talk of the Town and a run of stories that can only be identified with the *Reader's Digest*'s unsophisticated fixture The Most Unforgettable Character I've Met. This is usually a memoir of an elderly relative of the writer, or the writer herself in a more youthful phase in Beirut, Old Cracow, Philadelphia, or the Bronx. This stuff seems to demand total recall, but is inexhaustible.

Talk of the Town brings up E. B. White and James Thurber, *The New Yorker*'s two greatest practitioners. Between them they made the magazine what Ross really wanted: a therapy for neurotics who make up most of its circulation. White gave them his limpid sanity and his love of New York. Thurber gave them detailed proof of terrible feelings and fantasies, beside which their own paled into laughter. The secret of *The New Yorker* is that Ross had recognized his friends as neurotics and himself as their physician. The boorish manner was meant to have a bracing effect.

But the analyst died, and the 415,000 patients were left staring at naked defeat, impotence, and cruelty. Now look at the current jokes again. Their common trait is that one cannot imagine any possible sequel for the character *as given.* They present neurotic, or insoluble, situations; something has been added, or left out, to take them out of real life. Anybody can find one woman to replace another, but how can the sultan find even one, not to speak of twenty, if twenty rejected him? How can the man who could only peep over the edge of the boss's desk carry on any sort of business relationship?

To redefine sophistication, a healthy ego thinks he is superior to other people because his bits of experience and knowledge are the key bits. But *New Yorker* characters believe that their data are worthless. Thus, after *The New Yorker* has told its readers how to judge wines, it will run a cartoon of a suburban lady offering a wine with the tag derogation, "Its pretentiousness may amuse you." This brutality is fine in the hands of a good psychiatrist, but. . . . The audience is regarded as literally on the couch.

Several *New Yorker* campaigns have been fought against other people's "captive audiences," yet it treats its own as utterly captive. It will devote to a single piece a half, two-thirds, or all of one issue. In that of December 1, 1956, fully half the editorial words were given to a story and a memoir, both very good once you got into them: one cruel and defeatist, the other hopeful. Over two hundred pages of the issue were editorial and advertising mixed, doing a selling job. The editorial heartland of the issue—that is, editorial text without advertising—was only nineteen pages long. By contrast, *Town and Country* runs a solid block of forty-five to sixty editorial pages, *Vogue* the same or more.

Sophistication really breaks loose in *New Yorker* advertising. "Onward and Upward with the Lower Montgomery Olive or Onion Society"—a vermouth. A picture sequence is captioned: "This is a Dry Martini Olive—going down the Throat of—a Man who is Celebrating—the new Shave Lotion—that's dry as a Martini—and Just as Bracing!" "It's not as if we were going to call the law on you if you want to drink akvavit and tonic. . . . We're grateful if you buy a bottle. Buy two and use them for bookends"—akvavit. "If you like your ostentation undiluted . . ."—a tape recorder. "The Lord St. Audries writes . . ."—a cummerbund. Much of the writing, it may be noted, is defeatist—in the advertising yet! The futility of it all is developed by the existentialist poses of the models, part Dali, part ballet, part burlesqued Victorian portraiture. Women crouch under tables, men look up the barrels of rifles, everybody stares blankly. Often, on the wall behind the dry Martinis, is a gun collection—a dangerous combination for neurotics.

What has been described here is *The New Yorker's* inner dynamic, the culture in the laboratory bottle. It is all denied by the occasional highly intelligent writer, like Liebling, who ignores all the little psychiatric games and acts himself.

A juvenile sophisticated magazine coming up fast behind *The New Yorker* is a comic book called MAD which carries this fashionable mode of impotence and cruelty to a conclusion. Once children start reading it, they throw away all other comics, for MAD is an all-out satire on all other comics, printed and human. The draughtsmanship is extraordinarily good. In one issue a bludgeon job is done on Elvis Presley, Gunsmoke (my favorite radio program), Hollywood, mice, traffic police, bowling, Moby Dick, pulp magazines, and Disney. The effect is indescribable and to me distasteful—*The New Yorker* essence is too concentrated. The whole idea is implicit in an advice-department item. The problem is that the man loves to stuff birds, but also loves his wife who hates his stuffed birds. The advice, illustrated in awful detail: stuff your wife. The cover shows a gaptoothed boy, MAD's candidate for President; the back cover shows him, logically, from the rear, looking out at an audience of celebrities. He has big ears. MAD's circulation is reported at about 500,000.

Women's magazines (overlooking *The Bride's Magazine*, in deference to the unsophisticated groom) are not sophisticated at all in their readers' frantic desire to be told what will make them beautiful and chic. Yet V*ogue* and *Harper's Bazaar*, as well as *Glamour* and *Mademoiselle*, regularly publish very superior material as well as the prize short stories of the year.

The models must be described. A little while ago they were all gaunt, blaze-mouthed, narrow-headed girls with aimed nostrils. But *Mademoiselle*'s models, presumably college girls, showed their teeth, as if while beauty kept its mouth shut, eager intelligence kept it slightly open. Lately more and more of the models are showing their teeth, and a successful search is on for the Garbo type, which is slightly more brachycephalic.

The writing, too—"strange and wonderful," "flattering as mascara," "raffish jewelry," "demurely delicious," "precise elegance"— has lately undergone a change. It suffered from the need to get into a high key too quickly, assuming a reader so hysterical that such word combinations sent her instantly into a swoon of precious delight. Lately the sophisticated women's magazines have lowered their key close to plain talk. They can be read with great profit by a curious man. *Vogue* in its Spotlight and People Are Talking About tells you what, if you are already sophisticated, you are already talking about. This is really a kindly service.

Asking forgiveness, I must note that one associate of Frank Crowninshield's is still at *Vogue*, having bowed under the tidal waves of exquisite new words, having seen them all pass from Robert Benchley to Clare Boothe, and still kept her poise and continued to live in Brooklyn. I believe that the Crowninshield values are still high style in this field. Crowninshield either meant exactly what he said or very clearly didn't mean what he said.

In approaching the sophisticated men's magazines, I have to transit by way of the quarterly *Gentry*, which gives out no circulation figures but is probably under 100,000. It is a male attempt to replace the late *Flair* in the same—or modified—lavish portfolio style of fold-out art, paste-ups, curiosa, and almost anything one wouldn't normally run across. The first effect is of a convulsion of sophistication like a catalepsy. For example, there are Matisse cutout pictures of his old age, a handbill by Topolski, and a booklet of Fredenthal's sketches of Toscanini from a radio station soundbooth. But there is also a lot of solid stuff: Ring Lardner, Thomas Eakins, Kipling, Somerset Maugham on Henry James, and the last photographs of the defunct Weehawken Ferry. The editors seem to know that if you're looking for oddities, reality is the best place to look. *Gentry* is in constant danger of leaving the planet but never quite does it. After it has worn out its conversation-piece welcome, there is something more, I am glad to report. It costs two dollars a copy.

Esquire is too well known to need description. Rejecting *The New Yorker*'s impotence while keeping the cruelty (it officially hates women), it is doing very well at 778,000 circulation. Its format is essentially that of the old *Vanity Fair*, vulgarized by locker-room jokes, naked women, and a somewhat uncrystallized editorial policy.

The recent phenomenon of the sophistication business is *Playboy*, which has moved in a year from 393,000 circulation to a claimed million, and is still moving. Starting bawdily and naïvely, it has grown progressively subtler, having lately taken on A. C. Spectorsky, author of *The Exurbanites* and demonstrably one of the most sophisticated editors in the United States. A lot of young men, mostly college boys and G.I.s, were obviously just waiting for it.

The clue to its appeal, really very sophisticated, is to be read in the monthly foldout naked girl. Instead of being an unattainable and in that sense undesirable mannequin, as in *Esquire*, she is the girl next door or at the next desk with her clothes off and looking very well, thank you. One month the naked girl was the lady author of a story in the magazine.

As a male writer, I must protest unfair competition, but as an editor I must applaud a brand-new invention in eroticism which grew out of the free-wheeling, ebullient attitude of the editors. Essentially, *Playboy*'s subject is mating. But it likes to have fun with it, as in a touching love story of a pair of whales. It has its sights firmly fixed not on the outdoor man, but on a strictly indoor man (if not an indoor whale). Ruggedness is to be directed where it will do the most good to perpetuate the race. Sophistication here is primarily sexual, yet this is a subject on which, unlike the subjects of *Vogue* and *Harper's Bazaar*, nobody can really instruct anybody else. It is a treacherous subject, and I get the feeling that *Playboy* is trying to switch its readers to some firmer ground.

In this superficial survey I have omitted such specialized productions as *The Bride's Magazine, Gourmet, The Saturday Review, House and Garden, Theatre Arts,* and the admirably produced travel specialist *Holiday,* which does mankind the favor of disseminating

Perelman and Bemelmans. The place to end is with the most sophisticated and most indifferent magazine of them all, *Town and Country* (circulation: 1933, 16,000; 1956, 72,000). This and *The New Yorker* are the only general sophisticated magazines of today that existed in 1933.

Town and Country exudes such a tone of upper class that for a moment I was credulous when I read of a man who had been given for Christmas a diamond-set alpenstock when his wife could have had for less money what he really wanted: the Philadelphia Athletics. My credulity was not shameful because the issue of January, 1957, describes Venice, where the Communist poor really love the rich and in society one never introduces two people until one has privately asked them whether they want to be introduced. Nobody there reads the newspapers, and the only title of consequence is not Prince but *Nobil Homo* or *Nobil Donna*, the old Venetian titles. One should really dress (black tie) to read this. True, we also have to inspect Miami, Palm Beach, and Fort Lauderdale, but this magazine sells around 45 per cent of its pages to advertisers (more than *McCall's*) at a far higher rate per thousand of circulation.

The really interesting question is how many more or less sophisticated people, or aspirants, there are today in the United States. Adding the circulation of the magazines noted here, and excluding *MAD* as well as the other equally sophisticated magazines not reviewed, the total is over four million. The exclusions must certainly more than equal the duplications. Using the formula invented by Time Inc., one must multiply that figure by five (for readers of a single copy) to arrive at more than twenty million Americans who at least aspire to being sophisticated. I find this a formidable, instructive, and hopeful fact for America, even knowing that deadly serious people will reproach me for my frivolity.

If the vogue of sophistication is indeed on the rise, one can say it had to come: the mass life was too boring to last. But in the sophistications briefly examined here, one finds a repeated flaw. Each has a fixed attitude, a formula, a style from which nothing in the magazine can vary. As Malcolm Muggeridge wrote in *Time and Tide*: "I, or any other practicing journalist, can tell at a glance whether an article is suitable for this or that magazine." On such a system, sophistication will become as boring as mass conformism, in fact only a narrower sort of conformism. *The New Yorker* gives us an example, to everyone's great regret.

A fixed attitude exposed to life does not know how to survive. What all the sophisticated magazines need is something unexpected, something not in the prospectus.

The Gossip Columnists
(1956)

Every period wants intensely to know about its most interesting people, but all too often does not know who they are. Molière, for example, made the revolutionary discovery that in his time the ambitious bourgeoisie was far more interesting than the nobility; later and duller writers discovered the proletariat and peasantry; others have rediscovered miscellaneous aristocracies of wealth, power, sensibility, or mere decadence. Fortunes are made and lost in the search for the people who are, simply, interesting.

The syndicated gossip columnists of the current American press have this same old problem. Their solutions are the matter of this survey.

It is only fair to point out that Molière and Proust were not bound by some of the limitations imposed on the gossip columnist. A daily column of gossip is impossible for one human being to produce; but it is easy to compose it from the mail. Thus the columnist, by and large, must accept a cast of characters given him by companies and restaurants who hire press agents. Because most columns originate in New York City, the restaurants will be New York restaurants (or Miami Beach or Las Vegas). Secondly, the characters named must be presold or known at least by name to some fifty million people.

Who are these characters? Without wishing to put into this subject any more scholarship than it can safely stand, I have compiled categories of items for seven columnists, using three columns for each in the waning summer of 1956. If anyone is dissatisfied with the exhaustiveness of this monumental public service, I can only plead that it marks the absolute limit of my industry. The conclusions are presented on this page in tabular form. This table will blaze the trail for later and more conscientious workers in this overgrown field.

	Walter Winchell	Lee Mortimer	Ed Sullivan	Leonard Lyons	Frank Farrell	Dorothy Kilgallen	Bob Sylvester	Totals
Movie personages	12	5	33	11	10	15	9	95
Theater and night clubs	15	14	12	14	12	14	8	89
TV-radio personages	15	3	5	9	6	4	5	47
Society (including royalty)	1	5	15	8	3	6	..	38
Monaco	3	1	..	..	1	1	..	6
The Press	12	2	10	2	..	1	1	28
Athletes	4	4	6	5	1	4	2	26
Homosexuals	..	2	..	..	..	2	..	4
Law enforcers	5	1	3	..	..	1	..	10
Restaurant plugs	8	8	..	1	1	4	13	35
Slams at Democrats and Republican plugs	6	6	..	..	1	1	..	14
Records and ASCAP	7	1	9	2	4	5	7	35
Models	1	1	..	..	1	..	2	5
Writers	3	3	1	4	..	3	..	14
Unidentified and unknown	1	5	2	..	1	1	3	13

The table holds bad news for the intellectually somnolent. It cannot be read in one fast glance; the revelations embedded are too ramified even for full exploration here. Offhand, it would seem that movie, theater and night-club characters are the most fascinating people in America today. If true, this is a sorry indictment.

Actually, the high scores for this group derive from the columnists who work primarily from the mail: Sullivan and Kilgallen. These two do not stay up late much any more. Because they draw their main income from TV-radio, they rarely refer to their airwave competitors except sneeringly. Sullivan as a "performer" needs both show-business people and the press; his scores reflect the need. What he expects of society must have some simple explanation.

Winchell and Lyons obviously show the best balance, the most subtle and professional grasp of news interest; Sullivan is the most cursory, imbalanced, and generally amateurish. Winchell doesn't need anybody now. He has an antique habit of helping obscure people in show business whenever he can.

Sylvester, Farrell, and Lyons just get around. Sylvester seems to like the jive joints; Farrell is almost social in his wanderings; Lyons is almost literary, if one can count press agents and gag-writers in this profession (the former become the latter). These three represent a new type of columnist, indicating their editors' uncertainty about the old cast of gossip characters. They are essentially and ingratiatingly "guys on the make," minor characters in their own right. They tell true gossip, conceived as a small dramatic episode, joke, or memoir, rather than a bare juxtaposition of a male and a female name.

From the best sources I have a list of the New York saloons currently frequented by these people. The information should interest anybody who wants to get mentioned; it should be priceless to anybody who doesn't.

Winchell: Lindy's (comedians, gag-writers); Reuben's (miscellaneous); El Morocco (society, models, wolves).

Mortimer: El Morocco.

Sullivan: Le Pavillon (the Windsor set).

Lyons: Toots Shor (journalists, athletes); Lindy's.

Farrell: Weylin Bar (café society); El Morocco.

Kilgallen: Stork Club (advertising).

Sylvester: Toots Shor, Fourth Estate (fourth estate).

Only one or two of the columnists overdrink; several can't drink liquor at all.

Before we proceed to the subjects of American gossip, let us finish off the columnists.

Kilgallen. Her frank malevolence was at its best in her reporting on the Monaco wedding when she drew attention to the line of Grace's thigh, Rainier's titter-making medals, and Mrs. Kelly's "strutting" down the aisle of the cathedral. Kilgallen resembles a silly girl practicing to turn into an old witch, a sort of fangless Louella Parsons. Enough.

Sullivan. His malevolence is almost buried from sight beneath an awesome dullness and ambition. His current series in *Collier's* opened with a panegyric to the modesty of "the truly great ones," among whom he numbered John Jacob Astor II, Winthrop Rockefeller, Jack Dempsey, and Eddie Arcaro. By great, Sullivan means useful to him.

On the other hand show business, which has a long memory, has not forgotten that Sullivan has not often helped struggling performers with a good word at the critical moment. On occasion, in his powerless days, he often did his best to destroy the powerless and vulnerable performer.

Sullivan has a sound political sense of how to prove out his power, corresponding to his knowledge of whom to fawn on. He also has a reliable trick of inventing a feud in his column with a performer whom he wants on disadvantageous terms on his TV show. He has carried on noteworthy feuds with Kate Smith, Joe E. Brown, Frank Sinatra, Joan Crawford, and Gwen Verdon. Because the rest of the press fall for it, it usually works the way Sullivan planned it. The leverage he can apply to people in show business draws him magnetically, as if he were saying aloud, "How long has this been going on?"

The Sullivan face, a coconut with expression, has probably been more frequently insulted than any other in New York. In the old days Pegler, Broun, Frank Sullivan, and Jim Moriarty could not stand him; yet he boasts in his *Collier's* series that the friend of all these, Mike Romanoff, regularly sponged off him. I haven't the time or money to disprove this, but I don't believe it. In the same paragraph, Sullivan puts Winthrop Rockefeller in El Morocco when the boy was at Loomis School and Yale on a sharply limited allowance.

Sullivan's ignominious lust for power on the TV stage sets him apart from real show-business people, who when successful think themselves only lucky. As he levers and savagely defends his power, he is not above asking how he could just possibly parlay it, if things fell just so, into being President or Pope. His toadies have strange tales to tell of his ambition.

Negatively, the ambition comes clear in the story of the little TV repairman in upstate New York who made so bold as to paint on his shop front the name "Ed Sullivan TV." The little man's name was Ed Sullivan. The "great" Ed S. promptly sued the little Ed S.

Positively, the Sullivan afflatus can be read in his very recent public rumination on whether he, Sullivan, should forgive Ingrid Bergman for a seven-year-old adultery since regularized by marriage. Because Sullivan is not a priest, one must imagine that the thought gave him a titillation which he wanted to prolong and exploit.

Ingrid had flatly refused to appear on his show even before he invited his listeners to vote on forgiving her so far as to let her.

In case Jesus Christ's comment had not sufficiently covered the situation, a Catholic priest said:

I have never heard anything quite like it. It was distasteful to make a public issue of something that actually is between a person and her God. It is not the prerogative of the public to absolve or condemn an individual's action. Is Sullivan the one to say there have been seven and a half years of penance? . . . Miss Bergman's actions so shockingly exposed again by Sullivan are not public actions to be publicly chastised or condoned, or even forgiven in this mass whimsical fashion. . . . Only God can judge, not a popularity contest in which a public will vote against sin or for sin or whatever way Sullivan wishes to approach the matter for the sake of the program. . . . No matter what the vote of his audience might be, it cannot justify Sullivan throwing the first, nor the last stone. . . .

This admirable statement was quoted in the New York *Journal-American* TV volumn of Jack O'Brian, who loathes Sullivan as only one Irishman can loathe another. It helped inspire the typical Sullivan weasel: "The public voted 50–50." Ingrid Bergman was an especially ill-chosen Sullivan victim because she was always a Hollywood phenomenon: a truly moral woman who actually believed in love.

Winchell. By contrast, there is Walter Winchell, who created the modern general gossip column (but certainly not gossip, or the invasion of the American citizen's privacy). His recent return to action, after a vacation filled in by Mortimer, showed again what a professional of honor can do. Part of his strength comes from the fact that over the years he has given the timely hurrah to thousands of struggling members of show business when they needed it badly. He is known for never asking for any return for such notices; he often does not remember the talented people he has helped. He has no designs on the beautiful females among them. These people, many now famous, remember.

Winchell's gossip frequently exhibits the mark of a gentleman and a magnanimous man. When Louella Parsons was crowing that Rita Hayworth had become pregnant before her marriage to the Aly Khan, Winchell commented: "Gents'-room journalism." His imitators have unfortunately not noticed his decency in such matters.

Winchell's political sense, a sadder story, is bounded by his past admirations for the mob executive Frank Costello, and Joe Mc-Carthy, Sherman Billingsley and (the only one still in favor) J. Edgar Hoover. These smooth, tough gentlemen have impressed him the way Davy Crockett awes a small boy. He is of course on the Eisenhower bandwagon, but it should be remembered that he loved the elder Roosevelt and has never betrayed the great cripple.

He is about to take on a TV show. As usual, he is full of ideas, most of which NBC has turned down. But it will be a good show and might even put Sullivan off the air.

Lee Mortimer. Winchell's understudy is a limp and exhausted wraith seen only in a night-club haze, slumped over a table in an aristocratic droop. Despite his name, Lee is not a member of the great, extinct English house of Mortimer, whose name meant Sea Death. His own best gossip columns made the important discovery that a whole column about one trivial light woman might be more interesting than twenty items about twenty light women. These pieces about people named Candy Rococo seemed to promise something. However, under Mortimer, they died.

As Winchell's replacement, he unconsciously tried to destroy Winchell's livelihood by parading his own weariness with it. Thus: "Not Much of This and Absolutely Nothing of That"; "Was that whosis with so-and-so? (Only asking, I don't care.)"; "Last Week's Hot Nothings This Week"; "Little of This, Much Less of That";

"Times Square Trivia (And is it trivial!)"; "Little of That, Less of Nothing"; "Today's (or maybe it was yesterday's) John Jacob Astor item"; "I don't believe this item either but it fills space."

He has not been himself since the death of Jack Lait (the late Lait Show) who collaborated with him on the "Confidential" books based on information assembled from such reliable sources as deteriorated whores and cashiered cops. When I meet so much slander and hate, I want to know what the authors defend and love. Jack Lait, in a column in the New York *Mirror* of June 21, 1952, defended what he and Mortimer loved:

> Though he is a rascal, I get a twinge in my heart. . . . For I knew him long and well, during his big days, when he was the boss of Atlantic City, the supreme monarch in a glamorous domain. They broke him, the only big shot who was sent to the penitentiary by the New Dealers. [This term is invective.] Of course he was a Republican. He lived like an emperor. . . . He was a millionaire and spent like one. He gave to established charities as well as bums and hustlers, and he entertained in a fabulous three-story night club he had set up for a famous favorite. . . . Johnson had a unique understanding with the gangsters of the nation. . . . Guns were checked, feuds were suspended, murderous deals were made—but to be consummated elsewhere. . . .

The love object is Enoch ("Nucky") Johnson of Atlantic City, whose money came mostly from houses of prostitution. He frequently, while sitting at the table with ladies, imperially micturated without moving from his place. He gloried in cruelty and scatology.

Of good old Nucky, Lait finishes: "And now he is broke and broken, and if he wanders beside the surf with the loyal woman who married him when he was in his declension, only a handful of the aging faithful raise their hats to this toppled ruler. . . ." Boo-hoo.

As late as August 29, 1956, Mortimer's column awoke an echo of the beloved old Philadelphia-Atlantic-City midway with a salute to the night-club man who later married the "favorite," unnecessarily referred to by Lait, thus: "The most distinguished host on earth is Philly's 'Smiling' Jack Lynch. . . ." The title itself means nothing: Mortimer bestows it liberally on those douzepers of the night, Julie Podell of the Copacabana, Lou Walters of the Latin Quarter, and so on, and so on. The interest here is in where the bodies are buried and Mortimer's heart lies. Sea Death comes home appropriately to Atlantic City, so like the Norman coast where the name originated.

Sylvester. Bob Sylvester, along with Leonard Lyons and Frank Farrell, represents a new sort of columnist. Sylvester, the most interesting to me, is as refreshing as the New York *Post's* sportswriter, Jimmy Cannon. He is the New York *News'* hidden ace, along with the similar McHarry, in case of Sullivan's final desuetude.

Lyons. Leonard Lyons is clever and readable; I am sorry I do not like him better since he is at least a Democrat. His fellow customers at Toots Shor's and Lindy's ought to be amusing; they are journalists, comedians, and ballplayers. A recent column about a conversation among Hemingway, Jackie Gleason, and somebody else was meant to make a hero of Hemingway and was only embarrassing. Apparently a column about saloon life can make heroes of ballplayers but not of writers. Lyons gives one the feeling of a bright New York high-school boy amazing his English teacher. His fault is the opposite of Mortimer's. He is too sincere. Describing his world of hardened extroverts, he turns them all into introverts. They all prove to have souls and heavily oxidized ironies. The amorphous society that Winchell evokes does not take shape in Lyons.

So much for the gossips; now what of their subjects?

The most dramatic subjects are handsome young women whose pictures are on file in every American newspaper office. Yet it should be noted that the girls and women of show business probably have less sex life than the normal woman of thirty-five. Since they tend to exaggerate the importance of their favors, they are more moral than office girls. Hence most of the supposed sex life in the columns is strictly imaginary. Very sad, but very true.

Linda Christian has given us a serial story of some interest: the nude statue of herself given to her husband; the divorce; the gift of jewels by a playboy who hadn't paid for them; the fine settlement out of court; and now a canvassing of the English talent. Bobo Rockefeller, by doing the mambo in the right places, moved in on, and out from, the most amiable member of a millionaire family. For men who can afford it, it must be a pleasant sport to make famous their taste in women. The Texan, Sheppard, made his name with an Egyptian belly-dancer.

Grateful as we must be for these little stories, they are too ephemeral and lead to the question: "Whatever became of . . . ?" What is wanted are stories in which the bride and groom are both somebody, preferably not too rich. The Miller-Monroe wedding and the Monaco wedding seem to me honorable examples of such stories.

The current fashion is to regard anyone with an astounding mammary development as of intense news interest. Russell, Dagmar, Lollobrigida, Diana Dors, Jayne Mansfield, and so on, come and go, and some have talent. Jayne Mansfield is a natural. She has a bust and a wrestler, and the public is terrified to think what would happen if they met. The wrestler was publicized as a coward; but the bust is not.

The beautiful girls lose some of their drama when they marry; they regain it at the divorce.

The useful men are mostly young actors or hopelessly neurotic middle-aged ones. Most genuinely famous men are too old, rich or well married to be tampered with by gossip columnists. A fascinating man like Arthur Vining Davis can well defend himself. Apart from a few youths who inherited fame and wealth, the non-acting Romeos of the columns are generally faceless, identified as related to somebody else who is known. The ones with faces—Tommy Manville, John Jacob Astor, George Jessel, Billy Rose—are far from satisfactory either.

The great reliable geniuses at living like John Barrymore, Sr., Tallulah Bankhead, Marlene Dietrich, endow the press with a hundred million dollars' worth of public interest. The press is bankrupted when a John Barrymore dies. If it made any collective sense, it would have subsidized Barrymore and propped him up for a few more years, a few more editions. America has fewer and fewer of these figures who have given great energy to engraving themselves indelibly on the public mind.

As the great and gaudy characters have faded from the American scene, the gossip columnists have had to find somebody else whom they could honestly regard as the most fascinating people in America. They now and then betray their newest discovery. It is themselves.

Down with the Other Sex
(1958)

The relations between the sexes, even in those countries where the two are legally equal, are still attended with much pleasure, profit, and nourishment. Or so one would suppose, until one looked at the American women's magazines, and then at the men's magazines. In the women's magazines, one finds a world, infinitely real in its details but wholly imaginary in the large, which is run entirely by females, smug and miserable. In the men's magazines, these particular women do not even make an appearance; instead, the men are either out shooting polar bears or kicking Miss America out of bed.

Try as I will, I cannot organize these two worlds into one normal, heterosexual society. If I accept them both literally, the husbands and lovers in the women's magazines must be ghosts; and the houris and polar bears in the men's magazines are ghosts too. The two worlds are dream worlds in a dichotomy accepted by about half the population of the United States. Since dreams are always sacred, this is war.

The above sentence might be only the old cliché joke, were it not backed by some billions of dollars and the deep submarine tides of suppressed feelings in forty million homes.

The *Ladies' Home Journal* has been running a series of ads to prove that women do all the retail buying; the men in the ads are hopeless simps.

True, a men's magazine, is running a countercampaign asserting that it will be god-damned if women choose the brand of shaving cream, beer, whisky, shirt, tire, insurance, and so on.

Lady columnists have commented to this latter, "O.K., but don't crowd your luck."

And then, in October, 1957, came *Playboy*, showing claws, with the message that the big women's magazines are loaded with morbid pornography—how to arouse your impotent husband, how to stand off your hungry husband, and so on. *Playboy* gave chapter and verse to prove it. I don't think much of the argument, but I know blood when I smell it. And I don't feel that either antagonist has even begun to fight.

It is war, all right, and a truly shocking war. For it pretends to divide the population of this country into two great "homosexual" groups—homosexual only in its basic sense of "same sex"—that turn their backs on the reality of each other and sate their egos with unprofitable ghosts, in some way compensatory for the failures of the opposite number who reads the other magazines. Don't cry yet; this gets worse.

This sexual-social dichotomy is not entirely unfamiliar. In fact it reproduces the old-fashioned American middle-class party where the women and men huddled in separate groups, the individual thus confirming her or his status as one of the girls or boys. The expression of nonadulterous interest in a person of the opposite sex was impossible, because nobody would have believed in it.

This is the same cold war of the sexes conducted by the magazines, as distinguished from the hot and healthy heterosexual war. The cold war is Puritan or, on its other face, *roué*. It tries, even if not always successfully, to block a normal fearless exchange of affection. The two group-thinks, or party lines, are sick. The healthy individual must make his own way, in constant peril of running into a card-carrying party member in disguise.

The women's magazines typically—*McCall's, Ladies' Home Journal, Good Housekeeping, Household, Family Circle, Woman's Day, Everywoman's*—address a woman in a home, which also includes an adult male and some junior males. The woman, however, is larger than life, like a queen bee; the others are minuscule. The woman of course buys everything used in the house; the husband has the function of Her Majesty's Loyal Opposition, but without power; the chief end of it all is to keep The Government happy and the rabble quiet.

It may be coincidence, but in the stories the husband is impotent—and not only sexually. He just can't solve *any* problem. A *Ladies' Home Journal* serial (October–November) presents a husband who is utterly impotent to defeat a vengeful lunatic who sets out to rape and murder the husband's whole family. (This situation, very scary if taken on its face, falls apart under sensible analysis.) Another, in *McCall's* (September), has a husband virile enough to knock down another man, but he isn't subtle enough to see through the other's widow and murderous sister-in-law. His wife has to do it all.

Not only men, but all human culture, is judged on its assimilability by the American wife. Thus in the October *McCall's*, a story character actually says, "The man who put the first automatic washer on the market did more to further the cause of art than a whole generation of painters . . . gave leisure to millions of women so they could" [pursue the arts]. My own leisure doesn't help painting any; and I doubt whether a billion idle women will do it any good either; in fact a dozen or so of those wives may ruin husbands who might have done the arts some good.

Of course, besides being a genius as required, the wife learns in the women's magazines a great many things relevant to the home. These call themselves "service books" and are in fact that. They give innumerable tested and useful instructions on cooking, decoration, child rearing, housekeeping, dressmaking or dress buying, and gardening.

I have noticed, in the real world, that a woman does not live who is so degraded as not to think herself an expert on style, interior decoration, fashion (and usually gardening). Since the temperament of a genuinely feminine wife and mother is geared toward almost anything except a disinterested grasp of aesthetics, this claim provides one of the great running entertainments in life for men of taste. I have known three or four women who had real taste; the others have never paid any attention to my aesthetic opinions, to my great relief.

It would be suicidal to tell a woman that taste—the province of the women's magazines—is secondary, and a reflection of a view of life. There are many views of life that can produce an impeccable perfection—Assyrian, Gothic, the Adam brothers, Incan, Grand Rapids, if you know what you believe in and follow it through; in that case, you can even combine several styles. But a successful wife's point of view is the antithesis of aesthetic; and yet she has this manic delusion.

Therefore the women's magazines, whose editors know all this very well, must dispense advice on taste that is not exactly wrong; it is just nothing, except for an occasional accident. If you walk into a house that has been interestingly arranged without professional help, you have found a husband who participates in the family decisions, not a wife who reads the women's magazines.

We have veered from the magazine myth to reality, and here the women themselves know better than the magazine. (The magazine is only selling advertising, remember? Women Buy Everything.) Real women, fortunately, are fascinated by what real men think. This fascination, battered by the magazine propaganda, may be on the decline, but enough remains to be measured. Women are incredulous but fascinated to discover that a man can be so serious about a baseball team that he has to see the game on TV, even though his children are deprived. Women know very clearly what they are serious about—an area as sensible as it is limited. Their entertainment in life is to pry into the things men are serious about, especially when their comment is: "Crazy!"

As opposed to this reality, the September *Ladies' Home Journal* gave the successful wife a test: Does your husband (1) go along with your decisions? (2) confide in you in most things? (3) compromise rather than argue strongly?

Certainly the *Journal*'s advertising manager wants husbands whose wives can answer Yes to all three questions. But in fact I can hardly think of a successful husband, of the husbands I have known, who plays the game the *Journal*'s way, though a good many try to give that impression. Most husbands try to give the cues long before they come to "decision," "confession," or the need to "argue strongly." Let us draw the curtain on these last terrible scenes, where the *Ladies'* editorial policies spatter the wall-to-wall carpeting with suburban blood. The husband's, of course.

The pretensions of the women's magazines reached a small climax in October when *McCall's* assembled one hundred American wives for a "Congress on Better Living" in Washington, D.C. The first releases called it a "crusade," "unique probe," "completely uninhibited exposé." The ensuing revolutionary manifesto turned out to be a plaintive preference for bigger homes, smaller cars, bigger kitchens, dishwashers, more closets, more electric outlets, double beds, more fireplaces, and please stop calling us "housewives." The simple ladies finally blew up *McCall's* basic premise by confiding shyly that their husbands have a big say in the buying of everything, and even go shopping for home furnishings. The husbands cannot stand paper napkins and soft mattresses.

Like the healthy ladies in Washington, at least one women's magazine seems to submit to the winds of heterosexual reality. *Good Housekeeping* evidently does not despise men; the November issue even has an article, "I Am a Man Fan," which admires men because they like life simple and to the point. *Good Housekeeping* is in general edited without the irritating female braggadocio noticed elsewhere.

The readers of the men's magazines are divided by much more than sex from the readers of the women's magazines. The most astonishing difference, if the magazines reflect the readers' lives, is that these men are homeless.

The readers of *True* (2,228,000), *Argosy* (1,446,000), *Saga* (474,-000), *Cavalier* (352,000), *For Men Only* (315,000) *et al.*, evidently live off the land in the jungle or bush, or on the veldt, range or icecap, and spend their lives gun fighting, smuggling, pearl diving, detecting, and hunting and fishing for uniquely large and terrifying game. (The straight outdoors magazines make hardly any effort to be this exciting.)

The readers of the next group, typified by *Sir* (344,000), are equally homeless. They can still read, but their hearts lie in whorehouse life, harem slave markets, vice in ancient Rome, the leavings of Kinsey, crazy psychiatrists, speedways, and strip-tease joints. A tragic note is struck by the advertisements: "All Lonely Men! Regardless of Age!", "If You Are Lonesome," "Why Be Lonely?", "Tryst for Love."

After these, for readers who have completely given up on the printed word, are the naked-women magazines. But here it may be said that it is curiously difficult to be neurotic with pictures.

The readers of *Playboy* (circulation not given, but over 1,000,000) seem to inhabit a quite literate girl trap (but girls knew about traps before wolverines did) where an occasional omelette or casserole is whipped up and the hi-fi rolls on above the shrieks of love.

The common denominator of them all is guns and fast cars. The readers do not seem to need advice on how to shave or shine their shoes or clean up the place or—God forbid—garden. All they want to be told is: men are terrific.

A strange exception to the homelessness is found in *Esquire* (846,-000). In its recent, rather inscrutable, evolution, the naked-girl foldout has vanished, and the reader is somebody like Dave Garroway, Steve Allen, or Clifton Fadiman, with a library, wine cellar, hi-fi, sports car, and possibly even a wife and children. In the December issue are fifteen pages of a new libretto by Menotti and some quaint parlor tricks to amuse the guests after dinner. Much of it actually debunks typical men's magazine material: Mae West, "sick jokes," Westbrook Pegler, and so on.

The advertising reveals, astonishingly, that there is something else women don't buy: their own perfume. Any cosmetics salesgirl will confirm this. Women are too cheap to buy their own perfume, and limit themselves to toilet water. All the perfume companies advertise in *Esquire*.

This is very far from *True*, where you are faced with sure death on every other page. Raw courage sees you through. Or you are annihilated. It would make ideal reading for the Three Hundred before Thermopylae, or Custer's last hour.

For the modern man, the repetition of the Super-Colossal Peril grows characteristically very tired. Every issue is obliged to have its Johnstown flood, Chicago fire, Galveston flood, San Francisco earthquake, and an article on how to kill somebody with your bare hands. The supply soon runs out and has the gratifying effect of sending these magazines into the history books and out into the whole wide world. The aim is still to exhaust the reader's adrenalin resources. If a reader ever got in a real jam, where he needed the adrenalin in a hurry, he would find himself drained. He would already have made his fight in *True*.

Occasionally a story reveals the characters as charging around stupidly and cravenly; I was amused to realize that this performance interested me. I felt superior and contemptuous: emotions anybody would pay for. Why not a new magazine called *Coward?*

Unfortunately, this demand seems to have been met in a crop of magazines called *True Men, Champ, Mr., Battle Cry, Man's Action,* and so on. A recent series in the New York *Daily News* characterized these as a threat to our military morale. Along with the strip-teasers and the general violence are accounts of drunken, brawling, and cowardly American servicemen. One article is titled: American Soldiers Have No Guts! Another article claimed that WACs below the rank of major are prostitutes reserved for officers and visiting congressmen. The GI is consistently labeled a slob, sucker, pig. The heroes are, of course, our former enemies; and in this not unprecedented phenomenon there is a touch of magnanimity, as coming from the victors. These magazines seem abominable slop, but they will pass.

It should be noted that most public libraries do not carry any of the men's magazines, even those devoid of naked women.

The women have thus won, for now, the magazine war of the sexes.

A great law of life is that it is binary, or dual, or biological. It runs on two rails. Certainly there are conflicts in the dual arrangements; but they are not solved by cowards who propose the marvelous solution of simply eliminating one contestant. Surely, in the end, the women's magazines cannot really win; they will only drive the men's magazines to yet wilder frenzies. And if a lot of women are miserable, the blame must be equally divided between the two propagandas.

The whole picture has its pathos.

The Mass Magazines
(1957)

A magnificent free course in magazine publishing has been running for the past three months in full-page newspaper ads (in New York, chiefly in the *Times* and *Herald Tribune*). It described, at something under $3,000 a page, how great America's big magazines are. Most of it was addressed to advertisers, not to you. Nevertheless, it will be a public service to capture this splendid panorama of the present moment in magazine publishing by synopsizing the major theme of each ad as it appeared day by day.

McCall's, February 19th: "Togetherness" for 5,000,000 women.

Time, February 21st: "I know, I ken, I can." *Time* knows and hence can.

Life, February 25th: Picture of baby and pony. "Priceless. Warm. Human. Advertisements that make a lasting impression." 5,740,000 circulation.

Good Housekeeping, February 25th: "Picture of health"—over 4,000,000 circulation.

Time, February 26th: Hey, advertisers, *Time* readers buy anything.

Saturday Evening Post, February 26th: "News brought *into focus*." 5,100,000.

McCall's, February 27th: Sequel to "The Day Lincoln Was Shot"—"The Day Christ Died." "Tumultuous action, doomed Roman empire, tragic interplay, destined conclusion . . . you are there." (Better than Lincoln.)

S.E.P., February 27th: 5,200,000. Leads at newsstands. Best-read.

Parade, March 4th: Man with high-waisted pants—"too much coverage above the waste line"—attack on a competitor.

Ladies' Home Journal, March 4th: "Women have a world of their own." 5,600,000.

Life, March 4th: "The deeper meaning." 5,740,000. "Advertisements that make a deep and lasting impression."

S.E.P., March 5th: "Doesn't rush mere facts, photos into print. Really big stories—Is Don Newcombe a quitter?"

Newsweek, March 6th: "Continuing Study of Capital Appropriations. For management, and com-mu-ni-ca-tive people."

Coronet, March 6th: New invention—"triple-action ad" (also issued as a throwaway).

Time, March 7th: Baby climbing bookcase. "The need to know. *Time* readers are a product of natural selection." (They don't fall off the bookcase?)

Newsweek, March 11th: For people who can spell com-mu-ni-ca-tive. 1,100,000. Tops in 50 biggest corporate ad campaigns.

Life, March 11th: Jolly man and dog. "Jolly. Advertisements that make a deep and lasting impression." 5,800,000.

McCall's, March 12th: Ad revenue up 27.8 per cent.

Ladies' Home Journal, March 13th: "Gentlemen, what's in the *Journal* is none of your business: . . . Has 'hers' stitched right on it." 5,600,000.

Pageant, March 13th: "H-bomb hits St. Louis and doesn't go off." Tough fighters, good lobsters, Appassionata von Climax, naked girls. Yippee. 98 per cent newsstand sales.

McCall's, March 14th: Same as March 12.

Good Housekeeping, March 19th: Skip this lesson—dull.

Ladies' Home Journal, March 20th: Advertisers got 7,044,302 bonus ladies (divided by twelve).

Time, March 20th: "Baffled, but resolved to know."

Life, March 21st: 6,000,000 soon.

Look, March 26th: *Look* likes people. Looks like more people: 5,000,000.

This Week, March 26th: "For a super era a super magazine." 12,000,000. Thirty-seven newspapers.

Newsweek, March 27th: Still spelling com-mu-ni-ca-tive.

Reader's Digest, March 28th: "R.D. readers own forty-two per cent of dishwashers. Over half are women." 11,000,000.

Ladies' Home Journal, April 1st: Still a woman's world. 5,600,000.

Time, April 3rd: Atoms? *Time* doesn't know, but knows ABOUT.

McCall's, April 3rd: The most, the most, the most. Ever!

And so on.

This sequence looks at first like a poker game, with bets being called and raised on circulations, the pot being of course advertising budgets. The actual situation is that four magazines have newly arrived in the 5,000,000-class. *Look* did it by paying a million dollars for defunct *Collier's* circulation. *McCall's* and, in part, *Ladies' Home Journal* did it by splitting about two million *Woman's Home Companion* (also defunct) paid-up subscriptions, after weeding out duplications. The *Post* just got there. Meanwhile, *Good Housekeeping* keeps murmuring reproachfully that "healthy, natural growth is better."

If *Look* can hold on to the *Collier's* readers, it will really bother

Life. If the two big women's magazines can hold theirs, they will win back some ground from TV advertising. The *Post* is claiming the more intelligent readers, *Life* the warmhearted ones. (Readers tend to grow more simple and warmhearted as they grow more numerous.)

But these full-page ads are not really waging a small, internecine war among the magazines (though this must be returned to). The real enemy in the wars of the Guelphs and Ghibellines is TV.

These two ghoulish capital letters have struck a terror into magazine publishers that seems almost insensate. TV's actual share of advertising revenue has become a nightmarish question. Using exactly the same figures (always excluding enormous TV discounts to advertisers), very different results are published. One has TV getting 15 per cent of all revenue, magazines 9 per cent. Another has TV and radio getting 25 per cent of revenue, all magazines an approximately equal amount. Another gives the actual figures for 1956: TV network gross time $488,000,000, TV spot $397,500,000; general and national farm magazines, $723,500,000. But the TV figures are less discounts and the magazine figures are not all-inclusive.

What scares the magazines is that TV revenues are on the rise and include big budgets from the biggest advertisers. For example, last year the biggest spenders on TV spot were Procter & Gamble, Brown & Williamson (Viceroy cigarettes), General Foods, Sterling Drugs, and Philip Morris, all accounts that the big magazines could use. A still unkinder cut is that the big advertising agencies have tended to give over 50 per cent of their clients' billing to TV, a percentage far above its "just" share. The agencies may be attracted by the huge profit margin in collecting a million-dollar commission on a $50,000 TV film commercial. But the big advertisers, who typically have a huge profit margin to play with, themselves encourage this crude approach to their problems.

The magazines naturally want to go over the agency's head directly to the advertiser, particularly with their argument against TV; that is, that TV can only entertain, not say anything. TV may be all right for advertisers who haven't much to say, like the soap and cigarette people, but not for anything more complex than A plus *B*. Furthermore, the argument goes, you can't take a second look at a TV commercial, or keep it around the house like a magazine advertisement. And thirdly, since the TV ad yells at the consumer, it is as likely to enrage as win him, whereas magazine ads lie there politely waiting.

The magazines' weakness rests in that obscenity of obscenities, "duplication." When the *Woman's Home Companion* subscriptions were combed over, it was found that one-tenth duplicated *McCall's* subscribers and another tenth the *Ladies' Home Journal* subscribers. One-twentieth of *Companion* readers had subscribed to all three magazines. This is 25 per cent duplication. Add the unknown duplication of *McCall's* and *Ladies' Home Journal*, and you have between a third and a half; add *Life* and the *Post*, and you may have nearly 100 per cent.

Advertisers recognize duplication by roughly dividing space between the women's and the general magazines; but there are not too many advertisers who can pay the high advertising rates of magazines past the 5,000,000 mark, even if these reach from twenty to thirty million people—as many as a good TV network program.

On a one-shot program, TV can safely claim that it has almost no duplication. Nobody can look at two channels simultaneously, though one can switch in mid-program, of course, or switch to another channel next week. At one time, TV even let advertisers kill off competition completely. By guaranteeing that no competitive product would be advertised within fifteen minutes, TV let one advertiser freeze four or five competitive categories of products off the air for the best ninety minutes of night time. The trick was to buy two fifteen-minute spots half an hour apart and run commercials on four or five different lines of products. This was easy for P. & G., General Foods, and Colgate.

But in fact, ephemeral as slick magazines are, TV is still more ephemeral. Who is looking at any particular program, how many, why, for how long and to what purpose, are still unanswerable questions. A magazine can prove it gets into 5,000,000 homes, and *almost* prove that 20,000,000 people pick it up 100,000,000 times, more or less, in the week, or month, or longer that the copy lasts intact.

TV's challenge, however, has made the magazines search their souls. The apparent answer of the women's magazines, if we can believe the full-page ads, is that they are more feminine than ever. This seems to be the exact opposite of the fact. An investment survey recently completed says that the women's magazines, notably *McCall's*, are evolving editorially toward the general magazine. This can perhaps be more correctly stated as that women's magazines are trying to identify their audiences as a particular kind of woman who is also interested in general subjects. (The editorial content of *Ladies' Home Journal*, *McCall's*, *Woman's Day*, richly confirms this statement.) As *Time* said, the new woman buys just anything, not only P. & G. and General Foods products.

What has happened is that an undifferentiated mass of readers is no longer good enough to support a mass-circulation periodical. (*This Week* and *Reader's Digest* have the reader-mass, but not the advertising.) The developed relationship between reader and magazine is all-important; in short, the honor and integrity of the magazine are the key to its survival. This should always have been obvious; yet very few big magazine publishers have any but the dimmest notion of these great concepts. (Every new magazine is aware of them, but the vision fades.) They have flim-flammed the readers too long into sitting still for the advertiser's pitch; they have produced too many seven-day wonders, too many rabbits out of hats, repeated too many sure-thing stories too often, confirmed too many popular lies; and slowly that stain of skepticism has crept into the faithful reader's eye.

What to do? The answer is obvious. At least get honor and integrity into the full-page ads in the *New York Times*. The *Post* and *Time* seem to have best caught the point in the ads reviewed earlier. *Good Housekeeping*, an honorable magazine, seemed unable to get it across.

Some magazines that did not enter the course are to be found among the dozen leaders in auto-advertising pages for 1956. They are *Grit*, the small-town magazine; *U.S. News & World Report*, *Farm Journal*, and *Sunset Magazine*. These are all distinguished by reasonable honesty and reader loyalty. It should be clear that something is happening to reading and believing habits of Americans—and that the advertisers are profoundly interested in it. (No claim is made that the analysis given here is the final and definitive one.)

If, in some impossible future, consumer advertising were lost to general media entirely, the individual American would be far worse off than he is now. The immense, and generally awful, consequences are too complex and repulsive to be contemplated here. Such a possibility is only a reminder to magazine publishers that their hope and salvation is the individual citizen, with all his whims, rather than the advertiser who picks up the check.

It was not pleasant to have to write last June, "The existing press is primarily a vending machine. . . . It is unfair and irrelevant to criticize this vending machine because it dispenses Coca-Cola instead of truth." But another way of saying the same thing is the magazines' own description of themselves as "media" not for ideas, but for the merchandising of baby foods, detergents, and washing machines.

Slaughter on Madison Avenue
(1958)

Two great failures of advertising preceded and accompanied the present business recession. Neither the new long, high-powered, wing-swept automobile nor the sack dress * could be sold to the American people. These two awful letdowns unraveled America's first and third biggest industries, disgruntled the customers, and temporarily shook advertising's ulcered self-confidence.

"Campaign To Beat Back Attacks on Ads Urged," said a New York *Herald Tribune* headline on April 16th. An agency took a full-page ad in the *Wall Street Journal* on April 23rd to say, "Advertising makes possible the high-speed distribution that is the key to our economic system. Without it, capitalism as we know it would be impossible." (The "as we know it" is the important part of this.)

* Recent claims that the sack is catching on do not change the industry's loss of the critical November-Easter selling season. The writer admires the sack dress as an attempt to draw attention away from those two great disillusioners, the girdle and the bra, but he sees true sacks only on the rich, and modified sacks on working girls. Smart, middle-class women cannot afford a wasted dress. The sack never made the boat.

Advertising is indeed, as it urgently should be, under reappraisal by the American people. A few notes along this line have been contributed by me; but now I find that many of the same points were made better, earlier, and more politely in David M. Potter's admirable book *People of Plenty* (Chicago, 1954), about the "throwaway culture" that advertising has created. Mr. Potter pays advertising the (deserved, I think) compliment of grouping it with the other "instruments of social control." Of these, the church traditionally guides man as an immortal soul, the school as a reasoning creature, the free-enterprise system as a producer and earner. Advertising has its own theory of man; he is a consumer. The first three exhort man to greater and higher effort; the last pleads with him to make the biggest possible pig of himself. In its basic function advertising, unlike the other three, "has no social goals and no social responsibility for what it does with its influence." Potter measures the social influence of advertising in terms of money spent by advertisers for every separate American family (the figure for 1957: $350) against $152 spent (1951) on primary and secondary public education. Less is spent selling the two candidates for President in an election year than on selling soap.

The foregoing seems to me unanswerable.

The kind of responsibility advertising really feels, that is, to its client, is construed by advertising as a true social responsibility. Lately it has even taken shape, in the current "Buy Now" campaigns, as a patriotic responsibility. To these people, a recession very quickly begins to look like another Pearl Harbor. This is very funny, if we are right in thinking that the Admiral Kimmel of this disaster was advertising itself.

Thus, advertising has pitched the key of "Buy Now" on a level oddly reminiscent of 1942's "Hate the Jap." Boston has an official campaign to "combat loose recession talk." Cleveland has debauched Churchill's "V for Victory" into a "V for Values" selling campaign, renamed its main street "Value Avenue" and may, as a city, take on the *nom de crise* of "Valuetown, U.S.A." A New Jersey tire store trumpets, "Buy! Buy! Buy! It's Your Patriotic Duty." The Advertising Council, Inc., will spend over $10,000,000 on a "Confidence in a Growing America" campaign. The Public Relations

Society of America has circularized its members to squeeze only bullish news out of their companies. The American Management Association had an executives' mass meeting May 19–20 to exude optimism. Hotpoint (electrical-appliance) dealers wear buttons inscribed "Business is Good." Dallas ad men, much more patriotic, wear breast-pocket handkerchiefs saying "Business is GREAT!" A St. Louis bank actually advertised that there can be nothing more harmful than "excessive saving."

One does not have to be a satirist to get the strong reek of wartime propaganda, of the venal simulation of the survival desperation effort of the whole team where any dissent is disastrous subversion. Yet advertising got us into this mess (it can be argued); now the advertising commands us not to call it a mess and to buy our way out of it instanter. I expect soon to read of some poor little merchant strung up to a lamppost by a mob of infuriated ad men because he was suspected of muttering, "Business is lousy."

Since we all want to get out of the recession as quickly as possible, the laughs are thin and cut short. Still, to let advertising try to kid us out of a situation it may have partly kidded us into would not seem very bright. Indeed, advertising's frantic faith that it could do so is a neurotic symptom, if it is not the second stage of that sequence popularized by Toynbee from the Greek: get fat, kick wildly, death.

The present nervousness of ad men, however, may also be traced to the effects of the two healthiest subdivisions of advertising: market research and industrial design.

The first is described very faithfully in Martin Mayer's recent *Madison Avenue, U.S.A.* (Harper), and the most important of the seventy market-research organizations deserve listing here. Ernest Dichter and his Institute of Motivational Research look for the customer's "image" of the product in both Freudian and sociological senses. James Vicary invented subliminal advertising and discovered that people in supermarkets give fewer eye blinks per minute; he also tests new brand names. Alfred Politz, who has only ten big clients, gets the "right answers" by asking the ingeniously "right" questions and looks for the "controllable cause" of purchase. Market Research Corporation buys shopping diaries from 4,000 individuals daily, 7,000 households weekly. Arthur D. Little does operations research with the Theory of Games, mathematical formulas and electronic calculators. Daniel Starch tests every issue of twenty-four magazines on readers' recognition of, and susceptibility to, every ad in them. Gallup and Robinson, Inc., do more searching catechisms. Gallup's Audience Research also uses a free theater near Princeton, N.J., where audiences fiddle with dials to show interest. Schwerin Research Corporation has a Manhattan theater, using giveaways and questionnaires. Finally, the champion, A. C. Nielsen, produces the official TV ratings with 1,000 Audimeters (seventy always out of order), and also takes periodic audits of 700 drugstores and 1,600 grocers to get national sales figures. Terrifying, huh?

The advertisers and agencies have made Nielsen's TV ratings the final, official gauge of popularity of entertainment. Mayer complacently says, "How can 930 households state the actual habits of some 40-million-plus homes with television sets? . . . Well, oddly enough, it can—within certain predictable ranges of error. . . . Mathematical statistics, given its logical assumptions, is an exact science."

The foregoing quotation is possibly the most beautiful example of the scientific lie that could be found.

What is under discussion is a mathematical theory called the Theory of Sampling. The time has come when the individual in a democracy had better understand the rudiments of this theory, because the monopolists of the theory are perfectly capable of saying: "Why bother with elections? We can tell you what you think much more cheaply." These "samplers" are the most ambitious, foolish, and dangerous people in the United States.

Naturally I can report only what the mathematicians tell me. An engineer who works with the Theory of Sampling said, "Nielsen's ratings are not in the field of statistics at all; they are in the field of opinion."

A graduate mathematician tried to explain the Theory of Sampling. This, as he says, is a theory, on which an elaborate mathematics has been constructed. The theory, which must become an increasingly important technique in dealing with a mass society, generally works, if one plays by the rules. Nielsen and the others do not play by the rules. A "stratified sample" is one broken into homogeneous subgroups represented in the sample in the same proportion as in the whole. Common sense and experience will teach the proper number of subgroups. The difficulty comes in defining the significant subgroups. To test the apples on the sunny side of an apple tree, one sample may be enough. But nobody would generalize about all women after sampling one. It is assumed that each subgroup will show some deviation, one way or another, from the total truth, but it is hoped that the oscillation of error will constantly become narrower, the larger the sample used.

Nearly all the equations based on the Theory of Sampling use a figure, usually represented as *sigma*, standing for the "standard deviation of the sample." But Nielsen has no such figure and can never in this world get any such figure, because he can never know even roughly how many people were actually looking at anything at any time, and therefore what his sample's deviation was.

But what removes Nielsen's ratings entirely from the field of statistics is that, for all I know, there may well be more than 930 *kinds* of households in the forty-million plus. Suppose this pathetic total of 930 families decide one night to toss a coin as to whether to listen to Perry Como or his opposition. If the sample included an infinite number of homes, it would divide almost evenly, but with only 930 tosses of the coin, it might come out (taking the standard deviation or expected error) about 14.7 off, or 480 for Como, 450 for his opposition, or a rousing 6.6 per cent advantage.

Nielsen gets still funnier when we realize that even his few families are constantly changing: a young member who has dominated the TV-tuning falls in love, the big-league baseball races get tense, Father is laid off the job, and sonny takes a part-time job, the children are permitted to stay up another hour, or a good movie comes to town that night.

The truth about limited sampling is that the ordinary human being who gets around has been doing it since the world began, and may be better at it than the market-research boys. His biggest asset is that, having known the members of his sample a long time, he knows how to weight the data. A few, perhaps a very few, people have the gift of penetrating more deeply into the lives around them and really understand the true preferences far beneath the verbal avowals. Advertising's attitude toward such intuition is given in Martin Mayer's quotation of the three most terrible words in the business, "My . . . wife . . . thinks." Actually, ad men, as well as politicians and editorial writers, do far better to think of "The People" as the people they personally know than as a beautiful and fictional abstraction. As the Theory of Sampling shows, a mathematics of life can be developed if one uses a figure for "deviation" or error. But this should lead one to reduce the deviation, that is, to pick better friends or wives in the first place. Or perhaps we should pass a law against the Theory of Sampling.

As market research cuts in on the advertising genius from one flank, industrial design cuts in on the other, notably in the realm of *package* design, which is of course a kind of advertising, just as the very look of the new car or the sack dress on the street is a kind of package design or advertising, whether good or bad. Certainly neither has any functional, engineering purpose.

The package design does its work at the "point of purchase" and again in fitting suitably into the buyer's life. As for the first point, manufacturers now pay supermarkets premiums for space for their packages at eye level, from four to six feet above the floor. It has been found, in surveys, that women going into a supermarket say they are going to buy one brand, and come out with a different brand, probably taken because of shelf position, package design, color, or shape. In many products, such as paper towels, buyers don't even know the brand name. They have bought an appearance, that is, a package design. I do it myself; everybody does it. The actual package, speaking directly and brilliantly to the buyer at the key moment, is more eloquent than the half-forgotten advertising myth in the buyer's memory. To assist this great work, multiple packs are becoming more popular because they wrap round cans or jars in a flat surface on which a readable selling story can be told.

The interesting thing about the two hundred industrial designers who do package advertising is that they have some honor. They want the thing to look like itself, to be useful, and to cost less. They disapproved, from the start, of the new cars. They dislike "phony obsolescence" and like the genuine kind. They try to appeal to people's good sense and good taste; advertising appeals to almost anything else.

Perhaps the central criticism of advertising should be of its half-baked, shopworn sophistication, as if it were all a practical joke. This was nowhere clearer than in Martin Mayer's naïve and friendly survey. And what a joke! Some seventy-three companies spending $10,000,000 each (1956) on advertising, over half on the kitchen and bathroom, most of the rest on cars and cigarettes.

A quarter of agency executives are Ivy League; the dress is neat but not gray flannel or pink shirt. The salary scale runs: (1) agencies, (2) media, (3) clients. The order of status or prestige is different: (1) clients, (2) agencies and (3) media. The media's salesmen are the unwanted nags and indispensable town criers of the business. The agency's forgotten man is usually the media buyer. The copywriter ranks over the art man. Without a smile, Mayer reports the vast and various mumbo jumbo that surrounds an agency's production of an "idea." A combination of group-think, brainstorming, cost accounting, market research, pseudoscience, idea stealing, and blind hunch, the process is perhaps inevitable where uncreative people are part of the act of creation. The jargon can only be called philosophy. One agency seeks the Unique Selling Proposition (USP), another empathy, another the "brand image," another the product's "inherent drama," while the big agencies use all the jargons impartially.

I must tell Mayer that the best USP is the proposition that a product is the one thing it is not. Thus, the cigarette smoked primarily by timid men must be advertised as all-man, the ordinary whisky is only for "Men of Distinction," the plain, comfortable shoe is not comfortable but glamorous, the expensive, elite product is for absolutely everybody, and so on, and so on. Since the people who really want the product are never numerous enough, one must speak to the others who don't especially want it.

Advertising, according to Mayer, is tactically fascinating. TV is for advertising appeals and products that are fairly simple and of low interest. "Saturation" is achieved by hypnotic slogans or jingles, sometimes repeated 600 times a week on one station (Hit Parade cigarettes). Radio today is for people doing something else—driving the car or finishing the housework or reading the evening paper. The price of the peak hours, 8 to 10:30 P.M., is three times the price of daylight hours. TV costs four times as much as radio. The 150 stations affiliated with the three networks cover areas accounting for two-thirds of all retail sales. At the peak hours some 400 stations will be running the network shows. For this outlet, the network pays the station 28 per cent of its time charge and gives it the right to sell some sixty seconds an hour at the station identification breaks.

Mayer correctly describes TV as "the greatest selling medium ever devised," partly because it reaches that third or half the population that simply does not read (whether or not it can), partly because the TV commercial blasts into the viewer's mind willy-nilly while he is half-stupefied. (The only better advertising medium would be bedroom ceilings.)

It is not generally safe to be naïve about ad men; they are in too tight a squeeze between clients and media, market research and industrial design, ever to be naïve themselves; and they number some very polished jokers.

"To make people do things: that's the fun," one of them is quoted. You and I are the people he wants to have fun with.

Slaughter II
(1958)

Over the fat and smiling land of advertising (1957 volume: $10 billion plus), a cloud no bigger than a politician's hat came scudding in November, 1957. Taking dreadful shape over Baltimore, it had before the end of the year terrified St. Louis, Kansas City, and the whole state of Virginia; and it was still an untried baby.

It all began when Baltimore's Mayor Thomas D'Alesandro, Jr., who has firm command of his all-Democratic City Council, looked about for some new taxes to balance his city budget at a moment when he was also campaigning for the Democratic nomination for governor of Maryland. D'Alesandro is experienced, imaginative, and also impulsive. He slapped a tax on business inventories, to the special grief of the chemical-fertilizer companies. Then he proposed a tax on sewerage, a version of the old water tax.

Presumably in reference to the sewerage-tax proposal, the cartoonist for the great Baltimore *Sun* drew a lampoon of the mayor outside a pay toilet. The impropriety was a little careless. There is a story, so far not pinned down, that a reporter heard the Mayor say, "That cartoon will cost the *Sun* five million bucks." Since the remark fits too patly into the usual retroactive justifying legend, it can be taken with great reserve. It smells of newspaperman's bar talk, after the event.

Anyway, Mayor D'Alesandro suddenly had a new idea for a tax: a levy on advertising. The medium—that strange word means newspaper, periodical, or TV-radio station—was to collect from the advertiser an additional 7½ per cent of the advertising bill, add another 2 per cent out of its own pocket, and pay these surcharges to the city. The thing had a stark, revolutionary simplicity. For the first time, Government had noticed that a lot of money was moving around without doing the people any particular good—and was, indeed, aimed at eliciting vastly larger amounts of their money. How much thought the mayor put into what the money was doing, I do not know; but some of that can be supplied here, later.

Immediately, a thrill of sheer agony shot through the Baltimore business community. Ad men, merchants, manufacturers, and media men—incoherently muttering "Immoral!"—stumbled into battle stations. Their committee chairman, Wilbur Van Sant, harangued the quaking battalions: "The advertising-tax idea will spread like wildfire across the country unless it is stopped in Baltimore. We stand at the hinge on which this thing turns."

Don John of Austria, stopping the Turks at Lepanto, could not have put it better.

The battle cries ran down the long lines. The Baltimore *News-Post* (Hearst), which sells 232,000 copies daily, called the proposed tax "a threat to the free press." The Baltimore *Sun*, whose morning and afternoon editions have a combined circulation of 410,000 across the state, warned that the tax would drive business out of Baltimore. The mayor, a *Sun* editorial declared, had been growing steadily "more and more anti-Baltimore-business."

"Cry-baby nonsense," the mayor replied, unless the *Sun* had meant that "I am more interested in the average Baltimorean . . . than in adding to the already swollen profits of big business, of which the Sun-papers are a most prosperous part."

The hand-to-hand combat was joined at a six-hour public hearing which the mayor disdained to attend. Here it developed that the media men were too proud or too shy to argue their own case frankly (revealing a basic, vulnerable vanity in journalism that deserves closer examination). The merchants were no more articulate than usual. The ad men had to carry the attack. Apart from the theory that less Baltimore advertising meant less Baltimore business, the argument ran that advertisers would switch to national magazines and outside-Baltimore TV-radio stations, such as Washington's.

To this a city councilman answered, "Advertising rates have gone up continuously in the past ten years, but I notice last Sunday's *Sun* had 280 pages." A city witness calculated, "On a $2,000 page ad in the *Sun* the tax ostensibly is $175. But the advertiser is in the 52 per cent federal tax bracket and the 5 per cent state tax bracket. After tax deductions the actual net cost of the tax on that page would be only $65, which won't buy enough space in the *Sun* to cover a package of cigarettes."

Actually, the businessmen's sense of outrage seemed merely verbal and shallow; the real, unexpressed horror, as at a sacrilege, was reserved for the 2 per cent tax on the media.

The businessmen had found an odd ally: labor lawyers who argued that the tax on advertising might destroy some unspecified jobs.

The mayor, even in absentia, seems to have sensed the dynamics of the situation, as given here. He proposed to reduce the advertiser's tax from 7½ per cent to 4 per cent, but he left the medium's tax at 2 per cent. The ad men were not at all consoled. One said, "[We] were interrupted and insulted. . . . It was an inquisition." For the battle at the hearings had been a disaster. The mayor's men had done most of the talking. The spirit of Don John of Austria had not kept its appointment. The Turks had taken Baltimore.

Next day the Baltimore City Council approved the tax on advertising, to take effect January 1st.

In the following days I noticed with interest that the average citizen had never heard of the Baltimore advertising tax, but that a mention of it could bring a publisher, TV manager, or ad man to quivering attention. The episode was esoterica, though it should have been of concern to citizens everywhere.

The invective against the tax was all in trade publications: "dangerous and stupid," "foolish," "utterly and completely ridiculous," "utmost danger to the whole economy," "direct violation of the freedom of the press guaranteed by the United States Constitution."

By the time the tax became effective on the first of the year, fifteen suits had been filed in Circuit Court by Baltimore's two newspapers and three television stations, as well as several of its leading merchants. The suits contend that the new taxes are unconstitutional, arbitrary, discriminatory, and in restraint of trade.

The word "immoral," freely used in the early invective, has been dropped as a description of Baltimore's tax bite. (Anagram fans at least should notice that the word Baltimore is an anagram of Moral Bite.) Yet ultimately the legality of a tax on advertising must coordinate itself with the general morality of advertising in the life of American media. And this, as promised, will now be examined, in case Mayor D'Alesandro scamped it.

Looking at American media coldly, one must sooner or later come to the naked definition that they represent a "throwaway" culture. They are primarily a come-on to sell consumer goods, giving away entertainment and information incidentally, for nothing or for less than cost, like handbills thrown on one's doorstep.

TV and radio are, of course, "throwaways" in the literal sense. The same is all but literally true of the ten-cent chain-store magazines such as *Woman's Day* and *Family Circle*, which have their own distribution system. It is essentially true of the fifteen-cent Baltimore *Sunday Sun*, with its 280 pages, and of most other great newspapers.

What is not so clearly realized is that the glossy mass magazines are "throwaways" too. The average production cost of a Time Inc. mass magazine is forty cents per copy, *Life* somewhat more, *Time* somewhat less. *Life*'s circulation income (subscription 5,000,000, newsstand sale 1,000,000), is under thirteen cents per copy. The other mass magazines are selling at similar huge deficits. They are obviously not in the business of selling magazines, except incidentally. If that were all they did, they would all go broke overnight.

What is their primary function? It is, of course, to publish advertisements.

The operation might be described as merely renting the manufacturer of a commodity the magazine's subscription list and newsstand outlets for one mailing. But that would not describe what is happening. The magazine actually rents out its readers' faith in its editorial morals to Procter & Gamble or General Motors. To prove it, the magazine even binds the advertisers' sales pitch in with its own editorial matter, and delivers the combination as a package called *Life* or *McCall's*.

TV and radio even let the advertiser dictate the nature of the editorial matter.

The primary commercial function of the magazine, newspaper, or TV-radio station is thus to make a sales pitch. The preliminary jugglers and pretty girls are only to attract the crowd; the entrance fee, if any, is only to keep out the cheapskates who aren't worth talking to.

The consequent massive and lavish throwaway culture of America must inspire some awe. It dwarfs Rome's bread-and-circuses or the hope of heaven or Communism's wildest Utopia. This one is here, all for nothing or next to nothing.

The temptation is strong to agree with the Baltimore ad men, to say "So what?" and to "fall asleep counting your blessings." Much of the free entertainment is very good, even by cash standards. And when it is very bad, the people quickly tire of it. Why tax the geese laying these beautiful gilded eggs?

First, the operation is flagrantly taxable. Ultimately, Government will not be able to resist it.

Second, the throwaway culture is rapidly destroying its last remaining non-throwaway elements: books, theater, movies, night clubs, nonbroadcast sports, and many intellectual magazines. Gresham's law, or a variation, seems to be at work.

Third, it is probably dangerous and antisocial for anything to pretend that it is doing one job, and actually to be doing something different and opposite. A free press is a noble ideal, but a press that is merely free to the consumer is not what was meant by the flexible word "free."

A hired, gratuitous press cannot be, in the original sense, wholly free. A small example can be given. One year certain Detroit cars had an innovation that had the dazzling feature, if one steered first left, then quickly right, left, of going completely out of control. The idea of suing the manufacturer, lately revived in congressional hearings, under the Restatement of the Law of Torts, did occur to a few people. The press did not report these suits. People not bright enough to think of suing were not helped by the medium they depended on for moral information about their world. I know some people still scarred by that year's carnage.

Fourth, the free entertainment looks wonderful, but has little nourishment and less flavor. For all its mock heroics, it adds little to the people's thought or conversation. The talk gets progressively worse or dies entirely as all eyes glaze on the television set.

The corruption of the press by advertising hunger has been the subject of investigation for the past year by the International Labor Press Association. Labor is concerned about its own press. It doesn't like the boast that "an advertisement in the labor press is an automatic recommendation to the reader." It likes even less the racketeer blackmailing of businessmen into paying for a full-page ad saying, "Greetings from a Friend of Labor."

The taxability of a particular medium can most easily be tested by the question: Which is the means and which the end—advertising or editorial matter? If advertising is the real end—as financially it overwhelmingly is—one can see no objection to Baltimore's tax on advertising.

But there are differences among media. For example, *Family Circle*, at 10 cents, and *Good Housekeeping*, at 35 cents, have about the same number of readers and charge about the same for a page of advertising. Yet *Good Housekeeping* gives a good deal more editorial value. If ad rates mean anything, the advertisers seem indifferent to which of them makes a cheaper editorial effort; all the advertisers want is a shot at so many readers. This sort of cynicism suggests to me that I am actually the last man in the business to realize that the throwaway culture is already here. I feel stupid.

To determine whether any particular medium's advertising income is a means or an end, simply compare it to circulation income. If advertising income is the greater, it is an end.

It would be good to have a tax that encouraged the great, hard-working newspapers (such as the Baltimore *Sun*) to do still better by their readers.

The prediction that the tax on advertising would "spread like wildfire" from Baltimore proved a brilliant piece of prophesying. Almost at once, an alderman in St. Louis announced that he would introduce legislation for a similar tax. The Advertising Federation of America rallied its members against the new outbreak and at last account was doing well, "cooperating" with the city administration to find other sources of revenue. The threat flickered briefly in Kansas City. There was a rumor, unconfirmed, that the San Francisco City Council had written Baltimore asking for facts about the new tax. And then, at the end of the year, the mayor of Norfolk, Virginia, proposed that the new tax be applied to the whole state of Virginia by the legislature. Actually, everybody was waiting to see how the antitax suits made out in the Baltimore courts.

One nightmare was in the back of everybody's head. What if New York City should get the idea?

Slaughter III
(1956)

One of the most significant and quietly sensational stories of the year has remained relatively inconspicuous in the pages of American newspapers. The reason: the story was a lawsuit against an important advertising agency.

This treatment of an important news story brings into focus a basic fact of American journalism. In telling about a murder, adultery, drunken misbehavior, tax evasion, American newspapers seldom identify the criminal as an employee of any large corporate advertiser, department store, chain store, or, most particularly, any advertising agency.

The reader has no grounds for complaint about all this exquisite tact in his paper, because in most instances he does not pay for the publication. The advertiser pays for it. The citizen pays a symbolic tip to get in on a free ride. All he really has to contribute is his response to the advertising pages. You don't imagine, do you, that your twenty cents pays for the eighteen pages of four-color pictures in *Life?* Count the full-color advertising pages: in the issue I am looking at they come to forty against eighteen. That should tell you how you rate against the advertiser in *Life's* love-life.

The existing press is primarily a vending machine. "Freedom of the press" is 90 per cent a beautiful parrot cry by which we seek to identify ourselves with the Founding Fathers. Indeed, it is unfair and irrelevant to criticize this vending machine because it dispenses Coca-Cola instead of truth. Should the American people ever decide that it wants the whole news, it would have to begin paying for the whole magazine or newspaper. Meanwhile we must settle for what we get.

The lawsuit that the press ignored revolved around the advertising account of American Airlines (president: C. R. Smith), which rose rapidly from a trifling $7,000 in 1938 to over $4,000,000 last year. The selling of air travel was pioneered for American Airlines and to some extent for the whole airline industry by a man named P. P. ("Pete") Willis. In 1938, American Airlines gave Mr. Willis the power to choose an advertising agency. For the then small account, the agency of Ruthrauff & Ryan gave Mr. Willis a "lifetime, irrevocable" contract paying him $1,000 monthly and a third of all gross agency commissions on the account exceeding $18,000 in any six-month period.

On December 14, 1955, Llewellyn A. Wescott, Master in Chancery in Chicago Superior Court, ruled on the facts in a suit for an accounting between Ruthrauff & Ryan and Mr. Willis. Not a newspaper reported that the master had found that Ruthrauff & Ryan had tried to harass and "dominate" Mr. Willis, offering him small "loans" to be repaid at interest, trying to get him to sign cancellations of the contract, reneging on a plan to pay his back income taxes and ultimately suing him for $5,000, that the Bureau of Internal Revenue had returned. Mr. Willis launched his countersuit in November, 1954.

The Master in Chancery's report described the testimony of the company officers, F. Barry Ryan, Jr., and Ralph Van Buren, as follows:

I find that Mr. Van Buren's testimony must be disregarded in its entirety as being untrustworthy and unreliable. . . . Mr. Ryan, Jr., exhibited a reckless disregard for the facts in permitting himself to swear falsely to two affidavits. . . . Mr. Van Buren and Barry Ryan, Jr., betrayed the confidence and trust that Willis placed in each of them by displaying a lack of good faith and fair dealing. . . . I find that the statements of both Messrs. Ryan Jr. and Van Buren are unreliable and untrustworthy and should be disregarded. . . .

The full story appeared in only one American publication, *Advertising Age.* Soon afterward Barry Ryan, Jr., surrendered his job as board chairman to Paul E. Watson, uncle of the company's president.

Superior Court justices will normally accept the findings of Masters in Chancery. But on June 4, 1956, Judge Marovitz in Chicago reversed the master's findings and ruled for the defendants. This sort of news the press was able to handle, though still furtively and cryptically. In the back pages of the New York *World-Telegram and Sun* of June 5th, near the bottom of an advertising business column, was an item noting that Ruthrauff & Ryan were very happy that day because the court had "nodded favorably to them in the million-dollar action by Paul Willis in connection with the American Airlines account."

Included in the trial evidence was a letter to Mr. Willis from the man who replaced him as account executive for American Airlines: "I am not the type of person who turns around and cuts a friend's throat. . . . Throughout this whole mess, I have felt that our interests were more closely related than apart, yet you call me every kind of blackguard imaginable. In this racket that's comparative [*sic*] to two inmates on a penal jute machine calling each other crooks." The helpless immorality expressed in this pathetic letter reflects a world in which the immorality seems to some inhabitants conventional and necessary.

To explain this I am led to a brief survey of the advertising business.

There is too much money in it for too little effort. In the present phase, there is very little pioneering toward the creation of new American habits and a gigantic brawl to pander to established consumption habits. A campaign or layout costing perhaps $50,000 to create is duplicated in media whose billing runs into the millions, theoretically profiting the agency perhaps $500,000 at the 15 per cent commission for billing. One TV commercial may be repeated $10,000,000 worth (agency commission at 15 per cent: $1,500,000).

What kind of money are we talking about? In 1955 the billing in magazines, TV networks, and newspaper sections alone for the top one hundred advertisers came to about $2 billion. Add to that oddly limited statistic all radio and local TV time and newspaper space for all advertisers and a much better figure, according to *Tide*, is $8 billion. The pregnant 15 per cent of that figure comes to $1.3 billion in commissions. Some 3,000 agencies (excluding 1,800 one-man operations) divide it for an average of $444,000. Actually, only sixty-six agencies do $2.5 billion of the billing. J. Walter Thompson should keep about $35 million on its billing of $220 million; Young & Rubicam, $27 million on $182 million. McCann-Erickson and B.B.D.&O. should keep about $25 million. Next in order come N. W. Ayer; Foote, Cone & Belding; Leo Burnett; Benton & Bowles; Kenyon & Eckhardt; Grant and Kudner.

More interesting is where all the money comes from. A breakdown of that unsatisfactory $2 billion total shows the giants among the advertisers (figures in millions of dollars): General Motors, 44; Procter & Gamble, 42; General Foods, 30; Chrysler, 27; Colgate-Palmolive, 25; General Electric, 19; Gillette, 19; Ford, 18; American Tobacco, 17; Reynolds Tobacco, 15; Lever Brothers, 14; General Mills, 14; American Home Products, 11; Campbell Soup, 10; National Dairy Products, 10; Bristol-Myers, 9; Liggett & Myers, 9; Lorillard, 9; Distillers-Seagram, 8; Pillsbury, 7; Goodyear, 7; A.T.&T., 7; Swift, 6; Borden, 6; Kellogg, 6; Westinghouse, 6; R.C.A., 6; and du Pont, 6.

A lot of money is moving around. But do the advertisers actually let the agencies keep all of that enormous 15 per cent? If not, do the agencies bid competitively for accounts with promises of ever larger "kickbacks"? If so, where does the backflow disappear to? Is the United States Government missing out on its tax cut?

Constant flirtation by agencies with the accounts of other agencies is the present foundation of the advertising business. The "kickback" is a very seductive form of flirtation. Every week several accounts change agencies; yet there is rarely any sensible apparent reason for the change. However subtle the flirtation, in the minds of the two parties involved it has all the dignity of a trollop's wink.

The reason for this unattractive and unnecessary relationship is an odd one, and the whole vice of the advertising business. It is just the opposite of the trollop's practice of getting paid. In this case, the client—the advertiser—never pays the strumpet. He pays the business man at the other end—the newspaper, magazine, TV, or radio network. The poor trull gets to handle the money briefly and takes off her huge commission; but it is not morally her money for real services rendered. She passes it on minus her cut, and may even give back some of that to the heartless client to keep his favor.

This system is the disease that turns men into hucksters. The agency's charge does not really add a great deal to the cost of a product to the consumer. But the agencies constantly advise the manufacturers how to get more and more out of the consumer. The current conspiracy against the American consumer, disguised as a shower of free-enterprise blessings, is quarterbacked by the agency.

The days are past when every agency employed a few men solely to butter up the clients' sales personnel. They produced the tickets, reservations, women, and liquor, and sometimes have been known to secure a contract with a well-placed tape recorder. But if the practice is now largely extinct, there are certain interesting exceptions. One applies to the lower echelons of executives in the transportation corporations—automobiles, airlines, railroads, and shipping. The more conspicuous exception is the hard-liquor industry, some of whose proprietors today are Capone-era graduates now surrounded by C.P.A.'s as well as charcoal-gray hoods. Here again only the lesser executives can be so easily seduced.

However, there are many real friendships in the business. The social pal-ships flourish between the client's sales manager and the agency's account executive, or at a lower level between the agency's media buyer and a magazine's sales manager. In New York they can all be found lunching at Twenty One, the Stork Club, the Ritz Bar, the Cloud Club, the Waldorf Men's Bar, Christ Cella's, the Divan Parisien, and the Park Lane, often at their own expense. They may be telling the joke, six months late now, about the account executive who lost his account and whose hair turned charcoal-gray overnight.

Not a very good joke, it is hilarious to agency men because they read the agony beneath it. An account executive in the same situation, telling his hundred subordinates about the lost account, choked up and burst into tears. The best story right now is about Milton Biow who, on dissolving his great agency and throwing hundreds out of work, told them: "I've saved my money, old friends. Please don't worry about me. I'll be all right." This was really funny because Biow's whole career had clearly told everybody they need never worry about Milton Biow. A few days later, according to the New York *Herald-Tribune*, he was dining in Paris with Art Buchwald.

The huckster's love for the 15 per cent commission system within the advertising agencies seems to me to separate the men from the hucksters. *Tide* and the Association of National Advertisers generally seem to regard it as sacred. Others within the business have attacked it for forty years as senseless, humiliating, and obsolete. The Grocery Manufacturers' Association debates it at every meeting. The late Albert Lasker got around it by buying control of a company before he advertised its products. One agency, Cowan & Dengler, managed to do business on a flat retainer fee. The U.S. Justice Department recently got a consent decree against advertising associations for conspiracy to make the 15 per cent commission standard.

The hucksters' love for 15 per cent is compounded of belief that they are getting something for nothing and a groggy conviction that they are already running the United States. One agency man recently proposed to solve farm surpluses by "awarding wheat to McCann-Erickson, corn to J. Walter Thompson, cotton to Cunningham & Walsh, and butter to B.B.D.&O." Sometimes advertising men feel capable of repealing the law of supply and demand, or even the law of gravity, for a 15 per cent commission.

My own suggestion, if a percentage system is preferred, is that an agency, like a lawyer, playwright, novelist, or inventor, take a contingent fee based on a percentage of sales income rather than a percentage of billing costs.

Perhaps the present system is irresistible to the businessman because he, too, thinks he is getting something for nothing and if he gets a "kickback" he is getting it for minus nothing. It is tempting to analyze the attitude as the ancient and consecrated contempt that the man of business has always accorded the man of talent. The advertising talent does its work with such ease and enjoyment that the businessman finds it somehow obscene, hardly worth paying hard dollars for. Make no mistake about the talent in the advertising business. Compared to most other editorial work in America today, advertising offers more jobs, more scope, more research, more challenge, and more money. It draws some of the best people in the United States, along with the dull boys and the connivers. They certainly deserve an honest day's pay for an honest day's work.

But the commission on billing is not an honest day's pay. The only reason it exists now is that the advertising business started that way, under circumstances very different from the present ones.

In 1880 there was mass production in the United States, but the problems of mass distribution and mass consumption had not yet been solved. The chief consumer goods were "do-it-yourself" necessities such as sewing machines, bolt cloth, pins and needles, tools, rifles and revolvers, and the unique swindle of patent medicine. They were sold by drummers, door-to-door salesmen, peddlers, pitchmen, fairs, and local newspaper advertising. In this situation, the forerunner of the advertising man bought space in the newspaper and resold it for whatever he could get from the advertiser. Sometimes he helped to write the copy.

National advertising did not arrive until after the invention of the mass magazine by *Munsey's, McClure's,* the *Ladies' Home Journal* (1883) and the *Woman's Home Companion* (1893). Now the first advertising men, like J. Walter Thompson and Frank Presbrey, bought space in the magazines and sold it at a markup to the first true mass-commodity producers. The earliest fortunes were made by the patent medicines; the attitude that advertising was a bare-faced swindle lingered on, not in the minds of the readers but in the minds of the advertisers and agents. Oddly, the agents rarely went into the magazine business. They evidently liked the something-for-nothing illusion; the advertisers liked it, too.

American periodicals in 1908 numbered 5,136. In 1955 there were 6,092 consumer magazines, 8,525 country weeklies, 1,870 business newspapers, 1,765 daily newspapers, 2,698 radio stations, 412 TV stations and three TV networks, nearly all living on advertising revenue. The fleshpots were very enjoyable. In 1955, Time Inc. netted $144 million in advertising, the *Saturday Evening Post* alone took in $83 million, the Hearst magazines $119 million, Crowell-Collier $24 million, and U.S. newspapers $695 million.

Even at these prices, it is sad and unnecessary that the magazine be so servile to the advertiser. Any communications medium that can prove it has a relative monopoly on a particular audience may charge anything it likes, up to taking over ownership of the advertiser. The medium makes the mass corporation possible—not, as so many advertising people believe, the other way around. If there were no way to speak to the consumer, consumer goods would become local or homemade again. The trouble is that everybody in the act of selling, from the editor to the businessman, is ashamed of selling. They all think they are getting something for nothing, try to get something more for less than nothing, and end up with less than they are actually entitled to.

The consequent demoralization in American culture is most apparent in radio, TV, and magazines, in that order. Magazines do not accept much interference with their editorial matter, though they certainly do not intentionally offend the advertisers. Daytime radio, on the other hand, has long been ruined by the insistence of the advertising agency on writing and producing the whole program for its client, who is usually Procter & Gamble, Lever, or American Home Products. Hence the soap opera, the most abominable art form ever conceived.

The agencies are outraged that they have not yet got the same free hand in TV as in radio. Senator John Bricker's congressional investigation would challenge the monopoly that networks have in TV. Who would be behind the investigation? Who but the agencies? They have already got their hands, usually in collaboration with "talent-packagers," on such shows as the $64,000 Question (Revlon), Groucho Marx (De Soto), and the Kraft Theater, while convincing the naïve that they want no part of TV. The operation is as impudent as if a political dictator should demand to sit in on *Saturday Evening Post* editorial conferences or, worse yet, "package" the whole magazine.

The agency's dictatorship over what ought to entertain America is not necessary or even useful to the advertiser. The advertiser knows as much about entertainment as I know about dressing hogs. Until the communications medium throws him bodily into the street, he is going to dictate what the people want as long as he can.

And all this is a consequence of the American people's happy abdication of the burden of paying for their magazines, newspapers, TV, and radio. The occasional editor who still puts up a suicidal fight for the integrity of the American people's information sources goes unsung and unthanked. The tragedy is all in the closet.

Meanwhile, I must go on getting my pleasure from the advertising-trade publications. The Ruthrauff & Ryan story, which started all this, is not the only good one. In recent weeks Colgate-Palmolive and Mennen lost a patent case to Carter Products on the pressurized shaving cream they have been selling; Toni and Hudnut are at war; Liggett & Myers changed agencies to blended agony and jubilation; and Lucky Strike won its case against a man who claimed to have invented "Be Happy—Go Lucky." Above all, in April there was the crash of the once mighty Biow agency that had once handled $50 million in billings and lost half that in its last six weeks. Its trouble went back to Biow's testimony in 1953 in a tax evasion case against one Arthur Samish. But Biow went down fighting, obstreperous and inscrutable to the last. You miss these great stories in the newspapers and news magazines.

It must be clear by now that a great deal that is both important and invisible bears on the decisive influences that bear in turn on the American people. As I have said before, the invisible man is always unpopular; he has too great an advantage over the rest of us. But in this case the advertising man, who is the invisible one, is not the ultimate villain. Behind the visible pages of consumer-goods advertising, behind the loving gargle on TV and radio, stands the really invisible man, the one with the false face, the man of business who is being given these words for nothing, who did not and could not think of them, who despises everything about them except the sales they bring him, who despises the idiots who believe the words and at the same time cannot help believing them himself, who despises the sycophants who wrote the words for nothing and is constantly looking for new sycophants who will write shiny new words.

If the Revolution or Counterrevolution should ever come to America, I would not be surprised to find on the first line of barricades none but advertising men and women. I would have to be on the other side, but my heart would go out to them. Certainly if they wanted to change America, they would know well what it is they have to change. Finally, it should be remembered that the Republican National Committee is employing Leo Burnett's advertising agency, and the Democratic National Committee Norman, Craig & Kummel. The advertising people may have already decided on revolution—an invisible one, without the risks of the barricades.

III

Progress

The New Riches
(1955)

The Communists tell us that the "world crisis" is one of increasing poverty and despair, and some democrats believe them. Superficial observation, however, would seem to indicate it is a crisis of *decreasing* poverty and despair; one of newly awakened appetites rather than of newly starving bellies. But can we prove this by accurate measurement?

It may help to examine the world crisis as a complicated form of the kind of crisis that sometimes threatens at the end of the ice-cream line at a Sunday-school picnic. The harassed Sunday-school superintendent can usually see the crucial factors at a glance: What percentage of the picnic are still "havenots" and how fast is the line moving?

We must eventually try to answer these questions as they refer to the world crisis. But since modern society is a good deal more complex than a Sunday-school picnic, the questions themselves cannot be asked correctly until we have defined the nature of the "ice cream."

Between 1914 and the present, the "ice cream" did not significantly increase in quantity; it changed in kind.

The American multimillionaire of 1914 was regarded by kings and maharajas as the richest man in history. His riches were usually visible as large, very expensive apparatuses, as troublesome and inconvenient as they were conspicuous, designed for his exclusive enjoyment. The outstanding ones were: (1) two or more large houses; (2) one or more steam yachts; (3) a stable of horses for racing, hunting, or pulling a Victoria, brougham, four-in-hand, tallyho, phaeton, and dogcart; (4) a collection of high-priced paintings, sculptures, and antiques; (5) solid-gold faucets and doorknobs.

Yet the "ice cream" of 1914, though restricted to a very few, would not satisfy an average American today. The multimillionaire's yacht had a speed of only 15 m.p.h., his speedboat, 30 m.p.h., and his Simplex or Mercedes automobile only 50 m.p.h.—and his tires blew out short of a thousand miles. All his vehicles were in the repair shop a large part of the year.

His country houses in 1914 were fitfully lit by kerosene lamps whose cleaning, filling, lighting, and extinguishing took one servant's full time. His city houses did indeed have both electricity and gas mantles, in case either failed. His servants had no mechanical refrigerator, vacuum cleaner, electric iron, washing machine, toaster, oil burner, or air conditioner to make work easy and efficient. The houses were ill heated. The rooms used log fires; the cooking ranges burned coal. The iceboxes were filled daily by the ice man; the drain pans were emptied several times a day by a pantry maid.

It was actually to keep warm inside that the Rich Man, his family and servants ate as much as they did. The luxuries were wild birds: pheasant, woodcock, snipe, and ortolan (bobolink). The entrails of the smaller birds were cooked and eaten. "Never," says a 1914 cookbook, "draw either of these birds if you are preparing them for epicures; to have the birds served without trail [euphemism for entrail] would be quite shocking. . . . The birds must be served very underdone." With fish, a folded napkin was baked in the oven and the fish served on it. The Rich Man had no winter oranges or asparagus, no fresh fruits or vegetables out of season. For vitamins he had to depend on the apple barrel and dried or preserved fruit and berries, during eight months of the year.

He was even worse off for entertainment than he was for vitamins. He had a Victor phonograph with a horn, and a Mignon-Welte pianola. On big occasions he might hire a string quartet or a vaudeville act, usually a magician. He had theater and opera in a few cities, but he rarely patronized the soundless and colorless movies, which he considered suitable for children and tradesmen.

For his holiday, the Rich Man had the choice between health resorts and yacht anchorages. At some of these he was given horses on which to hunt, steeplechase, or play polo. He might swim, but his wife and daughters were required to use the breast stroke to keep their hair dry and look feminine. Sun bathing was taboo for the women. In practice, the Rich Man and his family spent most of their holiday sitting under the stern canopy of the yacht or on the front porch of the hotel, enjoying the "view." Here also they ate and drank to excess and took the laxative and sulphur waters.

The true value of these "riches" of 1914 showed their cruelest limitation when pneumonia, tuberculosis, streptococcus, typhoid, diphtheria, meningitis, lockjaw, venereal disease, yellow fever, diabetes, or pernicious anemia struck. The sequel was death, fast or slow.

The "riches" of 1914 were not only inadequate by our standards and restricted to the very few; worse still, they might all vanish overnight, if the Rich Man lost his money, for they depended on the labor of three hundred servants. The "ice cream" of 1914 was not only scarce and fairly tasteless; it was also very likely to melt.

The real revolution that was beginning in 1914 was, as has frequently been said, the extension and sharing of technology. When the Rich Man went to school, for instance, say in 1890, only 7 per cent of eligible American youth were enrolled in the high schools. By 1950 high-school students numbered 80 per cent of all eligible youth.

The old "ice cream" or "riches" have disappeared. The new "ice cream" is totally different in kind. The people today, in North America, and to a lesser degree in Europe, South America, and parts of Asia and Africa, do not generally want the old sort of "riches" —the steam yacht and Gothic castle. Nobody wants the three hundred human servants who hedged in and flattered the 1914 Rich Man. Nobody wants twenty rooms he would never enter nor the services of three hundred people who would probably dislike him. Nobody wants to meet a couple of hired snobs when he tries to walk to the bathroom in his shorts.

The new "ice cream" is so widely shared that it has become commonplace. Everybody floods his rooms with light by a flick of a switch; similar small gestures control the heat of the radiator, gas range, oven, toaster, electric iron, and tap water, the cold of the mechanical refrigerator, the suction of the vacuum cleaner, and the whirlpool of the washing machine. Few city people lay fires, clean grates, or empty ashes. There is no drain under the icebox. Any inexperienced bride can accomplish the essential work performed by the Rich Man's three hundred servants in 1914 all by herself.

The modern American eats better, partly because he gets better dietary advice from press and radio, such as would warn him against consuming the underdone entrails of wild birds. He gets oranges the year round from Florida and California, asparagus from Texas, avocados from the Caribbean, grapefruit, grapes, melons, peaches, lettuce, peas, and green corn in midwinter. Canned, frozen, and fresh, the staples and delicacies of the whole world are his at a reasonable price. He can even find Chinese, Mexican, French, and Italian specialties at his supermarket. Milk and unsalted butter keep in his refrigerator. A hundred special dishes, breads, and pancakes are made easy for him by prepared powders and mixes. He can even have the Rich Man's caviar, pheasant and champagne at a price, but he is not often interested.

Entertainment, once a luxury, has become the masses' monopoly. Everybody has his choice of the music, jokes, drama, and news of the world either aurally or, if he has television, visually. (And in India, for two cents, anyone can see movies with color and sound.) Holiday pleasures are available all or a large part of the year in public playing fields, pools, and beaches. In the time it took the Rich Man of 1914 to run his yacht up to Newport, modern man can fly to Europe or Hawaii and back, at rates of three to ten cents a mile. And his wife and daughters now sun bathe and swim the Australian crawl in one-piece suits.

Life itself is the most generally coveted form of "riches." Since 1914 a baby's life expectancy has been enriched by 18 years to a total of 68 years for a boy and 71 for a girl. The assassins of the Rich Man have been eliminated by penicillin, sulfanilamide, liver extracts, antitoxins, blood transfusions, brain and heart operations, and other miracles of medical science.

In sum, the modern American appears to have approached an ideal of true "riches," in the new definition.

This news seems to have reached everybody in the world, down to the last goatherd in Afghanistan. Yet, to all these people, "riches" still mean what they meant to the Rich Man of 1914. In consequence, the average American has been rotated into the role of the hated and envied object of revolutionary fervor. Many of the backward peoples credit him with vices and greeds once charged, often as unjustly, against the now obsolete Rich Man. The Communist caricature of the porcine, bejeweled plutocrat now refers, with astonishing irrelevance, to the modest, friendly, average American.

We cannot easily tell the backward peoples they are wrong until we know ourselves the real nature of the new "riches," the nature of the "ice cream" at our world-wide Sunday-school picnic. What we need is some scientific definition of today's "riches," not in terms of national wealth or national income or steel production or paid movie admissions, but in terms of the actual advantage a citizen of an industrialized society has over a citizen of a nonindustrialized society.

Such a definition is not as impossible as it might seem. One was worked out for the year 1950 by the mathematician, Buckminster Fuller. Taking the very conservative rate of 4 per cent efficiency in the conversion of fuels and water power into useful work, he found that, in 1950, the total amount of work thus performed in the world amounted to three and a third quintillion foot-pounds. Next he expressed this figure in terms of human work by dividing it by the total physical work an average adult can accomplish in a year, or 37.5 million foot-pounds. This gave him the number of human slaves that would have been required to do this same work had it been ordered done, for example, by the Pharaohs of ancient Egypt. These modern slaves are abstractions, what Mr. Fuller called "energy slaves." Using these calculations, he came up with the amazing total of 85.5 billion invisible men, 35 times the number of every man, woman, and child now breathing the air of this earth.

The world's envy of the American is of course derived from the uneven distribution of these 85.5 billion energy slaves. Mr. Fuller estimated that some 62 billion of them were working in North America in 1950, while only 2.5 billion tried to take care of all Asia. Asians had the use of two energy slaves per capita, every European had 27, and every South American 28.

In invidious contrast, North Americans had 347 energy slaves per capita. Each was thus 175 times as "rich," in the new definition, as the Asian and 13 times as "rich" as the European. An American family of four had 1,400 energy slaves, as against the scant 300 human servants of the 1914 Rich Man.

The 62 billion energy slaves of North America, however, must be regarded as working as one team rather than in family groups. In that sense, all 62 billion can be thought of as working for every individual American and also, fractionally, for all the people of the underdeveloped countries too.

America's 62 billion invisible men—the number is nearer 70 billion by now—release the human population from drudgery not only in North America but also, to a lesser extent, everywhere in the world.

To return to our Sunday-school picnic then, today's "ice cream" is clearly to be defined in terms of energy slaves. It will now be possible to take up the superintendent's two frantic questions:

"What percentage of the picnic are still 'have-nots'?"

"How fast is the line moving?"

Mr. Fuller has taken it that when the average family in any area has the use of 100 energy slaves—roughly 25 per capita—the members of this family may be said to have moved from the "have-not" to the "have" status.

As recently as 1900 the average North American had no energy slaves. Their creation began in earnest during the First World War and greatly accelerated during the New Deal and the Second World War. By 1940 North America had 22 billion, or 148 for every man, woman, and child. By 1950 the number rose to 62 billion, or 347 per capita. Today it is around 400.

Between 1940 and 1950 northern Europe climbed from 16 to 27 energy slaves per capita—and "have" status. The people of Africa and the Mediterranean basin increased their energy slaves from 10 to 13 per capita, thus passing the halfway mark toward "have" status. Asia held fast at two per capita but these were largely confined to Japan and a few mainland cities. Recent development programs in India, Pakistan, Indonesia, Israel, Lebanon, Turkey, the Persian Gulf, and the Philippines should soon send this last figure upward.

The true hidden history of the past fifty years is this progress of the world's people from "have-not" to "have" status. In 1900 the customers of industrialization were less than 1 per cent of the world population. To the Socialists and Communists of that period this number looked like a tiny coterie of dynastic and industrial kings and courtiers which could easily be overthrown by the 99 per cent of the world's "have-nots." The Communists and Fascists rose to power on the archaic standard that comfort was a strange and exclusive, hence wicked, luxury.

But by 1914 the percentage of "haves" had already grown to 5 per cent, the first crude services of the newborn energy slaves going to close to a hundred million people. By 1940, 20 per cent of the world could be counted among the "haves" and by 1948 the percentage rose to 25, or one-quarter of the world population. In 1952 the percentage of "haves" stood at 28, giving a total of about 700 million customers of industrial civilization.

The Communists can still persuade anybody with a grudge or an empty belly that the per cent of "haves" is not 28 but less than 1 per cent, as it was in 1900. But it seems likely that the truth will prevail when 51 per cent of the world's population have become participating customers of industrialization. On that day the majority will be among the "haves." Presumably this majority will then take up the problem of the remaining 49 per cent of "have-nots" as seriously as any community would attack a plague.

According to Mr. Fuller's chart of the percentage increase in the number of customers of industrialization, the 1900–1952 curve would cross the 50 per cent mark between 1967 and 1972. On the basis of this estimate it can be conservatively predicted that the chances are that industrialization will have reached half the population of the globe around 1970.

The critical period will thus come during the next fifteen to twenty years. Some of the obvious perils which could jeopardize the outcome of Mr. Fuller's calculations are that: (*a*) Communist power politics may succeed in leading the dwindling "have-nots" into a piratical seizure of the energy slaves; (*b*) the politically delicate operation of passing from "have-not" to "have" status may dazzle local leaders into attempting nationalist adventures that will serve Russian ends; (*c*) this danger is aggravated if, as hunger and greed unite the "have-nots," the "haves" remain divided by full stomachs, bad nerves, and ignorance of their overpowering strength in union.

However, the nightmare of Communism smashing the industrial

machine before the "have" majority has been attained in the world is probably *just* a nightmare, for the talent for team play inherent in industrialization is itself a mighty force.

Concerning the implication of these things for America, Mr. Fuller said in a speech before the Export Advertising Association of New York:

"The successful passage of these next twenty years is one requiring a new kind of foreign policy. In the first place, we must recognize that we have as yet no U.S. foreign policy and, in fact, never had one. Foreign policy means world policy, and world policy was made for the last five hundred years by international banking, headquartered for the most part in the United Kingdom. . . . In 1917 the old world banking management went out. . . . The old management did not send out any farewell notices, and all the world, including and especially the U.S., preoccupied with breath-taking domestic acceleration, thought that somebody was working out the big world pattern, as usual. Not until today have we awakened to the fact that we *do not* have any positive, comprehensive, long-distance foreign policy but only fortuitous defensive improvisations, waiting upon formulation of a policy of responsibility.

"World policy can only be made by one country at a time, and that country which *can* make it is, *ipso facto*, the world creditor nation and world energy value-master. . . . Whatever the U.S. calls out now signals the evolving *world policy*. . . .

"Twenty-eight years after the fact of 1917's world shift in mastery of credit (which determines 'who' and 'what' shall be given priority access to the integrated world network of resources and first-line technical advantages), that shift was formally documented for history in the British House of Commons on August 16, 1945, when Great Britain's Prime Minister Winston Churchill, world spokesman for those who had futilely sought to conserve the credit mastery as their supreme prerogative, said with honor and conviction, 'The U.S. at this minute stands at the summit of the world. I rejoice that this is so. Let them act up to the level of their power and responsibility; not for themselves but for all men in all lands, and then a brighter day may dawn on human history.'

"It is not a function of our democratic government to evolve foreign policy. It is government's function to formulate methods which will serve the American individual's competence and ingenuity in the expansion of industrialization in a manner responsible to the rest of the human family. The kind of factors I have been discussing [which have been paraphrased in the foregoing pages] are the kind of factors out of which you as enterprisers will have to evolve that truly new foreign policy."

World's Most Valuable Men
(1956)

Earlier we reviewed "the most interesting" people as indicated by gossip-column coverage. A much more significant category would be "the most valuable" people in the present industrial society. At various periods in the past, both titles might have gone automatically to kings and courtiers, great captains, saints, writers, politicians or, more recently, financiers. There can be little doubt that today these have all been superseded by the scientist.

Now and then various science executives, such as Admiral Strauss, warn the press that our "50 per cent shortage" of scientists imperils "all of our blessings, even our freedom." Maybe so. But no real progress can be made in this matter until we penetrate a little more deeply into the words "scientist," "research," and even "shortage."

Superficially, the United States (and Soviet Russia, too) is already a throbbing hive of scientists and researchers. The great corporations spent five billion dollars a year (tax deductible) on the industrial research pursued by nearly a million scientists, engineers, and assistants (the last figure is, if anything, low). Since 1900, when General Electric's laboratory was Steinmetz's barn, G.E., Bell, U.S. Steel, Esso, and so on, have hatched vast clutches of corporation scientists.

This year, G.M.'s new $150 million Technical Center at Warren, Michigan, drew press hosannas that seemed to answer Admiral Strauss's warnings of "shortage." The center has 5,000 "scientists," 320 acres and buildings done in chartreuse, royal blue, tangerine, lemon, and crimson; it also has luminous ceilings and "floating" staircases. It was stated that most of the program would be on product design and improvement, but part would be basic research and pure science, just for the fun of it.

These laboratories undoubtedly have a function in industrialization. Once a basic invention or discovery has been made, its potentialities can be explored by a team operation, the numerous dead ends exhausted and blocked off and the useful developments hastened. Until proved otherwise, it may be assumed that for this purpose a number of brains are better than one. The real question is: Who makes the *original* basic invention or discovery, and how?

Our definition of "the most valuable" scientist must be narrowed to the inventor-discoverer-scientist. All that the million others can do is to pick over his leavings. If this is so, some inquiry is justified into whether he is to be found in the G.M., G.E., Bell, U.S. Steel and Esso laboratories, whether his training or heredity "qualified" him, and whether he is the presentable, well-adjusted type that would impress the G.M. personnel office. The answers can only be found in a review of certified inventor-scientists of the past. To eliminate suspense, the answers seem to be in every case: No.

But it will be a revelation how wildly unsystematic the incidence of genius has been. Beginning in 1752, what sort of man invented the lightning rod and bifocal spectacles? The latter might have occurred to a lens grinder, but both were the products of a political-minded printer, Benjamin Franklin.

Was hydrogen discovered by a professional chemist? No. It waited on the inspiration of a dilettante nobleman, Cavendish, nephew of the dukes of Devonshire and Kent. (Professional proletarians ought to be warned that a good many well-born people have done thinking quite as brilliant as farm laborers.) The spinning jenny and spinning frame ought to have been invented by a weaver, wool carder, or tailor. Instead, they came from a carpenter, Hargreaves, and a barber, Arkwright. The practically limitless unpreparedness (in the formal sense) of other great inventors for the work which made them famous is shown in the table on page 119.

Who discovered machine tools, the knitting machine, and the modern process of tunneling? This one is no more unlikely than the others, but the inventor's career teaches us an ominous lesson.

By birth he was a Frenchman, but because he was an aristocrat during the French Revolution he had to emigrate first to the United States, then to England. He was a naval officer and architect, the great Brunel.

GREAT INVENTORS BY AVOCATION

Discoverer	Vocation	Discovery
Lavoisier	Tax collector	First list of chemical elements
Edgeworth	Country gentleman	Caterpillar tread
Priestley	Preacher and tutor	Oxygen, nitric acid
Bramah	Farm laborer, cabinet-maker	Water closet, hydraulic press
Bentham	Naval officer	Planing machine, explosive shell
Nicholson	Law clerk, pottery salesman, journalist	Roller printing press, electro-chemistry
Whitney	Unemployed teacher	Cotton gin
Conté	Garden laborer, artist	Graphite pencil
Murdock	Miller's assistant	Gas lighting
Appert	Unemployed gentleman	Canning of foods
Dalton	Farm laborer, teacher	Modern atomic theory, meteorology, concept of color blindness
Congreve	Law student, journalist	Ironclad warship
Young	Physician	Theory of light
Horrocks	Stonemason	Steam-powered loom
Fulton	Jeweler, painter	Steamship
Faraday	Bookbinder	The dynamo, steel alloys, solidifying and liquefying of gases
Stephenson	Stoker, clock cleaner	Steam locomotive
Brewster	Theology student	Kaleidoscope

Another great man, Benjamin Thompson, the accountant who created the science of metallurgy by first understanding the nature of heat, was lost to the United States because he was regarded as a Tory by New England patriots. The French Revolution cut off Lavoisier's head while it still had some good ideas in it.

I would hardly dare to suggest that masses of people are not entitled to their mob emotions, group thinking, and occasional revolutions. However, the price levied for these exhilarating exercises is invariably the loss of the group's most useful citizens, whether in Communist Russia, Nazi Germany, or the United States. Nobody can cast the first stone. Each of us is fond of his prejudices. The question is only whether we can quite afford our passions at such a price.

Whether or not we would have disliked Lavoisier, Brunel, and Benjamin Thompson, we want to know more about the habit of mind that made them great men. Oddly enough, I believe it to be the same habit that every ordinary man occasionally shares and intuitively understands. A man or woman sits alone in a room and simply thinks about his world. He does not have to believe anything that his society, his parents, or bosses have tried to hammer into him; he is not impressing his wife, children, or neighbors. He strips his mind down to its real fighting weight and wonders about the truth. People do this everywhere, though not especially in the $150,000,000 General Motors Technical Center, but the encouragement of the process varies in different times and places. In the United States today a man with an original idea learns that there are some groups where it would be foolish to voice it, but he is not afraid for his life, even at General Motors. In Communist Russia, an original idea passing through a man's mind is likely to scare him out of his wits because it may get him a ticket to Siberia. Yet even in America the pressures toward conformity are such that as people grow older and wiser they try to stop thinking, and corporate scientists especially grow older and wiser.

There is no use pretending that society is ever very enthusiastic about the original thinkers. The great men try to explain and justify themselves, usually in vain, and as a result a very high percentage of them become definitely antisocial. Cavendish disliked people so much that any maid in his house was automatically dismissed if he happened to lay eyes on her. Wollaston listened in silence to others advancing ideas he had already disproved. Many of the great men were virtual hermits. I conclude from this that as members of society we must face the fact that our indispensable benefactors may not like us any better than we like them. Why should they?

Moving up to this century in the list of important inventions and discoveries given in Clarence Streit's *Freedom Against Itself*, we find some extraordinary changes in the *apparent* process of invention and discovery.

The farm laborers, dilettantes, and craft apprentices *seem* to have vanished. Almost invariably the modern inventors have had exhaustive training in the great universities and done nearly all their work for corporate entities such as governments, universities, and profit-making corporations. They are usually members of a team of scientists living and working and communicating together. Typically, they do not look eccentric or act eccentrically. They wear well-tailored flannel suits, inhabit well-made houses with well-kept lawns, and spend a good deal of time on social, administrative, and educational duties.

Some of the inventors listed by Streit did not even exist as human beings. The monolithic brain of Corning Glass is credited with the invention of silica glass, the Standard Oil Development Staff with synthetic toluene, American Cyanamid with synthesized folic acid vitamin, Armour with ACTH. Nazi Germany's I.G. Farben is congratulated on its corporate invention of anti-malarial atabrine. However, Nazi Germany gives credit for the V-2 guided missile to von Braun rather than to the Third Reich, and the United States acknowledges Fermi, Zinn, and Anderson as having had something to do with the atomic pile.

Expressing the new view of invention, Streit quotes J. F. Lincoln, president of the Lincoln Electric Company: "You of course understand that there is no discovery that is made by an individual." This statement is a model example of how to develop a disastrously false principle from a minor truism.

Some inventions evolve as competitive and progressively improved models; sometimes it is hard to determine which was the "key" model. But most of the corporate "discoveries" of the past twenty years are routine developments of earlier revelations given only to individuals. These latter nearly always began as outsiders in the capitals of science.

The development of nuclear fission goes back to Einstein, the lonely Jewish clerk in the Swiss patent office; to Lise Meitner, a refugee; to the cyclotron of Lawrence (a product of South Dakota);

and to Fermi, the anti-Fascist Italian. The whole development of radio, radar, and television depends on Marconi, the Italian dilettante, and the vacuum tube of De Forest, the cranky individualist from Iowa. The jet engine (1937) is descended from the gas turbine —which is not even listed among the great inventions and was made workable before the First World War by the Armangaud brothers in Paris. Einstein and Steinmetz, in particular, began their careers as outsiders *par excellence.*

Listing of corporations as inventors must be read in the sense that no corporation or bureaucracy can think, create, or invent anything. Such listing is usually the whim of a vice president in charge of public relations. In fact, an idea from one individual brain, such as Franklin's, can bring into being whole unimagined industries and give employment to unborn generations of vice presidents.

Furthermore, any contemporary list of "great" inventions must be taken as highly provisional. Today's list will be unrecognizable in A.D. 2000. If, as some think, all motor vehicles of the future are powered by gas turbines, that will become a "great" invention. If Buckminster Fuller's hemispherical dwelling becomes a mass-production item, that will be another "great" invention of this century. And so on, as most of the present list is swept back into the drawer.

A recurrent phrase in scientific patents is "improvement of the art." An old saying has it that "a work of art will never be produced by a committee." That palace of creation, the G.M. Technical Center, is an attempt to substitute predictable solutions by committees for the old-fashioned, unpredictable explosions in the dark by individuals.

The lone inventor, without a corporation, is in trouble in America today. A headline of July 13, 1956, "U.S. Bars Inventor From Own Secrets," labels the story of congressional subcommittee testimony about a scientist ". . . who keeps coming up with secret and top-secret ideas. The results have been classified as secret and he no longer has access to them. But we can't seem to classify his head."

In the magazine *Mechanical Engineering,* Crosby Field writes, "In every one of the major lines I have pioneered, I have found my greatest obstacle to be the engineer [usually corporate], who always knows why a thing cannot be done, or if it can, why the doing of it is valueless." Mr. Field believes American science to be entering an era of decentralization.

This belief takes a lot of faith, when faced with the corporate palaces of research. Even the tax laws are prejudiced against the individual inventor and in favor of the corporation's hollow gesture toward invention. I have yet to hear of any government action to defend and encourage the priceless individual, the ordinary man doing his own unincorporated thinking.

He alone, never boards of directors, Cabinet officers, or faculty committees, chooses the subjects for investigation; he does so by a mysterious intuition. He alone senses the invisible doors to new worlds still unrevealed. He tugs at the doorknob and thinks the door gives a little. The future of our society trembles in that balance, as whole industries may be about to be born. The inventor-scientists do not even ask for our gratitude. All they really care about is "the improvement of the art."

The Unspeakable Germ
(1957)

The most fearful problem of industrial civilization is, in the long run, its refuse. Let us pass over the great industrial slag heaps, the sewage-fouled rivers and lakes, the noisome garbage dumps, and even the radioactive fallout and radioactive waste which are the refuse of the atom bomb. The garbage and the sewage represent something taken out of the soil and not returned to it, but instead disgustedly swept under the rug of Western civilization. It is not surprising that our soil has gradually degenerated, no matter how much synthetic fertilizer we pour into it.

If Western man were an incurable fool, we could confidently expect America to end as an ungodly, barren, foul-smelling mess, hardly fit for vermin. Still, the antifoolishness has a hard time making itself heard. Government has been no help, nor has big business, nor even the scientists. Indeed, these latter talk mostly rot, and not even good, nourishing, organic rot.

Into this dismal landscape, enter a smiling, open-minded countryman with the Yorkshire name of Stanley Fred Bulpitt. His father, Henry Bulpitt, had been an apprentice gardener for Queen Victoria and Edward VII and came to America in 1911. After working for various millionaire estates (Hamilton, Milbank, Mallory) in Tuxedo, New York, and Greenwich, Connecticut, he started the Brookside Nurseries in Darien, Connecticut, in 1925. The son took the two-year horticultural course at New York City's Bronx Botanical Garden. In 1944 he was stricken with agonizing acute myalgia and, with plenty of time to read, found the works of Sir Albert Howard on organic agriculture.

Soon the two Bulpitts were playing around with soil. By the time the father died, in 1951, Stanley had licked his own sickness and made some headway in the therapy of sick soil. In fact he was the only man in the United States in the business of manufacturing whole soil out of civilization's waste materials.

Basically, he did this by combining nitrogenous with carbonaceous materials, generally in the proportions of one to three or four. In the first group were green vegetation, various animal manures, slaughter-house blood, dried fish, fish emulsion, leather scraps, and ordinary garbage. In the second group were sawdust, wood chips, dried weeds, hay, dead leaves—and ordinary newspapers. The important factors in these combinations were bacteria, which consumed the nitrogenous stuff to grow and propagate, and used the carbonaceous stuff for energy.

Solely to give the combination structure, to let it breathe air and water, he added an inorganic material: sand.

At this point the city man may require a quick briefing in the present war being fought over the farmer's and gardener's heads by the great chemical companies and the "organic soil" champions such as Bulpitt.

The funny thing about the war is that the truths used by both sides were perfectly well known fifty years ago. Science knew then that plants need and take from the soil nitrogen, phosphates, and potash (as well as oxygen, hydrogen, carbon, magnesium, calcium, and iron). Yet an acre with as much as seven thousand pounds of each of the first three in the top foot of soil may not grow wheat or hay. The addition of still more of the three elements, however, seems to help. The great chemical companies (du Pont, American

Cyanamid, Allied Chemical, American Potash, Davison, Duval, National Potash, Tennessee) have made fortunes out of this crude chemistry by selling inorganic chemical fertilizers. They finance an increasing percentage of soil research in this country and abroad; and the schools do not like to annoy them.

It was equally well known fifty years ago that the soil's fertility depends on a myriad microscopic life in it. A single gram of good soil may have a population of 28,000,000 microorganisms. These change nitrogen into nitrates as well as into the protein which is the body substance of bacteria and the principal constituent of all mature composts or soils. Some bacteria can seize and use the inert nitrogen of the air. Some can "etch" sands, clay, and hard rock, capturing supplies of phosphates, potash, and the so-called "trace minerals."

But since all this became known, the word "germ" has become an unspeakably dirty word. And, of course, these priceless inhabitants of the soil, the bacteria, are germs (the word comes from the Sanskrit for "birth" or "creature"). The excommunicated and accursed germ has brought into being the great industries of the detergent and the germicide, so that these latter are worshiped as bright angels of virtue and godliness and life. But they are by definition and intent life-killers. They certainly annihilate bacteria, and we do not know what they do to enzymes, auximones, and hormones. However, the American heaven is a life without germs, without risk, without flavor, and without life. I have relatives whose terror of germs makes them boil anything not canned or bottled, eat off a well-deterged enamel table, and nearly give up eating entirely; but such people are now quite numerous and respected, even though continually ailing.

In such a world, people who talk about "organic soil" are anti-Christ and subversive. Meanwhile, in 1955, 22,000,000 tons of chemical fertilizer were dumped into the American soil at a cost of $1,363,000,000, and soil fertility continued its steady and ominous decline.

Stanley Bulpitt found himself in this war with an inherited nursery, a family, some compost piles, and no fear at all of life, that is, bacteria, that is, germs. With all the naïveté of a countryman, be began asking the orthodox scientists about the organic theories of the English Soil Association (publication: *Mother Earth*, Hyde Park Mansions, Marylebone Road, London) and the American Friends of the Soil. The scientists, as he says, "just walked away."

We must comfort him by explaining that whereas any science of the soil must be a science "of the whole," there is no such science in America at present. A truly qualified agrologist would have to be an ecologist, chemist, physicist, zoologist, bacteriologist, entomologist, mycologist, helminthologist, botanist, hydrologist, geologist, geographer, statistician, and a half-dozen more. But a number of these disciplines are in bitter dispute with one another; to combine them would bring on a schizophrenia.

It is therefore not too surprising to hear from Sir William Gammie Ogg, M.A., B.Sc., Ph.D., LL.D., F.R.S.E., Consultant Director of the Commonwealth Bureau of Soil Science and ex-President of the Society of the Chemical Industry, that after profound examination, he concludes that the chemical companies' fertilizers are the best ever and that "organic manuring" has simply not made its point.

But Mr. Bulpitt could see that organically nourished fields without any chemicals grew crops three times as big, healthy, and flavorsome as the chemical fields. Furthermore, insects thrived on the well-sprayed chemical fields and seemed to avoid the unsprayed organic fields. Bulpitt learned from the famous Haughley comparative test farms in England, the project of the Soil Association, that cattle fed on chemically enriched soil grew smaller and gave less milk with less solid-non-fat-content, and developed barrenness, malformation, and miscarriages.

Some of the differences, but by no means all, can be explained. Insecticides tend to kill all but the strongest individuals in a pest species, and may kill in addition the pest's natural enemies. When the shooting is over, the surviving pests run riot in what has been turned into a bug's heaven. On the other hand, healthy, organically nourished plants are almost impervious to the pests. Chemically fertilized fields of potatoes will be wiped out by microscopic eel worms on the roots; in the next field, an organic soil nourishes several species of fungi that have a genius for slaughtering eel worms in a gruesome but satisfying way.

In Argentina the progressive exhaustion of organic elements in the soil is given as the cause of hypocalcemia in cattle and of dental caries in children who consume the milk, wheat, and meat

These are empirical facts, but the word "empirical" has the subsidiary meaning of "charlatan" and is not in good repute. The mortifying truth is that there is a great deal about the soil and nutrients that we simply do not know yet. And the little we know may be yet more dangerous than ignorance, as is indicated by the primitive agriculturists of India and Mexico, who produce crops more flavorsome and less perishable, though smaller, than ours.

What is also needed is basic research, toward which ex-Secretary of Defense Charles Wilson of Detroit expressed the immortal opinion: "Basic research is when you don't know what you're doing." The epigram is perfectly true; but Wilson, accustomed to stockholders' requirements, could not know that it is only when you don't know what you're doing that you are brushing the mysteries of the universe, which does know what it's doing.

Bulpitt enlisted in the fertilizer war on the side of empirical research. To find out what industrial civilization is taking out of, and not returning to, the soil, he simply looked at what civilization throws away. Childishly simple. It was obvious that in a "package" civilization, about 75 per cent of most garbage is paper. He therefore tried throwing a few cans of garbage into an Agromat, with water, and chopping it fine as in a food mixer. Almost at once, it ceased to smell like garbage. What came out was ordinary mud.

Another great mass of trash is old newspapers. This wood pulp is a combination of carbohydrates, nitrogen, potassium compounds, and some other inorganics. Sounded good to Bulpitt. He chopped it up in a water bath and spread the mulch over his fields. The plants— delphinium, phlox, iris, thyme, sedum, bleeding heart, aster, columbine, English holly, and so on—grew through it. Later, he digs it into the soil. For these purposes, the cheap tabloid papers are best, and the slick magazines, with coated stock and colored inks, almost useless. The first year Bulpitt raked off the newspaper mulch, intending to throw it out. When he dug into the pile, he found it full of earthworms, a sight to gladden any nurseryman's eye. It is now one of his favorite fertilizers—"soil aids" to him.

When he makes a compost pile, his rule is to keep to the ratio of one to four in combining mainly nitrogenous and mainly carbonaceous material. The pile is never wider or higher than six feet, but can be built as long as one likes. Inside, it will reach a temperature of 160°. Air must be able to penetrate it. In ninety days, it is ready; at no time will it draw flies or smell.

This last boast was disbelieved by a customer, who agreed to pay for a compost heap of chicken manure and hay—if it did not smell. Bulpitt built such a sweet-smelling pile that the man gave a barbecue picnic beside it. However, the customer had his own men build an adjoining pile. To get rid of the chicken manure in a hurry, they made it 50–50 hay and manure, thus destroying Bulpitt's one-to-four ratio. This pile immediately swarmed with flies which, however, did not alight on the first pile.

Bulpitt is constantly trying out new combinations of the wastes listed earlier.

The final refuse of civilization is sewage. Several great cities—Chicago, Milwaukee, Pasadena—have tried to reclaim their sewage, processing, drying, and pressing it for sale as fertilizer. On this subject, Bulpitt is as radical as he is empirical. He tried some of it, costing five cents a pound. He worked two inches of it into eight inches of soil over an acre. But nothing would grow—not even crabgrass.

Why? For one thing, big-city sewage has far more industrial waste than organic human excreta. Its processing usually involves cooking at 1500° temperature and a heavy dose of chlorine. All bacterial life is thus dead on arrival. The sewage also has poisonous traces of zinc taken from the pipes. Bulpitt had to correct his sewage-treated acre with four tons of lime.

However, in theory, Bulpitt will agree that live human sewage would be useful, and might be reclaimed in towns and cities that have no important industries.

China has maintained its soil fertility for forty centuries—thirty-seven more than we—by dumping all fecal matter into the family pit in which lives a coprophagous pig. In the cities, the slops are dried, caked, and sold to the farmers. However, where raw night soil is used, the associated fatal diseases of hookworm, liver fluke, intestinal fluke, and blood fluke account for one-quarter of all Chinese deaths. This is a price no people would willingly pay to maintain the humus content of the soil.

If we can put aside both scatology and euphemism, the trouble with shit is that it is highly acid and greasy and tends to exclude air. Its evil smell and pathogenic menace might be eliminated by chopping it up, combining it with four times as much carbonaceous material—woodpulp, sawdust or paper-heavy garbage—and fully aerating it. The end product would be "clean" soil.

It should be emphasized that Mr. Bulpitt, an eminently practical man, does not concern himself with this last aspect of civilization's wastes. It is too loaded with popular sensibility and, even worse (and in consequence), politics.

For politics and prejudice have laid their clammy hand on Bulpitt. When word got around that he was using garbage for a compost, a neighbor half a mile away complained to the Darien authorities that the garbage smelled. I got within, not half a mile but half an inch, of Bulpitt's treated garbage, and it did not smell at all. The complainant was the wife of the president of a chemical company. You may not find this as interesting as I do, but these occasional patnesses in human affairs are so interesting that I am laughing. The chemical president's wife was blessed with a nose that would be the despair and envy of a champion bird dog. What a girl to shoot over!

For Bulpitt, the complaint was no joke. It ushered in half a year of anxiety and the threat of a jail term; and he with a wife and three children, and a lot to do. The complaint went to the Darien health officer, a Darien doctor. In January, 1955, the town prosecutor ordered Bulpitt to keep his garbage in a covered water-tight pit and remove it once a week between May 1 and October 1. He was fined $100 for refusal to do so, and was held in contempt of the state power. Continued refusal would mean a jail term. A local committee of seven was appointed to smell Bulpitt's garbage. Six could smell nothing; the seventh, the health officer, carried the prosecution up to the state sanitary engineer at Hartford. In July, 1955, Bulpitt's garbage compost was adjudged inoffensive by the state.

The health officer appeared again at Bulpitt's nursery and threat-

ened to start the prosecution all over again. Bulpitt went to the
Board of Selectmen and charged that the public nuisance was not
himself, but the health officer. The next morning the officer's resignation was accepted.

The story was never reported in the newspapers (granted, it is not
quite on a par with the Dreyfus case); it was all transacted *in
camera*. Still, the secrecy takes a little of the edge off all the prizes
Bulpitt's germ-grown flowers have won—Special Trophy of the New
York Florists' Club, Charles H. Totty Memorial Medal for Horti-
cultural Achievement, A. L. Miller Trophy, New York Horticultural
Society Certificate of Cultural Merit, International Flower Show
Special Trophy for Excellence, and the Belgian Begonia Growers'
Association Award for the Best Exhibit with Tuberous Begonias.

A man like Bulpitt cannot really do very much. He has kept alive
a small area of land and given some leadership to others. He was
able to dissuade the nearby city of Norwalk from installing a garbage
incinerator. The city fathers were probably glad of the excuse to save
their money; still, they may also reclaim their garbage.

To a nation that owns the inorganic atom bomb, a preoccupation
with organic soil and germs must seem very hick. It is a wonderful
thing to have mastered the universe even as one bankrupts one's
backyard. Death the one way will be spectacular; the other way it
will be ignominious, a nightmare of malformations, cripples, miscarriages, and mysterious pox. If the end is deferred a hundred years,
one can imagine that the public polls of the day will record that
some 50 per cent will welcome extinction, the others, being a little
weaker, having the usual "no opinion." To be extinguished "with no
opinion": what an end!

The Pesticide That Came to Dinner
(1958)

A pesticide is a marvelous poison employed by man to kill other
species he finds inconvenient. Over a hundred pesticides are now in
use; 30,000 more are registered for use. Since World War II, millions
of tons of these poisons have been dumped on the American land-

scape. Some, such as DDT, are very stable and stay around a long time. Some penetrate the skin of the fruit or vegetable. Some accumulate in the soil. Some affect the taste of the food. Some wipe out beneficial predatory or parasitic insects. Some actually strengthen the breed of undesirable insects, after killing off the weaklings for a few generations.

And of course the average American comes to consume certain quantities of these poisons, especially DDT. The best medical evidence is agreed that the average American now contains in his fatty tissue upwards of five parts in a million of DDT, a nerve killer. Since the DDT just stays there and new consumption is added to it, the American is slowly becoming a DDT bank. People with as much as 300 parts to a million have shown no immediate ill effects. Ten or fifteen years are usually required to establish long-term effects. For DDT, the time is almost up. This long-staying poison (The Pesticide That Came to Dinner) has now been accused by some doctors of increasing the American incidence of cancer of the blood, leukemia, Hodgkin's disease, jaundice, and aplastic anemia. These terrible charges are not brand new; they are six years old.

Yet the United States Department of Agriculture, and the state pest control agencies, officially love DDT.

This infatuation was the subject of a trial, last month and this, in Brooklyn Federal Court before Judge Walter Bruchhausen. The defendants were Ezra Taft Benson, Secretary of Agriculture, and the New York State Commissioner of Agriculture. The respondents were defended by federal and state attorneys. The complainants were fourteen citizens of Long Island, headed by Dr. Robert Cushman Murphy and Archibald Roosevelt, and represented by Roger Hinds and Vincent Kleinfeld.

Last year the United States had decided that the gypsy moth, a pest that had originally escaped from an experimental silkworm laboratory in Massachusetts in 1869, deserved massive retaliation. A crash program was to go into gear: the gypsy moth was to be purged, as Genghis Khan's generals purged Kharesmia, leaving not one stone standing on another. In fact, 3,500,000 acres, mostly in the Northeast, were sprayed with a variety of DDT designated as chlorophenothane. The fact that the moth was "light and scattered" on Long Island's two outer counties, Nassau and Suffolk, did not deflect the Government's mighty rage. It sprayed them too, all of them, instead of the few localities where the moths were lightly entrenched. It sprayed lawns, dairy pastures, ponds, washlines, children's playgrounds, baby carriages, from planes often flying as low as two hundred feet. This is a relatively congested suburban area, dotted with poultry and vegetable farms and well-tended estates. The overwhelming mass of sprayed acreage had no gypsy moths whatever. Vengeance was visited alike upon the just and the unjust.

The sense of the fourteen citizens' complaint was: "Cut it out." The complaint read, in part: "unless restrained, the defendants will tortiously" (legal word) "and illegally trespass upon the persons and property of the plaintiffs, and cause them irreparable damage."

The DDT, the witnesses testified, had indeed done some killing. It had killed fiddler crabs (which eat the eggs of harmful starfish which destroy oysters and clams). It had killed pond fish, even big carp, almost immediately. It had killed ground-feeding birds such as thrushes and sparrows, as well as chickadees and starlings. It had certainly killed many species of useful small insects, such as ants, bees, and so on. In all the constant, fairly even wars set up by nature, the DDT had intervened to wipe out one army and anoint its enemy the victor. The result might well be to launch a dozen new pests, much worse than the gypsy moth, calling for still further crash programs with yet more deadly poisons.

Furthermore, testified a biochemist, the DDT will stay in the soil up to seven years and contaminate all later crops. Furthermore, certain insects build an immunity to DDT and return to the attack refreshed. (For cockroaches, for example, DDT is now about as lethal as a dry martini is for humans; for bedbugs DDT is really lethal.)

Humans, however, said a doctor from Mayo Clinic (since they must live with DDT about three hundred times as long as, say, a housefly), have an individual immunity that *decreases* with continued exposure and consumption.

For the Government, on an executive decision, to do all this to the private property and persons of the sovereign power would seem unalloyed tyranny. It is, in fact, not even Socialism, but straight Communism of a kind that is becoming an increasingly victorious American heresy.

And so, as the Government brought in its witnesses, who would have to be Communist commissars, I paid a visit to the courtroom to get the image of the modern American commissar. These trials in nearly empty courtrooms, where the highly skilled legal actors are playing *as if* to all the appellate courts up to the Supreme Court, are at once thrilling and soporific. The chief Government counsel had the manner of an actor with a spear in his breast; the fact that he was nearly in tears would have reached to the balcony, had there been one, and will reach, he would hope, to the Supreme Court. The chief counsel for the citizens was a little Giant Panda; he delegated the cross-examination to his saturnine assistant, Vincent Kleinfeld—remember him. The judge, bony, gray and possum-eyed, had a kindly, apprehensive air.

The commissar I saw had a trick, while waiting for a question, of tipping his head back and closing his eyes dreamily, as if to convey that he could handle all this in his sleep. It was infectious; one of the court attendants took a nap.

The commissar, a thoroughly nice man (as perhaps Moscow commissars are too), testified that the executive decision to hit the enemy, the gypsy moth, had gone through channels, that DDT had never bothered human beings as far as he could see, and that DDT only killed those species of animal life that the Government told it to kill, so far as he had ever been able to determine.

Have I made his evidence ridiculous enough? I don't know how to get any more satirical. He might have said that the DDT was so patriotic it just couldn't have killed decent American fiddler crabs, carp, thrushes, and sparrows; but actually he didn't. He might have said that good frontier-stock Americans ought to be able to handle an ingestion of DDT; but in fact he didn't. All that he did was to issue the party line, with his eyelids disdainfully and patiently shut: America crushes its enemy—the gypsy moth; no second-guessing is needed or wanted.

There are two ways of dismissing the above story: perhaps the Government hadn't known what it was doing; or second, perhaps it won't do it again, anyway.

Taking the second first, the Government will begin this spring spraying 27,000,000 acres of the South, from South Carolina to Texas, as a crash program against the fire ant. The weapons will be a pesticide called dieldrin, two and a half times more lethal than DDT, and another called heptachlor. The fire ant nests in mounds two feet tall, sometimes occurring a hundred to an acre, and can very easily be extirpated specifically on the ground; but the Government will use indiscriminate spraying by planes, inevitably killing quail.

Since this pest is in the Deep South, a great deal of wonderful tall talk has already enveloped the fire ant. Some white Southerners on picnics have been bitten on the backside by fire ants; one such bite would more than justify a crash program to a Democratic Congress. There is a story that these fire ants are half-breeds between black and reddish fire ants, both smuggled in from Latin America; but Northern entomologists think they are native American fire ants, and that the immigrants are found only around several Gulf ports. As you can see, a certain satirical symbolism seems to ride behind this whole matter of pesticides, making faces. Anyway, Congress has appropriated $2,400,000 for the fire-ant war, and the states will add amounts up to $500,000, as in Florida.

As for the Government's other excuse, that it didn't know what it was doing, I have before me three volumes, dated 1951 and 1952, of testimony before a congressional select committee concerning the use of chemicals, including pesticides, on the national ecology. The chief counsel for the committee was the same Vincent Kleinfeld we have just met. The machinery does exist, under this democracy, and is actually used, to ventilate these terrible threats to the public welfare. The evidence ran to nearly two thousand pages; the seven honorable congressmen heard most of it; but what good is it? What is overridingly more important is that man has discovered a new weapon, and he tends to go crazy, whether it is a spiked club, a new car, or a hydrogen warhead.

In 1951–1952, all the necessary evidence was given to the Congress of the United States.

DDT, it was testified, is consumed by people on and in fruits and vegetables, and in the beef, milk, and butter of cows whose backs, barns, and silage have been DDT-sprayed. Newborn babies contain some DDT at birth and ingest still more with their mothers' milk.

To comfort hypochondriacs, it should be added that, as far as we know yet, most of us seem able to carry our DDT load without any apparent injury. Still, it is far from beneficial.

Chlordane, another chlorinated hydrocarbon, is five times as toxic as DDT, is stored by the human body fat much more rapidly, and causes rapid degeneration of the liver and kidneys. It is used on some food crops and in household pesticides (including the one on my own kitchen shelf). An added difficulty with chlordane, as with toxaphene, aldrin, dieldrin, and heptachlor, is that there is at present no satisfactory analytical method for finding it in food. Yet all these are in general and expanding use.

Selenium, in intakes as small as only three parts per million, will produce cirrhosis, and then cancer, of the liver. It penetrates the skin of sprayed fruit and also builds up in the soil, thence moving into the growing plant.

Phenylmercury compounds, a fungicide, are very poisonous and accumulate in the kidney. They have been used extensively on fruit and vegetable crops.

Benzene hexachloride (BHC) produces off-flavors in the canned product, and also has a toxic effect on the brain tissue of the consumer.

Arsenicals used as pesticides can definitely produce cancer of the skin, if as little as 0.19 gram is ingested.

Beta-naphthylamine, which is hardly toxic at all, will produce cancer of the bladder, if taken even in very minute quantities. (This is used in dyes, not in pesticides.) The champion chemical producer of cancer is probably acetylaminofluorene developed as an insecticide. It can put cancer into the liver, stomach, breast, thyroid, kidney, bladder, genital tract, external auditory canal, and occasionally the brain. Entirely by accident, some English scientists stumbled on the discovery of its great carcinogenic powers before it was used. This was a narrow escape. But since new and insufficiently tested chemicals are constantly going on the market, society is actually skating on a very thin sheet of ice.

Here again, some qualification is necessary. Some pesticides, if sprayed long enough before the harvest, will have evaporated or washed off the crop in plenty of time. Also, since the American public now demands nearly perfect fruit and vegetables, the farmer cannot sell his produce unless he kills off the bugs with something. The wormy apple is now unsalable in America. The pesticide, properly used, is indispensable to the job of feeding the world.

But the 1951–1952 congressional investigation fully brought out that the current infatuation with chemicals often approaches homicidal insanity. Apart from pesticides, a very few examples, out of many, would include: That the flour industry for thirty years used nitrogen trichloride, called Agene, which causes hysteria in dogs. That the Food and Drug Administration managed to seize and destroy frozen peaches sprayed with thiourea, very poisonous. That the poison, para-phenetyl, was used for fifty years as a sweetening agent. That lithium chloride killed some people before it was removed from the market. That mineral oil in food prevented human absorption of important vitamins. That monochloracetic acid, used commonly as a food preservative, was as poisonous as strychnine or carbolic acid (some manufacturers, mostly in the South, ignored this information for some time). That cheese wrappers made with dehydroacetic acid were equally poisonous. That "emulsifiers" are commonly used to offset lowered egg and fat content in breads, cakes, and mixes. That women were permanently blinded by an eyelash preparation using pyrogallic acid. And so on. And on.

Most of these many problems are now under control. In any case, a few deaths or outbreaks or blindings will bring summary action. But pesticides present the much more difficult problems of massive, slow poisoning of the whole American people and the possible dislocation and ruin of the whole ecology and economy to a point of no return. The pesticides have the support, not only of the great chemical companies, the farmers, and the great food distributors, but also of the unarguable fact that the bugs that want to eat our food are our enemies. These bugs, as well as such innocent bystanders as the poor fiddler crabs, carp, and thrushes, have no vote under our system of government.

And now it is a pleasure to point out that even corporations number their saints. One such is Beech-Nut Packing, which sets its tolerance of DDT traces in the raw foods it buys at practically zero. The witness, Dr. L. G. Cox, a Beech-Nut research chemist, noted that this policy costs the company about $100,000 a year and the goodwill of the farmers who, however, sell their condemned crops to other canners on the open market. He testified that human mother's milk averaged 0.14 parts of DDT per million, that 100 parts DDT per million killed a third of young turkey poults consuming it. Chlordane as a soil residue, he said, gets into carrots. Benzene hexachloride used on cotton was present in the next, rotated crop of peanuts, which the company rejected. The same chemical has also been found in Florida squash and celery, Pennsylvania peaches and spinach, South Carolina sweet potatoes and New York apples. The company has found chlordane on California celery and New York cabbage and carrots.

Beech-Nut makes baby foods and peanut butter; its scrupulousness is understandable but unfortunately unique. The witness did not think much of the so-called experts, who are usually economic entomologists. Some of these, he said, "who have been active in the development of certain ill-advised pesticide recommendations have tended to become chemical specialists rather than entomologists." He quoted another opinion on this expert: "He ceases to be a biologist and, in the majority of cases, becomes in effect, a mere tester of poisons or an insecticide salesman."

The response of the Manufacturing Chemists Association to such testimony was to raise a fund among its members to fight the bad news. The witness put the fund at $119,000 at that time. A meeting of the association did not let Dr. Roy C. Newton, vice president of Swift & Company, make the following remarks:

. . . It is not clear from the publications emanating from the chemical industry over the past two years that many of the members of this industry understand why a new material cannot be adapted to the food industry as quickly as it can to plastics, textiles, etc. . . . Running through this series of propaganda articles are many unsound premises [such as a sense of persecution; that since all foods are chemical, all chemicals are food; that anything, even salt, can be poison; etc.] . . . I have spent all my business life in the food industry. . . . I believe there is a real threat to the food industry. . . . [If] the Food and Drug Administration [is] prevented from carrying out its responsibility of protecting the public . . . there will undoubtedly be a surge of new chemical substances incorporated in food without adequate pretesting.

Such a program will lead to a disaster, just as surely as we are assembled here today. Such a disaster will reflect discredit to the food industry; incidentally, it will also reflect discredit to the chemical industry, but the principal damage will be done to the public. . . .

May we hope that part of the activity of the Manufacturing Chemists Association will be directed toward the education of its own members who may not understand clearly their responsibilities.

This voice, so much more grave and gentlemanly than my own, is surely entitled to the last word on the subject.

Knight in Two-Ton Armor
(1957)

By far the bloodiest of all congressional hearings—and possibly the least publicized—have just been released by the Government Printing Office, in 927 pages, for the House Committee on Interstate and Foreign Commerce. The subject was highway traffic accidents.

Everyone seemed to know the famous figures: 20,000,000 traffic-court cases a year, 9,000,000 accidents, 1,300,000 people injured, 100,000 totally and permanently disabled, and about 40,000 killed immediately, plus an unknown number who died later of the effects. The money cost was $4,500,000,000 annually. In the fifteen through thirty-five age brackets, one out of three deaths is caused by the motor vehicle, said one witness, who thought it incompatible with the American philosophy that we ignore our leading cause of death.

In the parade of witnesses, the automobile industry was brilliantly represented. Its claim that the horsepower race is not at all dangerous was corroborated, oddly, by a National Safety Council official. Ford, Chrysler, and American Motors engineers gave evidence of elaborate, intelligent, and sincere research into how to make cars safer for the driver and passengers. (General Motors was quoted as opposed to this endeavor.) The old steering post that could hit the driver's chest with a six-ton force even in case of a 15 m.p.h. crash (deceleration magnitude: eighty gravities) has been eliminated. Hurtling passengers will bounce off Ensolite-padded dashboards and be held inside the car by doors with improved locks; the foresighted will prosper in seat belts. Even General Motors, while insisting that power is what is for sale in an automobile, gave proof that it, too, is wondering what happens to the people when an automobile ends its career suddenly.

When a witness working on a Ford research grant at Cornell said that the first step toward highway safety was to get all the old cars off the roads, I thought I had had a preview of next year's advertising campaign for the new cars. If safety can be used to promote obsolescence, perhaps it will get sold.

Other witnesses filled in another reason why Detroit may soon have to embrace safety, willy-nilly.

Police captain, highway patrol: "The automobile is too fast for the person, the driver of today. . . . It is a weapon of destruction."

Supervisor of safety education: "We also recommend that automobile manufacturers place less emphasis on the higher-speed potentials and devote more emphasis to safety features."

Director, department of highways: "I am of the belief that the automobile industry could broaden its views and assume a greater share of the responsibility for driver and passenger safety. The power of sales promotion and advertising of the automobile industry might well be put to use in promoting safety on the highways. . . . With this change in attitude the industry might well consider real honest-to-goodness efforts toward designing safer automobiles. . . . [It] can do much more than it has."

Chairman, governor's traffic safety committee: "The manufacturer's defense is that it is reserve speed for emergencies. What emergencies? On today's graded highways, emergencies calling for such extreme power are so few they hardly justify the building of potential suicide and murder into every man's every-day vehicle. . . . Why design bumpers with bullet-like protrusions front and rear—veritable ramrods? . . . Why use so much chrome so placed on dash and hood as to blind the driver when the sun is at certain angles?"

Ex-chairman, judicial section, National Safety Council: "Automobile manufacturers must assume their proper share of responsibility for the attractive and destructive equipment they are willing to place into the hands of anyone who has a down payment and knows how to make an X. . . . Perhaps Congress ought to modify the existing excise-tax laws so that we tax motor vehicles on the basis of their rated, developed or advertised horsepower, whichever is the greater." He put into the record two automobile advertisements: "See this beautiful package of dynamite. . . . Meet the new

boss. . . . High-stepping strato-streak power-plant. . . . The blaz-
ing action of 227 horses is yours in a flash. Right here is the team
that puts you in a performance class all by yourself. You're driving
the one that's clocked from zero to sixty in ten seconds flat." "What
kind of a fool," the witness asked, "would want to drive an automobile on our public highways at 147 miles per hour, or accelerate
from zero to sixty miles per hour in ten seconds flat? These advertisements are designed to appeal to the highway idiot."

County coroner: "The manufacturers have claimed that a lot of
safety features have been installed . . . beginning in 1952 and 1953.
The study did not reveal any difference [in injuries to occupants] in
accidents to the automobiles of the vintage of 1940–49 and the
vintage of 1952 and 1953 . . . I believe that the automobile manufacturer must assume some responsibility. . . ."

Chairman, legislative study commission on traffic safety: "Our
commission made a trip to Detroit to study this problem. We returned convinced that the industry was giving only lip service to
traffic safety while continuing to build more and more horsepower
and speed in its products. . . . The industry is still putting sharp
pointed spears on the front of vehicles and calling them radiator
ornaments. . . . We legislate for the health, welfare, and safety of
our people. May it not be necessary to begin to legislate to get safer
cars on our roads? . . . The President's White House Conference
has been very helpful but even last year they took the word 'Action'
out of that so they wouldn't offend anybody. This is not a business
you can be in and not offend anybody." The witness cited a twelve-
year-old boy in Fort Wayne who had been impaled on one of the
aforementioned spears, which in the new cars vary between two and
five inches of working blade. The longer bayonets are on Chevrolet,
Buick, Ford, Packard—all at the height of a pedestrian's heart,
though such marksmanship is well beyond the average driver.

The unkindest cut to Detroit was a Chicago lawyer's brief in the
Chicago Bar Record that all victims of the automobile should sue
the manufacturer under the rule of manufacturer's liability according
to the Restatement of the Law of Torts.

The day seems near when Detroit will have to bow before this
gathering storm. Make no mistake, it is a real storm. The probability

that Detroit has already planned it that way was hinted at by the peculiar indifference of the new cars' designers to criticism of the 1957 cars.

There was a culprit, other than the industry, uncovered by the investigation. The driver, of course. Evidence was given of a man whose wife had to read the signs to him, of another filling out his accident card with the aid of a large magnifying glass, of others with one eye and truck drivers with one leg who used an iron bar to work the clutch pedal. All had licenses and, if they are alive, probably still have them.

The congressmen were evidently loath to interfere with state and local government in regulating license examinations, periodic re-examinations, traffic rules and signals, and so on, and so on, so that such evidence was as useful as a horror movie.

A conclusion of the testimony was that no one generalization or no one solution will cover all the drivers and situations everywhere. In urban areas, where the killed are chiefly pedestrians, the driver's only sins may be impatience and irritability. In rural areas, where the killed are overwhelmingly the drivers and passengers, the driver is essentially an unintentional suicide.

The situations in Ohio and Indiana were gone into thoroughly.

Ohio seems to have concentrated on publicity, education, school driving courses, and a driver file-card system. The legislature has refused to pass several highway safety bills. December is the deadliest month. Two-thirds of the deaths occur in rural areas. In the whole state, alcohol was a factor in 19.4 per cent of the deaths. Montgomery County (Dayton) in six months of 1956 had thirty-seven deaths caused by twenty-eight drivers. Of the twenty-eight, 57 per cent were in the sixteen-twenty-five age group and of these about 90 per cent of those examined showed 0.15 per cent alcohol in the blood or more, indicating either six ounces of whisky or six small bottles of beer. Two-thirds of the killers had had prior arrests. Here youthful drinking was the primary cause of fatal accidents.

Indiana, on the other hand, seemed to have successfully got those boys out of the driver's seat. It suspends about 40,000 licenses a year. The superintendent of state police said: "You can ask people on the street and they will say it is the drunken driver operating after midnight who is contributing to all of our trouble in the fatal accident picture. This is not so." He meant it was not so just then in Indiana. The Indiana drunks are so scared that, instead of December, October is the deadliest month, presumably on the way home from football games. A safety expert said sensibly: "We can have about as much traffic safety as we the people are willing to pay for in cash and in restricted privileges and mobility."

One congressman who had been generally quiet perked up at the alcoholic evidence and contributed that he had read, or heard, that four tablespoonfuls of honey would sober up a drunk: was this true? The state police laboratory lieutenant assured him it was true in some cases because the honey sugar (fructose) accelerates the burning of the alcohol sugar. Black coffee, it was added, does not reduce alcohol blood content at all; it only offsets alcohol's depressive effect. The congressman leaned back, satisfied. Perhaps we will get a bill compelling bars to add honey to all drinks.

Some witnesses tried to warm up the old story that the great killers are the railroads, but quickly sawed themselves off that feeble limb. A director of highway safety grew a little poetic. "The thing that is hardest to see in all the world, I think, is a freight train crossing a rural highway on a slightly rainy evening . . . If the track happens to be elevated a little bit the lights of the approaching traffic will shine under, and they are broken because the wheels roll past."

The fourth possible culprit was frequently given as Government, but the congressmen kept pointing out the democratic hazards of saving people against their will. About 30,000 drivers and passengers are killed a year: the reckless, incompetent, or unlucky drivers may not have to rest on the conscience of the state. They are largely the masters of their fate, playing a very large and relatively safe game of Russian roulette. Statistically, one can ride 400,000 vehicle miles before one has to be injured; one can spin the revolver barrel over five million more miles before one must be totally and permanently disabled, and then one has a chance through nine million more miles before one must be killed. However, any of these can happen the next time out, too. Remember, it's Russian roulette.

The pedestrian, however, did not agree to play any game and ought to lie on Government's conscience. Though only about 10,000 of him are killed a year, these are second-degree murders. On a main artery where drivers make a left turn to get on a bridge approach, I have seen an elderly lady bringing a child home from school intimidated by the cars for ten minutes until she was hysterical. Dozens of times I have seen cars whirl around a corner (to get out of the way of the following traffic) so that some pedestrian saved his own life only by mysterious intuition (crossing with the light at the intersection). The pedestrian does not get six million miles of chances in an exciting game; his murderer comes looking for him. Pedestrian deaths have declined, but this is because people's reflexes are getting better in situations where theoretically they are absolutely safe.

The best drivers take care of their passengers, but what is their record as against pedestrians? An indication would be given by the safety records of taxi drivers. Such statistics (broken down by type of vehicle) are hard to come by, but the New York City Police Department did a fifteen-month survey from August, 1954, through October, 1955, a period in which New York cabs, going 752 million vehicle-miles, killed thirty pedestrians and injured 1,795. The United States rate of killed per hundred million vehicle-miles is 6.4 fatalities, of whom 1.6 are pedestrians. The New York cabbies killed not 1.6 but four pedestrians per hundred million miles. This, though not good, is not as bad as it sounds, for most pedestrian deaths are in urban areas, such as that covered by the survey. My observation, however, is that cab drivers are far too proud of their genius at short bursts of speed, especially around corners. I have been in three cars that hit pedestrians. All three were taxis, at night.

Though the driver will be a pedestrian again an hour later, I think some of his subconscious impatience with pedestrians derives from the fact that he has spent up to $5,000 for his form of locomotion while the pedestrian gets around on an investment in a ten-dollar pair of shoes.

And so, of course, we have a fifth theory as to the guilty party on the highways. A Los Angeles judge named Pfaff wrote in *This Week* for February 24, 1957, "What we need to inaugurate is a 'get tough' campaign directed at the careless, *discourteous and law-breaking* pedestrian. . . . A pedestrian who crosses an intersection against the red light should be treated the same as a motorist who drives through it." Drivers who are convinced by Pfaff's peculiar legal concepts ought to be able to deposit 20,000 pedestrian corpses on Pfaff's front lawn this year. This odd judge not only overlooks the relative weights and speeds of pedestrian versus car, but seems ignorant of the pedestrian's sovereign right as owner of the highway versus the merely licensed and controlled right of the driver to be there at all. Pfaff is probably more dangerous as a driver than as a judge. Keep him, Los Angeles, but take away his driver's license.

This sort of murderous frivolity (always expressed as virile efficiency) underlay some engineering testimony at the hearings, but not the enforcement testimony, as the quotes given above show. We are all pedestrians, except for the babies, the bedridden and wheelchair cases. In medieval times, the armored knights at full gallop had every legal, as well as impact, advantage over the serf on foot. I had thought those days were gone, but they seem to have returned to Los Angeles.

The kind of thought that was not aired at the hearings, but is central to them, was the fact that it is economically absurd for an American citizen to spend a third of his income on his car and use up the equivalent of a barrel of petroleum every week in order to commute twenty miles to his job. One train can carry a thousand of them to work. This fact is currently invisible to the American public, and will remain invisible until the very day it becomes plainly and horribly visible. The automobile as now used is an extravagance that no ecology can afford; nor can this one. Some future day may well see 120 million cars on the American roads, and the oil reserves down to one year's consumption. The day after will see perhaps thirty million motor cars, mostly trucks and buses.

On that day, with car owners a voting minority, Congress will doubtless get very serious about highway safety. For the present any bill that comes out of the hopper will be a model of tact toward the driver and the industry.

Darkness Under the Dome
(1958)

In the charm war with Russia, the natural arena is the so-called international trade fair which has become increasingly popular among the underdeveloped countries. Here the local people can see for themselves what the two competing worlds have to offer. Our own participation in these endless fairs makes an instructive story. Here is a working test of what our Government thinks is charming about America, how charming our mass-produced merchandise is to other people, how capable Russia has become at duplicating it, what is America's real charm and power, what in general charms whom. If it seems sometimes that the present American Government cannot charm beetles, it may be because we are at present infatuated with our own merchandise, and imagine that anybody else would be too.

The trade fair was not fully understood, as late as 1954, by our concerned agencies, the State and Commerce departments. That year, when the great Milan Triennale invited us to exhibit, our Government sneered that this was a matter for private enterprise. A little magazine called *Interiors* did invite Mr. Buckminster Fuller (truly private enterprise, at both ends) to install one of his geodesic domes at Milan, and in fact this won the Grand Prize. If the reader is not long since familiar with the geodesic dome, I will describe this object later.

On August 1, 1956, another little trade fair was to open in Kabul, Afghanistan. The strategic importance of Afghanistan was formerly well-known to the masters of the British Empire who had not, however, bothered to pass on this crucial information to the new masters in Washington, who seem to have been unable to work it out for themselves. For 2,500 years Afghanistan has been the door to India, and the only door overland. The Russian passion to push the Turk-Sib railway into Kabul had been blocked by the British for a hundred years. The British ambassador's palace in Kabul is still bigger than the king's, but the British have ceased to care.

By themselves, the Afghans are interesting people. They have had a dozen emperors and kings of India. They were the tribesmen who poured into Kashmir and gave Nehru an excuse to send in his troops and instigate the most volatile unfought war on the agenda, not against Afghanistan but against Pakistan. They are born to the mechanics of mobility. They are superb mechanics. They take a piece of junk and turn it into a beautiful rifle. They buy exhausted, third-hand American taxis and make them run with hand-made parts. Seeing this, the Russians paved a good stretch of Kabul highway for the Afghans to race on. A little later, Russia was allowed to push its railway into Kabul; tomorrow, India and the world. The slumber in Washington was still sweet and untroubled.

And then came the cables from the American ambassador in Kabul describing a most peculiar interest in the Jeshyn Fair by the Russians, the Chinese, the Czechs, and the East Germans. Why, the exhibits of the two greatest Communist powers were to cover 32,000 and 22,000 square feet. In Kabul, of all places! And the Jeshyn Fair was to open in two months.

What to do? A miracle was required. The growing American philosophy is that miracles are produced by corporations. But what was wanted was far beyond any existing American corporation to deliver. It was to complete a large building in its component parts within one month, load them on a single DC-4 plane and deliver them in Kabul prepared for erection in a day or two. Since America is lucky enough to number individuals as well as corporations, the Department of Commerce was lucky enough to find a South Asian expert named Jack Massey who was smart enough to know about Buckminster Fuller. Both individuals. As usual, in a genuine emergency, the individual has to be found.

After consultation with his staff, Mr. Fuller said that he could and would do it, at cost. And at a minute fraction of what any other structure would have cost.

Before the month was up, the dome was delivered at Raleigh, N.C., airport—a 100-foot clear-span frame of aluminum tubes and vinyl-coated nylon skin. It was approved, packed on the DC-4, and flown to Afghanistan.

In Kabul it was erected by a few Afghans in a day. Its materialization, immense and gleaming-white, was stunning to the Afghans.

Some came inside, fell on their knees and prayed. Others said that it was merely ancient Afghan architecture, for indeed it applies the same universal principles as the nomad's yurt, made of interlaced saplings and sheepskins.

The dome was the sensation of the Kabul fair. It outdrew the huge Chinese and Russian exhibits, which were four and three times as big, by heavy margins. The number of visitors, 202,000, was equal to the population of Kabul.

Every testimony was that this last-minute victory in the charm war was won by the dome, not by the merchandise inside. This latter is exceedingly interesting as showing what American bureaucrats believe to be America's charm: the Borden talking cow, Lionel toy trains, bouncing ball bearings, a cranky hi-fi set, a TV screen on which the Afghans saw themselves looking at the screen, and movies of American football games and drum majorettes.

America is full of better things than these. The electronic gadgets of automation, for example, open up the world of applied brain and spirit. A lot of modern children's toys are quite fascinating. But merchandise, simply as merchandise, means nothing without a local production and distribution system, or a big import operation.

The dome was different. The Afghans were so delighted with it they kept climbing up the frame and sliding down the taut, suspended skin, with whoops. They were doing so when the king drove around the dome several times, and had his police drag his subjects off their slide. The King conveyed to the United States ambassador that he would be happy to accept the geodesic dome as a gift. The request should have been granted at once. But the Department of Commerce had no budget item to cover it. The king was refused. The Russians at once consoled him with a plane worth at least $150,000, five times the cost of the dome.

The Fuller dome, I should explain, has evolved over a period of thirty years out of a quite complicated mathematics describing the tensions on the surface of a hollow sphere. Being based on sound universal dynamics, the structure is incredibly strong, though it looks fragile. It is the basic component of the Defense-Early-Warning line of radar stations and of the Marine Air Force's mobile installations. It is as typically and individually American as the first Model T Ford car—the simplest and best way to do a difficult thing.

The Kabul dome was packed up toward the end of 1956 and flown to another trade fair in Bangkok, Thailand, then in the middle of last year to another in Tokyo, to go in 1958 to still another in Osaka. In Thailand and in Japan, as in Afghanistan, the people said, "But that is our own traditional architecture, industrialized." The Japanese are building a half-dozen of their own. Since Fuller has no Asian patent, they need pay no royalties. One in Tokyo is, however, called the Fuller Dome, in honorable apology.

The dome was by now basic propaganda, and the Department of Commerce invested in a fleet of them to be flown about the globe. Two, of 100-foot clear span, were at the Casablanca and Tunis trade fairs in the summer of 1957. One of 114 feet was the center of the fair at Poznań, Poland, our first entry behind the Iron Curtain, in the summer after the Hungarian rebellion. In this political climate, the dome must have revived some of Europe's faith in the continuous American revolution of fresh, untrammeled thinking. Later the Poznań dome was flown to Istanbul, Turkey, while another went to the fair at Salonika, Greece. One of eighty-four feet at the 1957 Milan Triennale won the Grand Prize again from a jury of seventeen nations, to round out the story. Other domes covered American exhibits at the trade fairs in Calcutta, Madras, and Bombay, India, and in Rangoon, Burma.

A comparison is insistent between the charm of the geodesic dome and of the rocket missile. Certainly the development of the rocket was equally individualistic until Hitler took it over for the V-2. Afterward, the Russian and American corporations took it over. Since it seemed competitive with manned aircraft, the American effort could not be much advanced by the young air generals who could not help regarding the missile as something aimed at shooting boy generals out of the air and the aircraft companies into the red. Russia's air generals had no claim to having "won the war" and no prestige. Thus, the Russians beat us into the sky with the satellite. The charm, as we can still painfully remember, was instantaneous and universal. Our own satellite four months later seems to me to have been the more charming by its relative lightness and efficiency. And it was put up by what was formerly the heavy-handed branch of the services, the ground army. Yet here again the job was saved by individuals, by Wernher von Braun and the court-martialed Colonel

Nickerson. When the Russians put a dog into their second sputnik, they even put the concept of an individual into the sky, and into the minds of men.

This sequence strikes me as very interesting. The present government of the U.S.S.R. is the enemy of the individual, quite frankly; yet it takes an individualistic invention and projects it as individualistic charm and has an immense success. I begin to remember again the many charming feats of Adolf Hitler, such as the Volkswagen and the Autobahnen, not to speak of the V-2. These fellows, it seems, can always outcharm us.

We need only move on to the trade fair in Zagreb, Yugoslavia, in September, 1957, to read a climax in American and Russian policies in the charm war. The American exhibit had no geodesic dome this time, but it had a lot of merchandise, admiringly reported by the American press. Contributed by the Chain Stores Association, it was assembled in a reproduction of a typical American supermarket crammed with frozen lamb chops, spinach, and ice cream, the putative contents of the American belly. Since the Yugoslav beholder had no way of getting any of this, he either regarded it as a sort of museum exhibit or a personal insult. The message was: "Eat your heart out."

Life in particular said that it found this propaganda for the American way of life simply splendid. Since propaganda is a subjective matter, I do not want to sound cocksure about anything here. Nevertheless, for myself, I can say that I have a very limited interest in how well somebody else eats—somebody I don't know and probably wouldn't like anyway. The consumption of food, as all fiction editors know very well, is beautiful in babies, still charming in children, acceptable in teen-agers and repulsive in adults. Try to sell a story about gluttony. My thought is that our Zagreb exhibit was about as offensive as it is possible to get. It had no mark of brain, spirit, abstraction, or hope; it simply presented a marvelously refined bestiality of the belly. Yet this is the level of our foreign policy, because it is also the level at which corporate advertising works.

Am I subversive if I say that America stands for something very different? We were once a masculine, ascetic, roving, adventurous people who created new solutions as fast as new problems arose.

And in fact that same personnel is still here, though in the shadow.

The ruling personnel of America had their total failure rubbed into their noses, right there at Zagreb. There was of course no American geodesic dome. And so the Russians now proceeded to raise over their exhibit a vividly colored geodesic dome, of aluminum tubes, but of canvas instead of plastic. It was, of course, as it had always been under the United States flag, an enormous success.

Tragedy Writ in Water
(1956)

The worst blows taken by the United States in the last years have not been political, but physical; and they have all come from the same source—water. Flash floods in New England and California. Southern droughts, sinking water tables, virtual civil war in the Southwest over water rights, vast erosion in the Mississippi and Colorado basins: the whole country seems to be in this jam together.

As a great planning people, we ought to be able to plan our way out of this net of disaster. Yet we have hardly made an effective start, despite all the warnings.

The reason for our failure may be that our thinking about water, both by expert and layman, is shot with fallacies rising from some of man's oldest and deepest instincts. Starting at the bottom, the indicated fallacies follow:

1. Primarily because people hate to get wet and dislike drowning, they tend to feel that the world has too much water, rather than too little. The opinion is understandable. The oceans hold some 300 million cubic miles of it—eighteen times the volume of all land above water. This total cannot diminish, except to turn into ice or vapor. Some of the vapor blows across the land, carrying an estimated (remember that word!) 24,000 cubic miles of water a year to the land areas. The ensuing rainfall, sleet, and snow are what make men build tight, warm houses with cozy mortgages. The human opinion is that a rainy day is a "bad" day. Worse ingratitude can hardly be imagined.

Oxygen, which is eight-tenths of water by weight, but not of course by atomic count, is one of the rarest elements in the entire universe. In the universe it is a collector's item. We are fantastically lucky to have it. Oxygen as water and air is what primarily differentiates our planet from the moon and Mars and the other deserts in the sky. If there is one blessing for which alone man should get on his knees and give thanks daily, it is oxygen.

2. Nobody, in his own opinion, uses much water personally. If a suburbanite in the Northeast with a lot 50 feet by 100 collected in a tank the rain which fell on his property over the year—about three feet of it—he would "own" 500 tons of water. Ample, he would say. But in fact the city American uses for his personal requirements in a year about 4,000 tons, the rural villager 1,000 tons, the suburbanite something between. The American family uses an average of 10,000 tons a year personally. And everything Americans use or consume uses still more water. We really survive on such facts as that an acre of grain needs a seasonal 650,000 gallons, an acre of cotton 800,000 gallons, a ton of finished steel 65,000 gallons; a ton of viscose rayon 200,000 gallons, a ton of bromine five million gallons, and the hydroelectric power plants of the United States need a trillion gallons a day. The industries that need the most water are precisely those that most intimately affect the average consumer: oil refining, metalworking, paper manufacturing, chemicals, distilling, and rubber. And industry could use most of its water up to fifty times over, if it would clean it, but it generally takes the same attitude as the individual citizen: there is always plenty more—until an area is utterly exhausted and fouled, and the plant moves on.

The total American use of water for domestic, irrigational, industrial, and power-generative purposes has been estimated at 200 billion gallons a day.

3. People tend to think that only the local rainfall and stream-flow affect them. The grim fact is that every local water situation is intimately controlled by events a thousand and more miles away, as New England may now agree after water disasters that were spawned in the tropics. All sensible expositions of the water problem have to deal in billions of gallons, millions of acre-feet, and thousands of cubic miles of water. Before any local situation can even be described, a repulsively huge picture has to be sketched in.

4. Every American is committed to the absolute, inherited, and

inbred knowledge that God gave America more of everything than anybody else. Hold onto your seats. Not water. The United States is among the least favored in this respect among the world's great populated areas. The explanation is simple. The winds north of the equator blow generally clockwise off the oceans. The United States thus gets its original water winds down along the Pacific coast and up from the Caribbean and Gulf of Mexico. The Pacific winds run into the Cascade Range and drop virtually all their water in the narrow belt west of it. The Atlantic winds miss most of the Great Plains.

The disfavored zone is the home of America's favorite entertainment form, where never a discouraging word is heard. Though it be treason to reveal it, the whole Rocky Mountain plateau and its eastern slope constitute a leading candidate for the world's next great desert. Progress in this dismal direction is already well along. The cowboys may soon turn in their dogies for camels. The sandstorms may bury the transcontinental roadbeds and overland communication between the two coasts of the United States. The consequent injury to the free peoples of the world, in spite of all that air freight and the Panama Canal could do, would drown the screams of Arizona real-estate agents.

5. Any child "knows" that all water finally flows back into the oceans. Any river, while fulfilling this necessary function, is a true beauty of nature. But it also represents by definition a failure of the land to hold on to the water given it.

Unlike man, the land tries to hold on to the water. The grasses and trees, the valleys and ponds and soils, incessantly trap and hold the priceless water. The Great Lakes alone bank a volume of water that could cover the whole United States under a ten-foot sea. There is, however, another, greater, invisible lake from coast to coast—the underground water table. Some say it holds enough pure, filtered water to cover the country under several hundred feet of the best water you ever drank—in other words, over half a century of normal rainfall.

The surplus of water is represented by the rivers. But this is the only water most people mean when they think of fresh, clean, inland water. This is the water that Government and private entrepreneurs especially love to play with.

The history of our rivers is so tragic as to be outlawed from parlor conversation. City civilization has made a river an unspeakable, untouchable and, of course, undrinkable wonder of civilization. Man's habitual horror is always, as Arthur H. Carhart put it in *Water—or Your Life*, to use the river as a "convenient extension of the sewage system." He estimated that in 1950 American cities and industries poured two-and-a-half billion tons of sewage into once-live streams. Coal mines alone dump in a year several million tons of sulphuric acid into the nation's rivers. The bed of the Schuylkill River, a once-idyllic river flowing through Philadelphia, became so foul that its slimes generated enough "marsh gas" to run efficient gas stoves. (In this case, a few private individuals dug out the slime and restored life to part of the river.) Most American rivers passing great cities end as great sewers of death.

Clearly disgusting as this is, a far more disastrous mishandling of water lies in our ruin of watersheds from which the rains drain into the rivers. Water has a consuming vice: it is in a tearing hurry to run back into the oceans. The result? Since Americans began plowing the ancient sod of the plains, it is estimated that the waters of the Mississippi-Missouri system, running majestically to the Gulf, have been carrying with them every year an average of 400 million tons of topsoil—an inch of topsoil off 5,000 square miles, or the area of Connecticut. This process, repeated over the United States, had ruined by the 1930's an estimated 150,000 square miles of American land, mostly lower-grade pasture land—the combined area of North and South Dakota.

If a foreign enemy had seized that much of the United States or a traitor had betrayed it, no American could rest until it had been avenged and rewon. But though the equivalent of two great American states has been detached from the Union, so far as useful purposes are concerned, the political calm is terrifying. Even to mention the loss of two states on the floor of the United States Senate is regarded as something of a bore. Since the total American loss of topsoil per year equals an inch off 70,000 square miles, or the area of Missouri, it is fair to predict that we shall permit the permanent secession of four more states—the 300,000 square miles now seriously endangered.

It may be asked where the kidnaped states have gone. They have gone where the vanished empires of Babylonia and Assyria went: out to sea. The rivers of Babylonia built a delta 150 miles out to sea where the coast line of the Persian Gulf runs today. The Mississippi has built a delta nearly as long, as have also the Nile, Ganges, and Brahmaputra, Indus, Yangtze, Rhone, Volga and, with the help of the grateful Dutch, the Rhine and Meuse.

So runs the rivers' revenge. Even the domesticated little streams of the Northeast have lately shown a wild and murderous streak.

6. More and more people are replying to the ruined and ill-tempered rivers, "The hell with you. What about all that ground water?" Of course, they at once start tapping the ground water faster than it is being replenished. The fresh-water table sinks rapidly; if the wells are near the salt seas, the underground salt water pushes in and ruins everybody. Carhart gives the figures showing that Savannah, Georgia, has lowered its water table thirty-two feet below sea level; Long Beach, California, seventy-two feet below sea level; Texas City, Texas, to 102 feet and in spots to 165 feet below sea level. Low water tables and small runoff have already affected over a thousand American communities, among them New York City, Philadelphia, Memphis, Mobile, and Peoria.

7. The next-to-last fallacy about water is that it can be regarded and treated as a fixed or static asset. Water is always in movement— evaporating from lake and forest, or condensing down as rain from clouds, or being sucked up into a rye plant by its 14,000,000 root hairs, or being breathed out by leaves into the air again, or rushing down rivers and hydroelectric penstocks or creeping through the rock strata or cascading down plowed furrows or pouring out of the faucet or being thirstily gulped down an animal's throat.

8. "I own that pond," says a man in the unchallenged belief that water can be owned like anything else. This is the worst fallacy of all. It is not that it is wicked or antisocial to try to monopolize water, though that, too, may possibly be claimed. It is that water does not give itself to anybody in fee simple. It permits itself only to be used for the moment, and moves on to another place or form or condition.

Imagine a water miser who took a glass of river water and, to make certain it would always be his to have and to hold, locked it in his safe-deposit box. In the dark and silence, the organic vegetable and animal material would go on growing and propagating in the glass. Invisible bacteria would be born and die until they had consumed all the free oxygen. Day by day the level of the water in the glass would sink from evaporation. The miser would come back to find an empty glass stained with a very faint scum. He would run to the bank manager, to the police, but not even the F.B.I. could give him back his glass of water. If he still thought he had ever owned that water, he would have to cry, "I've been robbed!"

Crazy as he sounds, most people are just that crazy, but on a very much larger scale.

So much for the human fallacies about water.

Let us look at one American river—the Colorado, the main water resource of about half the Rocky Mountain plateau, one-tenth of the United States, and about eight million Americans, including those of Southern California.

The Colorado, with an annual average flow of only five cubic miles of water, beautifully demonstrates a useful function of rivers in serving as a water pipe to transport surplus water from where it is to where it isn't.

The river is born in the melting snows of mountain ridges, trickles through the pine and spruce, hastens past the aspen and pinon-juniper, and tears into the dry canyons of the sagebrush country of Utah and Arizona. Finally it slides across the sloping deserts of Arizona into Mexico and builds its own huge delta in the Gulf of California. In this last run, the rainfall is often only two inches a year.

Over 70 per cent of this priceless watershed is owned by the United States Government which, after due and careful thought, has spent billions of dollars on its development. Hoover (or Boulder) Dam provides the hydroelectric power that makes Los Angeles an important industrial area. Parker Dam downstream supplies the Los Angeles area with fresh water at the rate of 675,000 gallons a minute. Colorado River water irrigates 2,676,000 acres in the whole basin, plus 416,000 acres in the Salton Sea basin of the Imperial Valley.

Over fifty Colorado River projects are now operating, and fifty more are planned.

And what is the state of this great watershed, the equivalent of four great American states? In 1951 the President's Water Resources Policy Commission reported soberly in a 792-page document that over half of the basin was "land with severe to critical erosion including development of deep gully streams and extensive sheet wash." All Arizona and the part of Colorado included in the basin were about two-thirds eroded. In Arizona over half the topsoil was gone from 25,000,000 acres. In Utah, 11,000,000 acres were gullied. The worst erosion of all—how much worse can you get?—was reserved to New Mexico. As one reads the report, the word "erosion" becomes the most terrible word in the language.

The report says judicially that "even in its natural state the basin had achieved only a precarious balance." But reckless Government permission to private entrepreneurs to harvest timber and graze herds of cattle, horses, sheep, and goats on the precious watersheds has destroyed much of the natural cover. The precarious balance has long since collapsed.

But what of all the marvelous Government projects? The great dams are not quite so marvelous as they look. Lake Mead, the reservoir behind Hoover Dam, is being filled every year with 199,000,000 tons of sediment from upstream. Furthermore, the priceless water stalled behind the dam evaporates in the desert sun at the rate of seven feet a year. Furthermore, the accumulated fine silt and the fluctuating water level have destroyed fish life. Furthermore, the flooding of the forest slopes has drowned the winter forage havens for wild game. Other projects have destroyed essential marshlands for migratory waterfowl. In the upper basin, the processing of gold, uranium, and vanadium is pouring poisons into the river. Everywhere overuse of the water results in infiltration of salts from the alkali soil and ruins the water for human use. Though river navigation was one of the professed major purposes of Hoover, Parker, and Davis dams, there is no freight traffic.

Perhaps the irrigation projects redeem it all? Beginning around 1916, shrewd realtors in various irrigated areas sank wells in marginal zones and did a brisk selling business in land. The get-rich-quick process continued until the whole water table had sunk so far that 2,000-foot wells were required to reach it. The President's report comments with appalling calm, "The end result of the dissipation of the ground water resources will be abandonment of a considerable part of the agricultural economy, with the distress and business failures which accompany such abandonment." Since schools, stores, churches, and homes had followed this unscrupulous speculation in water, the "abandonment" is never pretty.

The fight to "own" water here is too desperate for morality. It breaks through all laws and agreements. Many people circumvent the law restricting one owner to 160 acres of irrigated land by assigning 160 acres each to husband, wife, several children, uncles, brothers-in-law, and even grandchildren. Since every American taxpayer paid for the project—and can never be repaid by the landowner—this is a raid on the United States Treasury. It looks worse when we see that an average of only twelve acres of rich irrigated land seems enough for each of 19,000 families on the Salt River project of the Colorado system.

The fight for water has turned state against state. California has a complicated interpretation of the Colorado River Compact among six states—"the law of the river"—which manages to "prove" that California owns all Arizona's Gila River water. The argument has its real base in that three-quarters of the 8,000,000 people using the Colorado's water live in California.

This fact, paramount so far, is about to run head-on into national defense. For in the sparsely inhabited upper basin lie various minerals, such as uranium, which must be processed, with a heavy use of water, on the spot where they are mined. Here also are the country's largest undeveloped deposits of coal and oil shale. Something has to give when Imperial Valley jumbo asparagus and Darryl Zanuck's swimming pool run into atomic fission and national security.

It may be a comfort to know that American businessmen and officialdom have not savaged our American real estate quite as badly as the Russians have manhandled the area southeast of Stalingrad as far as Central Asia. However, an act like Secretary of Agriculture

Benson's recent reduction of soil-conservation services was a good try for the booby championship—a virtual liquidation, if I read the factors correctly, of two more American states.

The only hope for the American property, as for spiritual values, is here again an enlightened citizenry, requiring of its Government control of water resources that tries to balance all the conflicting values of water suggested above.

This is a great cause—actually greater than antinarcotics or anti-Communism or anti-inflation or antivivisection—this resolve to restore all forty-eight stars to the flag. Such a cause gives the word "patriotism" its original and reputable meaning.

All Alone in the Supermarket
(1958)

The supermarket may be said to give half the people of America the most regular, satisfying, ennobling, and masterful experience that they can confidently look forward to in any given week. In great cities many women regard the local supermarket as the only stable social force in their environment. They cash all their husbands' checks there; everything on their kitchen shelves is transposed from there; they gossip about the surly girl at the cigarette counter; they pride themselves on wangling six items past the "express" checkout limited to five items; they delicately bump their carts on the Achilles tendon of the other customers and indelicately rebuke those who bump them. In the supermarket they feel that indispensable justification: they are doing something important, functional, respectable, American, and godly. It is incredible but true that a quarrel in a supermarket has a tone of the sacerdotal about it.

I work at home. I live near a supermarket. I am in and out of it several times a day.

Some sort of market research discovered that supermarket patrons blinked less often than normal as they wheeled the cart under control, steered it imperiously down the aisle, began to peer at the stacked shelves and piled the cart with commodities to match the unpremeditated sugar plums suddenly dancing in their heads. The

unblinking consumer is not embarrassed by having to voice her
desires, perhaps discreditable, to the other human being, the clerk.
She sees, she desires, and a moment later the coveted thing is buried
in her cart, all but secretly. In this way she buys as greedily as if she
were stealing.

This little fact is worth several billions of dollars a year in the
consuming economy of America and, as the idea spreads, of the rest
of the world. Its terrible power is that of leaving a woman alone
with her desires, not for herself exclusively but for her loved ones.
She has this dream of how good she is to her family—a noble dream,
which makes the world go round. But here it is diffused and debauched into a consumption of overbuying and hence of waste.

The supermarket proprietors are not fiendish enough to have
devised this foul plot against the soft underbelly of the American
consumer; they just stumbled on it. It works, and it will inevitably
keep on working.

The old-time shopping list is virtually extinct. If you see one in a
supermarket, it is almost invariably in the hands of a man who is
bucking the smooth flow of traffic because he is actually looking for
a specific item he has been sent for. His wife doesn't trust him
to do what she does.

A supermarket may carry 15,000 items, brands, and sizes. It is
estimated that 70 per cent of all sales are "impulse buying." In
consequence the woman's total purchase is so huge and heavy that
most women have their own additional, personal cart to drag the
monstrous orgy home.

We are told that that is the marketing for the whole week.
This claim is undercut by a syndicated column, released to the
papers on June 13, 1958, which fairly represents the American
housewife's opinion. It gave the maximum length of time that
certain foods will keep in the refrigerator (not the deepfreeze) as
follows: 1–2 days—chopped meat, fresh sea food, poultry; 4–5 days—
fresh meat, cooked sea food, milk, cream, soft cheese; a week—fruit
and vegetables. According to this table, much of the food has to be
consumed, or thrown out, well before the end of the week. And these
figures are about the same used in America before there was universal
refrigeration. Remembering the old winter-long apple barrel, one

must smile at that week for fruit. The modern system certainly produces Lucullan garbage cans.

Furthermore, this bounty is not cheap. For California lettuce, it was testified, the farmer got 5 cents, transport to New York City cost 9 cents more, and the final 15 cents, making 29 cents, was added in New York. Other figures, if you'd like two sets, have the farmer getting $403.17 for a market basket costing the consumer $997.21. "Distribution" used to mean primarily the salesperson, but at the supermarket there is no salesperson. The labor is out of sight of the customer.

This formidable institution, which began to spread only in 1932, may easily prove to be America's most universal and powerful export. How the various peoples adapt it to their own *mores* will be a fascinating story in a few years.

England already has 175 supermarkets (defined as having over 2,000 square feet of selling space) and is adding five a month. It had to wait until 1954, when rationing was lifted. The cooperative movement runs half of the supermarkets, chiefly in the industrial North. The private chains include Premier with sixteen and Fine-Fare with twenty-two. There, success is represented by weekly sales of 20 shillings ($2.80) per square foot of selling space (not far off the American figure of $2.74, as against the small grocer's 76 cents), and a wage cost of 4 to 5 per cent of sales against the former 7 to 8 per cent. The British supermarkets go up to 8,000 square feet, whereas the American reach 100,000 square feet.

Supermarkets have already infiltrated the Continent—France, Germany, Switzerland, The Netherlands, and elsewhere. The largest in Europe is the Eklöh in Cologne, containing 23,000 square feet of selling space. The American firms that have the advantage in Europe are those that already have plants there: Heinz, National Biscuit, Corn Products, and General Foods.

The supermarket exhibited by the United States Department of Commerce at the 1957 Trade Fair in Yugoslavia has been bought by the Yugoslav Government to equip the first of sixty supermarkets, this one of 10,000 square feet. Israel is to get twenty, with Canadian, United States, and Israeli capital. The opening of the first, in Tel Aviv, on August 28, 1958, was attended by a riot of small shopkeepers and pushcart peddlers. One could hardly imagine a more reasonable riot, or one more futile.

Supermarkets are also proliferating through Latin America and Australia.

Canada is acting as if it had invented them. In the Winnipeg area there is a price-cutting, giveaway, building war among Safeway (thirty-nine-store chain), A & P (five), Loblaw (ten to come), Dominion (six to come), Shop-Easy, and 1,400 local independents, which have pooled their advertising and buying. And still other un-named chains are itching to get into the fight.

Returning to the United States, the food situation is awesome and not at all what one would think, though this is another subject on which everybody is obviously an expert.

According to the statisticians, the American today buys more food than ever—$48,000,000,000 worth in 1957—and eats less than ever in his history—only 3,200 calories today as against 3,500 calories in 1909. (How the statisticians know this I cannot imagine, nor what is meant by a figure of 4.2 pounds of food a day per capita. Does this mean food bought, put on the table, or ingested? I guess that it doesn't mean dehydrated food, or include the weight of the can or package. Readers might try weighing a few meals.) Well, those are the figures.

How this food is conveyed to the United States consumer is a desperate story which explains the Israeli riot. In this country there are usually around 350,000 stores selling groceries (a very liquid category, so that you can change the figure any way you want). Ten per cent of them do less than $10,000 a year gross business. These are barely living, even though the proprietors eat off their own shelves at wholesale prices. Two-thirds of the food stores do $10,000 to $100,000 a year gross business. But their share of the total retail food business is less than a quarter. Still, they keep alive. Supermarkets—both chain and independent—number around 27,000 (depending on how you define them) and get most of the rest of the business. The supermarkets, including one-store, two-store, and three-store independents (the chain designation starts at four stores) have clearly cornered the American food market.

The situation of the small independent retailer (not just food) has been studied very thoroughly. One set of figures shows that in 1955 the United States had 1,865,000 retail stores. But in the immediately preceding eight-year period, 991,200 had gone out of business, 1,052,000 new entrepreneurs had taken the plunge, and there had been 2,067,400 transfers of ownership. Cold statistics can seldom have disclosed more heartache, insomnia, ulcers, vain hope, and black anguish. The source (Victor Lebow for Babson Institute) was convinced that the American small retailer was in an "atmosphere of catastrophe . . . steadily intensifying crisis."

This statement is put into a more correct perspective by a book that should be read by anybody trying seriously to fit into our economy—*Little Business in the American Economy*, by Joseph D. Phillips (University of Illinois Press, 1958). Here, with figures generally based on 1939, it appears that the atmosphere of catastrophe is perennial in little business in America.

Of all independent small retailers in 1935–1936, 91 per cent had an annual net income under $2,000! Of all business in 1941, 329,000 enterprises were born and 328,000 died. About the same numbers went in and out in 1905. In the years between, the variations were not dramatic. The higher number of deaths occurs generally in fairly prosperous periods.

As to what is nibbling at the small grocer, a distinction must be made between chain supermarkets and independents. For some years the chains have barely increased their percentage share of total food business. But new, well-financed independents, often offering a better and more varied type of food than the chain, have increased their share of the business from 22 per cent up toward 30 per cent since 1954.

A definite division along class and intelligence lines seems to be taking place. The better class uses, with some discrimination, the independent, "luxury" supermarkets. Political liberals seem to me to carry the trend one reactionary step further and have returned to the butcher, baker, and small grocer. The masses generally do their mass shopping in a dream at the chain stores. (I use a chain store, A & P.)

This drama has a fourth character, the great nationally advertised-brand packer. The chain stores are applying a slow squeeze on the packers, but the existence of the independents and the small grocers saves the big packers. A & P, Safeway, American Stores, Food Fair, National Tea, Giant Foods, First National Stores are themselves listed as "packers" by the United States Department of Agriculture, putting them under the friendly auspices of that office and releasing them from the harsh inquisition of the Federal Trade Commission. (But new legislation may modify this arrangement.) As packers, these chains compete directly with the famous packers, buy their own cattle, sheep, and hogs, fatten, slaughter, pack, and ship to market. A quarter of all Colorado's cattle is handled by two chain-store packing houses. The percentage of cattle going to the great markets is rapidly sinking each year.

Chain stores, as well as the regular packers, also supervise contracted farmers' operations to the end of obtaining for market mass-produced broilers and fryers to specifications; lean bacon; big, firm heads of lettuce, and so on, and so on. Naturally, the chains use their own brand names on their products, but they also ask the regular packer to put their brand names on part of his product.

One effect of all this—not our subject here—is that the farmer is becoming a one-crop specialist in an assembly line, dependent on one buyer who also supplies him with all his needs and even keeps his books. Another is the heightening of the creeping war between packers and chain stores, which the Government will doubtless referee. As things stand, the packer's weapon is national advertising which, he hopes, will make the consumer *demand*—yell, scream, and stamp for—his product. He can also advertise in the chain store by packaging his product seductively.

The chain store is fighting on its own home grounds. It can give its own brands the best shelf position and cut prices—for example, today the large A & P instant-coffee jar is 95 cents, while Borden's equivalent is $1.05, and the A & P coffee is moving.

In reprisal, the packers may reduce their prices to the independents. They may increase advertising, especially in local papers in co-operation with the independents. They may get into the retail business themselves, at least to the extent of improving trade credit to small grocers.

If the chain stores followed the monolithic line of least resistance, they would stock nothing competitive with their own brands and cultivate the undiscriminating mass-type shopper who never knows what's going on. (On the other hand, one of the big chains—Safeway —has recently opened in Manhattan its first supermarket specifically addressed to the epicurean élite.) The packers might see an incentive to market more varieties of more highly differentiated products, aimed at the more discriminating consumer.

There is some support for the theory that the American consumer is growing a little more sophisticated. He might some day even demand food as fresh as his grandfather got. In that case, an independent supermarket could outstrip its competitors, at least in season, by contracting with a farmer thirty miles away to bring in fresh stuff every dawn. To people who have always eaten chain-store eggs, it is a shaking experience to eat an egg laid the day before. Corn and potatoes harvested the same morning would turn modern city consumers into religious fanatics. The same applies to really fresh new peas, asparagus, tomatoes, and all the rest of the edible flora.

Ultimately, the supermarket is judged on food. And food, perhaps wrongly, is judged on only one quality—taste.

The Morality of Money
(1959)

Just over there are ten $100 bills. They show no marks of individual ownership. You do not know the peculiar history that makes them "belong" to somebody else. They are an abstraction that might as well be added to your bookkeeping as to that of the somebody else. Somehow these ten bills float through the air and arrive in your pocket. Now you are magically in a position to obtain $1,000 worth of other people's real goods and services. And you are a thief.

The very existence of paper money, a very feeble symbol of wealth, turns real wealth into an abstraction that nearly invites an immorality about money. When wealth is respected and feared, the society is highly moral about it; when wealth is abstracted into mere dollar bills and ledger accounts, it becomes contemptible and thievable. As everyone knows, this is the present situation. It is even odd that the epithet "thief" still has a force that makes a man cringe. Who are in fact the important thieves?

The spectacular thieves shoot their way out of banks, creep in windows by night, rob strangers at the point of a gun, and otherwise comport themselves in crude, conspicuous, and inefficient ways. In a good year these bungling hoodlums manage to collect about $500,000,000 in cash and property, and sell the property for a fraction of its value.

The unspectacular thieves, without even owning a gun or sneakers, steal three times this every year, quietly and intelligently, for an estimated total of $1,500,000,000. These are the embezzlers, skilled, inconspicuous, and efficient.

The embezzlements discovered are only a fraction of those now taking place, and only a fraction of those are covered by fidelity insurance, usually as a "blanket bonding," which does not require investigation of individuals. Still, the insurance companies paid out over $57,000,000 in 1957, up two and a half times over 1956, and the trend is still up. A dozen claims were for over a million dollars each. Employers rarely send the embezzlers to jail, if they can make some restitution; the insurance companies are much tougher. There is an old Arthur Train story of an embezzler whose lawyer advised him to lift $125,000 more before he confessed; then the lawyer offered the bank $100,000, keeping the rest for his services to all concerned. In a single fiscal year, the F.B.I. has handled 1,641 bank embezzlements, half by bank officers, as against a mere 600 violent bank robberies. Embezzlement is more than a hobby or avocation.

It has been said that there are 210 illegal ways to separate a bank from its assets, and the rarest and worst way is just to pick up the money. Manipulation of cash receipts, in other words, occurs in only 13 per cent of known embezzlements, manipulation of inventories accounts for another 15 per cent, and the rest, or 72 per cent, involve manipulation of cash disbursements, the best way.

The techniques of embezzlement are derived from the business fact that every money transaction is authorized by a specific piece of paper, or several pieces. All the embezzler has to do is use the same piece of paper over and over, or falsify it to meet his needs. Embezzlements are said to hit hardest at laundries, bakeries, chain stores, the entertainment business, labor unions, and almost any sort of branch operation. This dishonesty is given by Dun and Bradstreet as the primary cause of 10 per cent of business failures every year. This figure will seem very low to any small retailer, who knows that his survival depends on finding an honest man or woman.

Obviously important as this subject is, only one man has gone into it with scientific care and dispassion—Donald R. Cressey in his thesis *Other People's Money* (Free Press, 1953). He limited himself to people who had accepted a position of trust in good faith, *then* criminally violated the trust, and been convicted and jailed. His question then became just the one we all want answered: Why?

He defines a hypothesis which held good for all the embezzlers he examined, in repeated interviews in a number of prisons. This must be quoted exactly as he gives it: "Trusted persons become trust violators when they conceive of themselves as having a financial problem which is non-shareable, are aware that this problem can be secretly resolved by violation of the position of financial trust, and are able to apply to their own conduct in that situation verbalizations which enable them to adjust their conceptions of themselves as trusted persons with their conceptions of themselves as users of the entrusted funds or property."

This definition is obviously descriptive of a twentieth century, not a thirteenth or eighteenth century, man. One can almost see the transition of the "good boy," the scoutmaster, "the responsible family man," into the state of moral disorder and the role of cheat, rather than that of thief. He has lost the grasp of wealth as something owned by another and substituted mere figures in a ledger, which have no moral meaning. And who is here who will judge him?

That fascinating "non-shareable problem" can be literally any problem known to man or woman. The popular view that it must be "bookies, babes, and booze" is overwhelmingly wrong. On the contrary, a man tries to be a little more important and respectable than he can actually afford, and then he embezzles, often philanthropically.

The "verbalizations" in the definition must be, and are, pitiably banal, such as that the biggest people in the business cheat a little here and there, and that the embezzler is only borrowing the money for a few months, and has mentally all but repaid it. The sad day comes when he faces the clear truth that the amount is too great for him ever in any probable life to repay. Then he becomes reckless.

There have been waves of embezzlement, one of which may now be in course. Another was among United States Army paymasters during the Civil War, usually blamed on the gambling houses in Washington, D.C. Purchasing agents for large corporations are another sensitive spot, and are almost never prosecuted.

The embezzlers who blame their crime on a helpless defect of character are, according to Mr. Cressey, generally the absconders, whereas the true embezzlers blame the crime on a situation which unpredictably and through no fault of theirs got out of hand. In the jail cell they are still virtuous, and their statements are sometimes enough to bring tears, as quoted by Cressey.

Incredibly, this opinion is confirmed by a bonding company official who wrote to Cressey: "The average embezzler is no more crook than you or I. As a result of circumstances, he finds himself in some position where, with no criminal intent, he 'borrows' from his employers."

This remarkable but well-founded statement leads us to start our thinking about money and embezzlement all over from the beginning.

The first question must be: How old is this crime? Through most of human history since wealth came into being and society became stratified, the upper levels of society have subsisted quite frankly and legitimately on embezzlement. Everybody surrounding the king, favorite, first minister, lord treasurer, great barons, rapidly became very rich. The feudal system was based on an open invitation to embezzlement. Technically, the inferior baron should have passed on all surplus income derived from the properties in his trust to the superior baron, up to the king. In not doing so, he was embezzling, but without wrongdoing or guilt. However, courtiers who had lost favor were beheaded for this guiltless crime, under whimsical or avaricious kings. Historians do not make much of this matter, because the great barons did not fill out detailed financial statements or income-tax returns, and the data are hard to come by.

It is amusing to notice that in English law embezzlement first became a crime in 1529 in the reign of Henry VIII, who wanted to do all the stealing himself, and that it was directed at "servants and clerks." But since the servant's possessions were those of the master, it was necessary to define embezzlement as the transfer of the wealth of the servant *qua* servant to the servant *qua* thief. As late as 1824 a London banker with the lily-white name of Fauntleroy was hanged for separating his bank from $1,500,000, and he too felt no guilt.

The word "embezzlement" is derived from a French word that became in English "bezzle," meaning drink to excess, gluttonize, revel, waste in riot, plunder ("bookies, babes, and booze"), and not at all characteristic of the average embezzler.

It would not be surprising if the attitude toward embezzlement has changed, along with the attitudes toward wealth and money. From a society where wealth was sacred and even the money, not being paper, had real value, we have evolved a system where paper money, notes, mortgages, stocks, bonds, checks, bank accounts, and so on, stand for wealth.

We have tried to repeal the unwritten right of people in power to legitimate embezzlement, and forgiven the small embezzlements of "servants and clerks." (But not in Soviet Russia.) One can nearly sympathize with a corrupt political boss or union leader who has not noticed that the old rights have been repealed and finds himself in the dock answering impertinent and unhistorical questions. His defense usually must fall back on accountancy.

Wealth is now bookkeeping; embezzlement is bookkeeping; and the embezzler typically steals only to keep his personal books in order, not out of any old-fashioned love of money.

The embezzler is in this failing, just like the rest of us. The love of wealth and money, and the awe of it, in the eighteenth or nineteenth centuries cannot be found anywhere today, excluding a few cranks. Money is necessary to most people; but it is a kind of coupon in the small denominations, and in larger amounts, a cleverness score in a game, like a proof that you won the four-horse parlay. "Score" is in fact gamblers' slang. You may think this is the normal way to think about money, but it would not have been normal in any other century. The modern attitude toward money makes a comedy of the Communist theoretical hatred of capital money. Our own industrial democracy has gone much further in eliminating the love of money, by indulging it rather than forbidding it. Here the whole matter is bookkeeping; the Certified Public Accountant has inherited the earth. Success is not in how much income comes in, but in how well you keep your books. The wages are only a fringe benefit; the important rewards are the respectability and credit rating, and the services of the accountant who pays the income taxes and any garnishee judgments that may have been levied. Some banks have even taken over the function of wives, and pay all monthly bills. You never have to look at your money.

The foregoing has been essentially an exculpation of the embezzler.

And still the fact remains irreducible: the embezzler is a crook. He is cheating with his life and his fortune and his sacred honor. We may be touched by his inability to share his problem; we may sympathize with his verbalizations; we may even agree that the money he steals is not a compelling representation of wealth. But we must acknowledge that he has missed some of the key signals as to what life on earth is all about. Sometimes one must be hard-hearted, even toward oneself. The embezzler gets too wet-eyed about himself.

The honest man still stands up, even in the twentieth century. He will scuttle the "verbalizations" and the "unshareable problems" before he scuttles his right to say (to himself), "I am an honest man." The thievery must appear to him as an abdication of dignity. The last and strongest defense of a social arrangement is the individual's opinion of himself.

But this rather doctrinaire opinion runs afoul of the results of lie-detector tests described in Cressey's book. Of the employees of some Chicago banks, 20 per cent of those tested were shown to have taken money or property. But the percentage of embezzlers in a cross section of chain-store employees was 75 per cent. And if we can take the word of the bonding-company official, this clear majority are not very different from you and me.

It would be good standard journalism to say now that business morality is probably going to hell, perhaps. What one can say is that the old immoralities are more widely shared, take new forms, and are nearly respectable. The example is set by business leaders.

If they do not steal from their own companies, they have no qualms about stealing from their competitors. Thus we have businessmen who plant radio transmitters in the chair upholstery of the competitor's president, tap his phone, stare into his board room with a telescope and read his lips, bribe his telephone operator, buy and study his wastepaper, and so on, and so on. These eminent gentlemen record one another's conversations at distances up to sixty feet, with devices like the Magnemite ($349) built into an ordinary brief case with the microphone in the lock, the pocket-size, two-pound Minifon tape recorder ($290), the Dictet ($294), or Midgetape ($250). The most assiduous thieves are in the automobile, advertising, and oil-prospecting businesses, but any business is in trouble if it defers filing a patent claim until the product is pefected. The name for these obscene shenanigans is I.E., or Industrial Espionage. One motor company has a counterespionage force that has recruited thirty ex-F.B.I. men.

In such a moral climate, what price embezzlement?

But a great moral force stands over all. Who else should it be but the insurance companies? More and more, every risk is insured, including accident liability, fidelity, and industrial espionage. The risks increase, the premiums increase, until the insurance companies decide to put a stop to the immorality. They then take on the role formerly monopolized by the Church, that of guardian of public morals.

The insurance companies are far from reluctant. For it is an eternal phenomenon of the ages that the guardian of morality has always had a peculiar tendency to grow enormously rich. In the Age of Faith, the Church owned from a third to a half of western Europe. In Utah even today, the Church of Latter-Day Saints does relatively as well. But the real monopolists of wealth are the insurance companies. The great ones count their assets in the billions of dollars, which by every equitable agreement should long since have been divided, in mutual companies, among the policyholders.

The reason for the pyramiding wealth of the insurance companies is the same as for the former wealth of the Church, and comes in two parts: (1) people hope and plan to be a little more moral than they actuarially turn out to be; and (2) people have an irrational fear of the future.

Leaving out the fear of hell-fire, the insurance company sells policies on the unmentioned assumption that the insured will have forty continuous years of solvency to pay up his policy. I wish we had the figures on the percentage of lives that can show this level of performance. It is certainly not a high percentage. Two or more years intervene when depression, war, labor troubles, prolonged family sickness, educational requirements, bad investments, or sheer boredom makes it impossible or undesirable to pay the premiums. The insured borrows back a fraction of what he had paid in, and loses the policy. The insurance company shovels the difference back into that vast underground hoard, along with the broken hopes of all the generations of foolish optimists, not so different from the knights who sold everything and went on the Crusade. In Church or insurance company, the guardian of morals piles up the billions while some god laughs.

In this context, I would advise the insurance companies to read what happened, on Friday, October 13, 1307, to the officers of the Knights Templars, then the richest institution in Europe.

But might I also piously suggest that somewhere in the insurance companies' actuarial tables on embezzlers, honest men, robbers, pawnbrokers, engineers, philanthropists, atheists, and churchmen is actually revealed the face and expression of God?

IV
The Empire Builders

Women and Also Men
(1959)

For some forty years now, women have had equal rights with men in suffrage, employment, education, inheritance, politics, and misbehavior. There has been a huge gain in economic energy output, lady novelists, mass magazines for women, and illegitimate birth rates. To what further frontiers the ladies have carried their victory is a matter that begins to be discussible.

For those who still think there is nothing to discuss, one must quote a Mike Wallace interview with a Dr. John A. Schindler, printed in a New York newspaper owned by a woman. The doctor said: "The American woman is a good deal smarter than the man. . . . The dominance of the home and the family by the woman is a very good thing. . . . Look at the male character—its being aggressive, hostile. . . . I think the present trend [of feminizing men] is a very good thing. . . . Tyranny is masculine, democracy is a feminine concept. . . . [When we are unable to distinguish between the male and the female of the species] it will be wonderfully good for the human race. It's something that's coming; it's here. Accept it."

Speaking competitively, any man would be delighted if the rest of the men were feminized. This might have been Schindler's sly game, but he sounds as if he'd already taken his own advice.

Seriously, this remarkable doctor compels us to redefine the male and female principles, so that we know what it is we are abolishing on the one hand and glorifying on the other. And there can be no cockcrowing in these definitions.

The male principle, as I tentatively isolated it, is that of wasteful and reckless experiment, risk and creation. The female principle is

175

that of compromise, conservation, monopoly, complacency, and results.

These findings were concurred in, to my surprise, by Buckminster Fuller, the engineer-philosopher and a chivalrous old-school gentleman who would never hurt a lady's feelings. Mr. Fuller took his proofs from other species and from prehistory. He had found that male wolves, foxes, tigers, and birds hunt over a much wider range than the females. The male of many species of birds migrates ahead of the female, picks the home area, chases away other males, and sometimes starts a few experimental nests. The female then arrives, vetoes his nests, and starts her own. After the eggs are laid, the female has a good reason for not going far for her own food; she wants to get back before the eggs have cooled off.

In the home area the female is superior. Although she didn't get there first, she has learned it better and she is conducting the serious business there. After the family gets on the move, the male is naturally superior. He has "been around" more than the female, seen more of life, had more experiences.

The two ways of life make a lot of otherwise inexplicable differences between the sexes quite understandable. The female's concentration on the home area very naturally brings out certain predictable traits. She tends to become monopolist and to have an acute and angry property sense. She tends to believe that her kind of life, her beliefs and values, are the only possible correct ones. She tends to become complacent and self-righteous and unable to accept criticism or contradiction. Her justification is that she is organizing her life, values, and home area for the greater happiness and convenience of the whole family group. It is interesting that as she ages, she generally gets nearsighted whereas the male gets farsighted; each retains longest the abilities that that one needs most.

Mr. Fuller sees primitive man as having brought home each new trophy with the bewildered question, "Hey, Mom, what do we do with it—skin it, milk it, or bury it?" and Mom decided, along purely sensible and conventional lines. As she thus organized the family group, she invented the first factory and the first principles of industrialization. Left to herself, she would have gone on doing things in the same way until the end of the world.

But the experimental, irresponsible male was the ruler. When he fell into a hole, he saw that a game animal might fall into a prepared hole. As he played with flexible branches, he came closer to the snare and the bow and the yurt. As he moved rocks around, he discovered the inclined plane and the lever. He was always engaged in research. To what end he did not know.

In such a world, the female raising the family and keeping the home is obviously indispensable, whereas the male is by and large dispensable. The device for dispensing with him was warfare. The percentage of the enemy males killed by, say, the Aztecs or the Zulus, was hair-raising. The only superiority of the hydrogen bomb is that it can't choose between males and females.

Real civilization began when the male became indispensable too, valued for his creative gifts. And so arrived Egypt and Jerusalem and Knossos and Athens.

This real male was not a monopolist. He was not a board chairman of General Motors—this is obviously a female function. He had a property sense only competitively, that is, to prove himself superior to his neighbor or his enemy. He could not take money or possessions with the awful seriousness of the female. He was "worldly," that is, respectful of ways of life other than his own. He was not especially complacent or self-righteous, except in time of national emergency. He was not much of a home body. But how he liked to travel!

Civilization seems to flourish when the male principle is paramount, the gifted males become indispensable, and the female's home area continuity can be taken for granted.

"Tyranny," said the fellow Schindler, "is masculine, democracy is a feminine concept." Enough has been said to indicate that this peculiar doctor has exactly reversed the truth. Tyranny is obviously feminine; democracy is a strange, rare, risky experiment that only real males could have devised.

Whether freedom is male or female is a question that is all but answered in the asking. The male, although he can sometimes be herded into armies, parties, and gangs, has very strong nervous resistance to being confined, crowded, or pushed around. He wants to be able to move around, see what's going on, investigate the next valley, the next trout stream, the next woman.

On the other hand, even emancipated American women love to wear slave bracelets. They viscerally love the idea of being a slave.

Their whole dream of happiness is a confinement in a home, a certain pleasurable pushing around by one specific somebody and then slavery, if not to the poor American husband, at least to the children. They hope either to enslave or be enslaved; all they ask is that the opposite-number slave or master hang around the house at night. Who would dream of asking them to fight for freedom? To a woman, freedom spells "old maid."

Every modern record shows that women have always voted well to the Right of their male associates. In the last Spanish elections before the civil war they did so with disastrous results. After they got the vote in the United States, they helped to vote in twelve years of isolationism leading inevitably to the 1929 crash. Isolationism within one's home area comes close to describing the female principle. And there is a case for describing Harding, Coolidge, and Herbert Hoover as women in men's clothing running the world. Khrushchev and Mao look to me like women in men's clothing.

This war between the males and the women in men's clothing is tragically apparent in the new book by General Gavin, evidently a true male, describing the Army's dealings with the Secretary of Defense, Charles Wilson, a former General Motors man. Wilson, stingily housekeeping in the Pentagon, could, as a trained woman in man's clothing, invariably outconnive, outdissimulate, and outmaneuver the poor males of the Armed Services.

Stalin could not get along with the male chiefs of the Soviet Air Force; he constantly had them in jail. Khrushchev could not get along with Zhukov, and the latter has disappeared. The females always won, because they had first taken care of the home area. The most female figure in recent history was Hitler—not in my opinion a homosexual, simply another woman in men's clothing.

The women actually in government today are satisfactory because they try to think like men: but suppose they acted like all-out females. "Hell hath no fury like a woman scorned." Translate this into foreign policy. Further, when a woman knows she is absolutely in the wrong is the time she chooses for her most violent tantrum of self-righteousness. As self-anointed custodian of the moral law, a woman cannot admit to certain kinds of error. Finally, women like to be defeated occasionally. Thus they would embark on wars they expected delightfully to lose, as distinguished from men's wars which the poor fools usually expect to win. The ancients invented a woman-run world—the savage warriors called Amazons, on the Black Sea.

A good deal of what is said here was said earlier, though in a rather different accent, in May, 1957, by a Frenchwoman, Nicole, who was after all talking about France, whereas I am talking about America. There is a difference: France lost World War II: America won it; but Nicole's contempt for her male compatriots is overmatched by the American woman's contempt for her male compatriots. The modern woman is so full of euphoria that she does not even care whether the menfolk win their wars.

Nicole wrote: "Whatever they may do or fail to do in our twentieth century, Women, in a word, are invariably right. . . . They can admire a man only if he really deserves their admiration. . . . The Western man . . . is so occupied with his own subjective problems that he has utterly failed to notice that his world is being stolen from out his very hands."

If her plan was to antagonize men, she succeeded. In reply, it might be said that men do not really need a woman to applaud their victories or deplore their defeats, but they have too often, in defeat, seen the female face suffused with joy, overlaid with the phony compassion, as if the man were an idiot. Women are fools to take men for fools. In self-defense, the modern man had better develop an implacable self-confidence, iron nerves, and a pretense of deafness.

The Nicole sort of contempt incites to rape and wife beating of which there is still far more than Nicole evidently knows. The female proves nothing by inviting sadism, which the male should eschew less out of kindness than self-respect. It is the female who wants heat, uproar, and battle in the home; it is the male who, after he is housebroken, wants peace, pleasantness, and periods of silence. Recently, an adulteress being killed by her lover realized this fact too late, and with her last breath was heard to call out "Tommy! Tommy!" for her husband. But nowadays the cry of the female, in the words of a very old joke, is "Do something!" It is the voice of one who admits she herself cannot do anything important alone, and pleads for action, even if it is atrocious. Too many women today despise gentlemanly husbands who decline to strike them, and finally find one who has no objection to breaking their jaw from ear to ear.

Why are modern women so troublesome? The answer may lie in the truism that the cruelest people in the world are the weak. This can be seen, if it needs proof, in the first emancipated generation of any suppressed minority, heavily stocked with snobs and bullies. Weak woman is loaded with hostilities, mostly taken out in talk. Watch a woman with umbrella or supermarket cart. I hear people threaten to destroy somebody else, and, excluding some drunks, the speaker is always a cold-sober woman. A man, on the other hand, before he tries to kill another man, has to consider the possibility that the other might kill him. Women don't ever seem to think of this: but this thought happens to be the fulcrum on which human society has balanced for uncounted millennia.

A woman one likes is a unique and priceless creature. Each of her mannerisms, when one is in the mood, is a delight. She modestly exhibits just the edge of her self-love and her desire to please, and one could eat her. We could easily do without the atom bomb and the automatic toaster, but as this strange, amiable animal lifts her head to listen and looks out of the glossy soft eyes, how can one say a word against her?

Inside her head are some quite remarkable qualities not generally noticed. In my observation, most females have great courage and far more loyalty to other women then most men realize. Courage goes with a kind of hardheartedness. And loyalty to women goes with sentimentality. The female has both awful sentimentality and a terrifying hardheartedness.

All this fits in perfectly with the female's basic rôle in life, as defined earlier. It is all corollary to the female function. Before the female can give, she must get. She is accustomed, from earliest prehistory, to defending the home while the male is off prowling in the next valley. She is a natural expert at building up a local propaganda, call it Nazi or Communist or soap opera. Her home area, in the truest sense, is herself, her own body, and later her womb, where her child has its first home. The male's home, on the contrary, is never his body (unless he's a homosexual); it's his brain. The female's secret plan is to get the designated male out of his own brain and into the sublimated womb she can so excellently furnish for him and the children.

The writer on this subject is usually terrified of offending one or more females associated with him. The present writer is in the happy position that all the females associated with him already regard him as impossible. These remarks will not lose me a single female friend.

In the American mass magazines for women, a vast, engulfing propaganda tries to persuade the American woman that she is the strong, wise, loyal, honorable, cultured, clever member of her marriage. A good many women are inevitably persuaded and try to transmit the propaganda to 40,000,000 husbands with a degree of success that must range from 100 per cent to zero.

The victory of the female principle—compromise, conservation, monopoly, complacency, and results—has been achieved subtly, progressively, and overwhelmingly, that is, femininely. The male principle—experiment, risk, and creation—is nearly in hiding, championed by a few of the young and, ironically, a few superior women. Otherwise a riskless conformism is the rule. Certainly the female principle governs American foreign policy. It runs the large corporations and has even penetrated into the laboratories.

The female victory could quite possibly be viewed as final and complete. In that case, the decadence would already have arrived. But I cannot agree. The true male principle is still undefeated. The eternal war against female monopoly and complacency, against smug error and tyranny, against conformist mediocrity and the apparently safe *status quo,* is not over yet.

The writing is too clear on the wall. Our world will die with the female principle. Mankind has known numbers of such civilizations, but never for long. The feminized males were not even interesting to the females. Their pleasures were the last of their race. And curiously, as Nicole warned us, it was often the females who betrayed them to the barbarians.

Once Upon a Time Inc.
(1956)

To win all one's arguments is a dream that has always fascinated mankind. It is why people become tyrants and shrews and teachers and priests and even novelists. Communism and Fascism both bask in this dream. The art of winning arguments was based on name calling in the seventeenth century, on rational aphorism in the latter eighteenth, and on pseudoscientific philosophy in the nineteenth.

Today "facts," delivered impassively, have taken command in the American press. Gone are the frankly prejudiced thunderings of the early press lords. The tone of every current mass magazine and large newspaper was set in the early 1920's by a young man named Briton Hadden, now long dead. His partner was Henry R. Luce and his organ *Time* magazine, both very much still with us. His early successes at winning arguments, all arguments, slowly drew the exasperated attention of other editors and they adopted a similar impregnable, factual position.

The extremes of opinion about *Time* and *Life* are explained by an unnoticed gap between Hadden's dream and the commercial fact of the magazines; the one sold to Time Inc. employees, the other to the reader.

The dream was that an eternal truth exists this week and can be expressed in five hundred words by a talented writer after he has read the week's New York newspaper clippings. This dream can be understood, but nobody in his right mind can entirely grasp the grandeur of Hadden's and Luce's original concept that every Monday night was the end of the world, wrapped up in a red cover. In a lowered voice they would overwhelm the chaos of Mencken's twenties. "Make up your mind," they growled at the writers. Of a story that referred back to the Crimean War, Hadden is said to have demanded, possibly in jest but more probably not, "I want to know this time what was the crime." This was *Time's* period of tough-talking college boys and speakeasy props, one of whom perfected *Time's* one-line jabberwocky picture caption and, having fulfilled this ordained function, died of an alcoholic hemorrhage. The magazine sounded as if Luce and Hadden were trying to amaze and shock somebody they never mentioned. But the dream was strong stuff for a number of high-minded young men of the twenties and thirties, who honestly wanted to see whether an eternal truth could be stated every week.

The commercial fact, on the other hand, is no dream. The format is such that all the "credit," a word Luce likes, goes to the corporation, never to an individual. Every story in *Time, Life,* and *Fortune* (with a few irrelevant exceptions) is miraculously devoid of two things generally considered indispensable: (1) sources; (2) an author. Only the Frankenstein speaks, and he made it all up out of his own head. The performance is obviously sheer magic, and the American reader is duly impressed.

This anti-individual and antitraditional miracle has implications and revealing exceptions, which will be returned to. On the lowest level, the miracle involves a legal larceny that for years enraged newspaper men. This was, in practice, Time Inc.'s exploitation of the modern legal principle that all knowledge, and especially all news, is public property. From this, Hadden and Luce developed the revelation that the talent and legwork of every reporter and writer on earth were theirs for nothing—and in a hurry. Since they had to boil it all down to limits that could be printed and read in a week, they had no time to argue.

This was one crime that Luce, after Hadden's death, felt he had to expiate to move into journalistic respectability. And so he subscribed to the United Press to establish his legal and moral right to at least that much information. He also set up his own network of news offices around the world. This apparatus looks impressive, but its absurdity is that, should hard times return and compel its abandonment, the content of the magazines would hardly change at all. Most of the writers still get three-quarters of their material from the New York *Times* and *Herald Tribune.* The apparatus supplies about an eighth or tenth of fairly low-grade information, though the actual wordage in cables can swamp an editor who takes it seriously.

Add to the free raw material the individual talent—and you have the greatest low-cost invention since the tin can.

A capable *Life* writer has repeatedly produced twenty pages or more in a single issue and averaged between five and ten pages a week over a period of years. At a salary of $200 a week, this production works out at a text cost of about $27 a page (of course excluding picture costs) or the same as the page cost of a tiny intellectual magazine with perhaps 15,000 readers.

This rate of work probably has no exemplars today. Since wealth accumulated, Time Inc. has tried to give its readers some slow, thoughtful writing. But much as cheap money drives out dear, fast writing will always drive out slow writing. The writer who can bat it out this week, today, now, by the time the Century leaves Grand Central Station, is still the one you will read next Thursday.

Fast work has its risks. Time Inc. does not knowingly plagiarize whole sentences from its invisible sources, but one day a free-lance writer spotted in *Life* a complete page lifted without quotation marks from his latest book. He sued and collected $5,000 out of court. It happened that his book was the only existing source on the subject (a combat area in World War II). In copying out his material, the lady on *Life* assigned to do the research had neglected to put quotation marks around her "research." The *Life* writer, taking it as her material, had used it straight. The Frankenstein spoke out of his own head, as usual, but this time in an arrangement of words that already belonged to a human being with a name and a lawyer. If only the writer had rearranged the words a little, they would have been Luce's for nothing.

The faceless writing of Time Inc. has come to dominate current American culture. The American reader realizes that the individual writer is, if not exactly nonexistent, at least inconsequential to the point of ignominy. The assassination of the individual writer by *Time* has come to permeate the whole American press. Even in slick magazines that permit signed articles, the reader hardly notices, nor long remembers, the names, except those of regular columnists who for the most part deal with personalities and opinion. Furthermore, other editors have followed Time Inc. practice in removing all individual human personality from the story as published. I suggest that this may be the reason why it is almost impossible in America today to hear a "great" writer, a great voice speaking individually. (Yet *Life* recently had the gall to complain editorially of the absence of great writers.) The Voltaires and Chestertons and

Menckens have been edited and mass produced out of voice. Only faceless Frankensteins speak.

Not only Time Inc., but American magazines generally, omit the names of books or other articles that can be followed up if the reader gets really interested in the subject. This, says the magazine in the brisk, cold Time Inc. voice, is all you need to know right now; if there's any more, we'll give it to you. Renew your subscription. The fashion of faceless writing has even penetrated to the book world where a happy breed of editors is busy tweaking the eyebrows and pimples that gave the manuscript its human identity.

Time's real success began about 1931, in the depression, and *Life* proliferated in November, 1936, in the recession. In the national confusion, self-doubt and flirtation with Communism, it was good to read in *Life* and *Time* the untroubled absolute truth. Hadden's ghost was winning another argument, as Luce took the bows. In addition, Time Inc. was bright enough to report the most obvious scientific discoveries of which at that period government, business, and the military were disgracefully ignorant.

This may be called the Silver Sty period of Time Inc., ludicrously marred by the first appearance of masked Communists and Newspaper Guild brawlings.

The thirties saw the work of some thoroughly reputable and even distinguished men and women who deserve listing: Davenport, Larsen, Martin, Busch, Gottfried, Billings, Matthews, Grover, Fraser, Hodgins, Schroeder, Kay, Fuller, Vind, Schwind, Kennedy, Peyton, Underhill, Barnett, Butterfield, Piel, and others.

The editors, writers, and researchers were the elite of Time Inc. They had the acknowledged power. They could and did overrule the advertising side. They once outraged even the Ford advertising account and just as it had been wheedled home again, insulted it afresh. More than one, basking in the supposed power of the word, refused an executive promotion. Some, especially on *Fortune,* exploited and strained their prestige by wearing sneakers to interview tycoons, by disappearing into clipjoints for weeks at a time, by introducing sofas into the office and taking naps, by brawling in saloons. But such eccentricities are by no means inconsonant with spiritual power. Tactically, of course, no group of writers as such can ever accumulate power; on the contrary, every member of the group risked his power weekly in his work and bequeathed the credit for risk and intellect to the Frankenstein, which gobbled all. Yet at the late thirties' rare editorial meetings—a practice then already doomed —the assembly exuded the feeling of power held in check, courteous but arrogant, busily cerebrating but sullenly silent. Most novels about Time Inc. reflect this conceit. However, the creation of such a group was in fact Luce's masterpiece and, probably, his subsidiary dream.

What could have destroyed it? Why did it not live as long as the editorial traditions of the New York or London *Times?* What happened?

The answer is Luce himself. He was never the group's leader, only its boss. In consequence, he was frightened by it as he tried to fall asleep at night. He grew jealous of any writer's growing prestige, on the excuse that an empire builder was rearing his treacherous head. Such a man was presently removed to meaningless activities, to another publication, to promotion work, to a leave of absence, or encouraged to go away. This evidence of Luce's jealous impotence lies behind most ex-Time Incers' unfriendly comments about Luce. A few others, however, give as Luce's motive for destroying his own masterpiece his rarely avowed belief that he can, while remaining invisible, make Fate dance to his tune. Since Fate, especially in the person of the Ambassadress, has seemed to call the tune instead, a wry expression has come over Luce's face in the more recent news pictures.

There may be another, parallel, reason for the decay of Time Inc. In the thirties the top editors—Luce, Billings, Gottfried, Matthews— were almost unbelievably unsophisticated, heirs to a more innocent American tradition. Sophistication entered Luce's life with a bang after his second marriage. Sophistication oozed on into the magazines with the move to Rockefeller Plaza and the importation of such sophisticated promoters and "idea men" as Dan Longwell, Alex King, and Willi Schlamm. Before Luce could destroy the old creation, he needed something to fill the void. Sophistication was tagged for the job. Of the new boys, Longwell quickly cut down King and pushed Schlamm into a Graduate Faculty limbo. A portent in this period was the promotion of an undistinguished writer, who had the merit of having been born in France, to publisher of *Life*. At first a little shamefaced with the other writers, he incredulously realized that his career coincided with the transfer of power to the hucksters, and presently he was one of them.

The 1956 editors and writers—if one may risk generalization about a fleeting present that may itself be transitional—are journeymen workers, easily controlled by hucksters on one hand and lady researchers on the other. They certainly do not alarm Luce. Perhaps he is now leader as well as boss—but of this I know nothing.

The present period may be described socially as the Toots Shor era. Intellectually it is the corn-fed or children's hour. In terms of famous employees, in an evolution that would leave Hadden gasping, it is the Age of the Photographers. For these latter, in apparent violation of the Time Inc. formula given above, are allowed to sign their work. The incongruous fame, in an office of anonymous men who actually give them orders, often goes to their head. The model of this new kind of grandee may be given as Eliot Elisofon; he is said to imagine himself Alfred Hitchcock, who also makes pictures.

However, to a sensible reader, the name of the man who snaps the shutter is trifling, as Luce has realized, beside the question of who certified the words.

This latter question asks itself in every issue, in every story. An almost perfect example, because it represents an ideal toward which Time Inc. constantly strives, was a pleasant, unsigned story in *Life*, issue of October 10, 1955. This purports to tell in word and picture how far or fast various creatures can jump, run, fly, or swim. The story tells us that the great gray kangaroo jumps just four inches farther than Jesse Owens. "Says who?" the congregation must respond. The story says that every impala, or the world's champion impala, jumps a foot farther than a mounted horse. "Says who?" It says that a fox, running at forty miles an hour, would nose out all the greyhounds, bison, and giraffes in the world. "Says who?" It says that the Canada goose, crow, and wild turkey all fly at speeds between fifty and sixty miles an hour. "Says who?" responds the now fascinated, but proportionately skeptical, congregation.

The Frankenstein implication is that *Life*'s editors and lady researchers went out and chased impalas, kangaroos, and wild turkeys with a stopwatch and tape measure; hence the Frankenstein knows what it is talking about. Or the impalas and turkeys timed themselves and mailed the results to the Time and Life Building. The most interesting part of the story would be precisely these details of who recorded the times and distances, and how, and with what difficulties —and how inaccurate the figures really must be. But *Life* cannot tell this real story or it shatters the Frankenstein illusion and breaks its monopoly on impalas and turkeys whose addresses are unknown to *Newsweek* or *Look*.

A similar test can be applied to virtually every story in *Time* and *Life* by any reader who will trouble to use his wits.

An apparent exception is given by the lists of scientists' and experts' names at the end of such current features as "The World We Live In" and the like.

It will be noted that the scientists' books are not listed. Furthermore, if I know scientists, they told *Life*'s researchers a great number of contradictory things, so that the published compromise among their disparate opinions represents no one of them accurately. One scientist tells his friends: "I don't know why they gave my name. All I did was tell them to read my book, and now I tell my classes not to read that issue of *Life* or they'll fail my course." But obviously he was flattered by the inclusion.

These stories were signed "Lincoln Barnett and the Staff of Life" in the republication in book form. The latter half of the signature must have been insisted on by Mr. Barnett.

When Luce or a stand-in gives a modest and honest man like Barnett such a subject as "Man" or "The Universe," he has two peremptory, if implied, commands. One is, "Make like Carlyle"— or Darwin or Toynbee. The other is, "Work God in, preferably in the King James version." The fact that the classy Presbyterian writing of "The World We Live In" has excited no parodies and no hilarity is a serious defect in literary America today.

Viz: "Below the sun-spangled satin of the waters there loomed a fabulous world. . . . The great continental platforms loomed rocky and bleak. . . . From such shadowy beginnings . . . the wondrous procession . . . down eons of terrestrial time . . . the ciphers of some arcane code-script . . . untold ages past . . . these wondrous laws of nature. . . . A few glimmerings of light in the dark abyss of time . . . echo the words of Paul, 'God hath chosen the weak things.' "

The stories are loaded, not exactly with errors, but with self-destroying compromises between irreconcilable and unprovable hypotheses, all issued as solemn and holy truth.

The pretentious fraud descended to farce in the current "Epic of Man" series because in this case—November 7, 1955—artists were required to dream up the human faces on the ancient bones. The result is that Chancelade Man (14,000 B.C.) is certified by *Life* to have been Willie Howard. Abbeville Man (600,000 B.C.) was recognizably Boris Karloff. Acheulian Man (300,000 B.C.) was unmistakably John Garfield. Mousterian Man (170,000 B.C.) must have been a nephew of Ernest Hemingway and Jo Davidson. Neanderthal Man could go on TV tomorrow as unshaven Ed Sullivan. These people are all shown as no hairier than Clark Gable and, in final climactic error, several expose the turned-in toes of men who have just slipped out of pointed shoes 600,000 years ago. A reader genuinely interested in the great subject is once more afforded endless merriment. At the end comes again the hollow boast implied in the list of scientists, but no real sources, no books to read, no way to discover the real story underneath the Frankenstein story.

The effect of Time Inc. on Time Inc. people is an absorbing, unwritten, but necessarily provisional story. In general, it can be said that they are as nervously exhausted and as affable as hucksters on Madison Avenue, two short blocks east. Any statement of mine that many of the top people dislike themselves is clearly subjective. Time Inc. people keep themselves apart from the New York literary world. Generally they don't know "anybody" or if they did before they were hired, soon stop seeing "anybody" but other Time Inc. people and other Toots Shor customers. They have their climax of euphoria at Senior Group dinners (I assume this has continued) where the year's bonus is announced (I hope this has continued). As salesmen have come to dominate Time Inc., the outpoured love at these dinners must be suffocating. Because Luce has heavy eyebrows, Time Inc. people never let the barber trim their eyebrows.

A curiously valid generalization is that a man begins to have trouble with his wife about a year after he joins Time Inc. The writer can have been happily married, but he becomes intolerable or contemptible to his wife in that employ. Time Inc. women who support their husbands, on the other hand, seem happy. Of the third sex, very, very few have ever appeared. One lesbian even reformed and married.

Neurosis, yes, but no suicide for working Time Inc. people. The suicides are instead ex-Time Inc. people: the tragic and inscrutable cases of such ranking writers as Goldsborough, Wickware, Balliett, and perhaps some others, all apparently courageous and fruitful men.

The explanation may lie in the pretense of toughness that Time Inc. demands. The individual actually comes to believe he is tough. He is deluded by the intellectual cruelty of the Time Inc. formula. Time Inc. is in fact a sort of overcompensation for sensitive people as long as they can keep on taking the drug. On the job they haven't time for suicide. But a while after they have been detached from the apparatus, they begin to feel pain again.

What is worse, a term at Time Inc. gives a writer a conditioned reflex that automatically produces an eternal truth out of a fast reading of the material. He has perfected the technique, and worse, the habit of the snap judgment. Even if he leaves and revolts against the Time Inc. reflex, his sole aim in life becomes the opposite and equally useless ambition to get his name signed in print to the most eccentric and personal opinion he can conceive. Thus, he thinks, will he defy the Frankenstein. He has, in essence, mislaid his sense of perspective about himself, the world, and his writing. He is lost until he can get over spelling it "cigaret" and give it that more thoughtful "ette." He must get used to not mastering and dismissing a subject in a week and never again thinking about it. He must learn to do his own research. He must get over being in debt one full year's income. He has to learn ordinary human values all over again.

Not many ex-Time Incers have achieved the metamorphosis back to human identity. Their stories—which I do not know—must be fascinating indeed.

Nebuchadnezzar II
(1956)

The autonomous government of Robert Moses, who has never been elected to anything, is richer and more powerful than a good many nations and several Western states. Though its authority rests only on thirty years of appointments and reappointments by New York mayors and governors, it is oddly free of the customary American system of checks and balances. It issues its own revenue bonds. It collects its own taxes in the form of tolls. It raises its own uniformed army. Within the huge ramifications of its various spheres, it is one-man government nearly as absolute as a Latin American dictator's, openly based on the same proposition that always makes dictatorship "necessary": that everybody else is an idiot or a scoundrel.

Robert Moses' considered opinions of his fellow citizens are given in his current book, *Working for the People* (Harper's), in the list of people he is against: "demagogues," "crackpots," "party bosses," "radical unionists," "ignorant editors," "reactionary tycoons," "uplifters," "reformers," "do-gooders," "taxpayers' groups," "eager-beaver political amateurs," "visionary planners," "sociologists," "ultra-modern, long-haired designers," "federal planners," "partisans," "enthusiasts," "state planning bodies," "virulent, vicious troublemakers," "irresponsible mudslingers," "doleful bankers," "muckraking commentators," "civic secretaries," "sour critics," "Lewis Mumford, Frank Lloyd Wright and their followers" and "goon union leaders."

Deduct all these from the population. What remains are Moses men and of course Moses. It is obvious that Moses is indispensable.

The people's desperate need for Robert Moses is revealed less by the list of his offices than by the offices he never bothers to visit. On the important New York City Planning Commission, one member says that Moses attends "darn few" meetings, another says "none in eight years." As Coordinator of Construction, he cannot very well get into his office, which is listed as Post Office Box 35, Triborough Station, New York 35. The *New Yorker* magazine has reported that he never goes to his office at the Arsenal in Central Park where as New York City Park Commissioner he is supposed to earn the only salary, $25,000, he is credited with collecting. But there is no doubt that he has a real talent for absentee administration.

The real Moses consolidation of powers only begins to be visible at his Babylon, Long Island, office on the former Belmont estate, where he is dictator-president of the Long Island State Park Commission and dictator-chairman of the Jones Beach State Parkway and Bethpage Park Auditorium. In the warm months these latter yield substantial revenues to the Moses empire. During those months, Moses puts in a Thursday-to-Monday weekend at the Babylon office (he lives nearby in the summer), surrounded by his certificates of appointment and the tiny silver trowels that memorialize old triumphs. But at Babylon the curious and awed investigator has not yet really caught up with Moses.

The big-power ganglions feed in to still another office, tucked away on Randalls Island in New York's East River. Here Moses is dictator-chairman of the consolidated Triborough Bridge and Tunnel Authority. This fuzzy title conceals the fact that this office runs and collects tolls and revenue from not only the Triborough Bridge, but also the Henry Hudson Bridge, Whitestone Bridge, Cross Bay Parkway Bridge, Marine Parkway Bridge, the Midtown Tunnel and Brooklyn-Battery Tunnel and garage. These great properties are currently out of the control of the people of New York, though by paying tribute they may have the use of them.

The Triborough Authority has a new and somewhat baffling enterprise—the housing and convention-hall development known as the Coliseum on Columbus Circle in the heart of New York City. The reason for the Coliseum's hiding under the Triborough's ample wing may be that by that dodge Moses would not have to submit the plans to the city art commission, a capable and patriotic body which probably falls under the heading of several of the epithets listed above. Though the art commission has legal jurisdiction over buildings on city land, the plans actually were never submitted.

However, even the majestic Triborough Authority is dwarfed by new dreams of empire.

The latest expansion is heralded by the new function of still another Moses office—at 270 Broadway, New York, which formerly served only the dictator-chairman of the State Council of Parks. In 1954 Moses became dictator-chairman of the New York State Power Authority, charged with redesigning Niagara Falls and the St. Lawrence River. Its office promptly moved to 270 Broadway. From here is conducted his major current fight. From here he expelled from the Power Authority the unsympathetic trustees and substituted his own men, conspicuously aged William Wilson. The names of Moses men—Wilson, Howland, Blakelock, Chapin—are likely to appear in the interlocking units of the empire as the "virulent, vicious troublemakers" disappear.

The prospect of Moses, unsupervised, unchecked, and unaudited, running wild with Niagara Falls and the great St. Lawrence River is, to put it quickly, disquieting. He announces in his new book that he expects to flood a certain amount of the St. Lawrence shore and sell power to the Aluminum Company of America under a contract that in the view of some experts conceded far too much to ALCOA. While tapping a great economic potential, Moses is in an unassailable position to ruin some of the most beautiful and most widely appreciated country in North America. In any case it will forevermore look like Moses. As the poet Melville Cane has written:

> The bird who in the waning light
> Was wont to call: "Bob White! Bob White!"
> Now cries instead: "Bob Moses!"

Power, in the hydroelectric sense, is a new field for Moses, but he is conducting this new fight for power, in the older sense, along his customary lines. These range from violent bluff, "or else" threats, a publicity barrage against politicians, do-gooders and greedy private interests, to protestations of unselfish humility and insidious infiltration. As usual, he asks for no salary. As usual, he asks only to be allowed to give the people the benefit of his rightness. After the job is finished and the income and power begin to roll in, the man in possession is Robert Moses; and he stays and stays and stays. He pocketed parks in 1924, bridges in 1934, tunnels in 1945; he has never unpocketed anything.

An example is the Triborough Bridge. It was opened in July, 1936, with a promise that tolls would cease when the bridge was paid for. It had been built, "at relatively small cost to the city," on a Roosevelt-Ickes PWA loan of $44,000,000—rewarded with a stream of Moses insults at Roosevelt and Ickes. I don't profess to understand bookkeeping, but the announced construction-fund balance and receipts in 1938 added up to $25,000,000. Just about the week this is published, the total of toll collections on the Triborough Bridge alone will be passing $100,000,000 for the twenty-year period. It is now running at the rate of nearly $12,000,000 a year. The whole Authority's income is about three times that every year. But in 1953 it was announced that the bridge tolls would be pledged for nine years to the end that "the crossings can be returned to New York City by 1973." I don't know what this means, but I don't believe any part of it.

At a Marine Parkway Bridge opening at Riis Park on July 3, 1937, Moses responded to the usual compliments by saying that he didn't yet understand the true nature of the five Authorities he then directed, "but they are great for getting things done." He evidently understands them better now. They are great for getting all sorts of things done, some of them a surprise to the people who give Moses the jobs.

The "Authority" as a device in government is, to say the least, interesting. It is essentially an escape hatch from political-constitutional government which is always limited in the jobs it may undertake and the revenue bonds it may issue in a given year. With every such undertaking, Presidents, governors, and mayors find themselves harried by all sorts of people and interests. The Authority, on the other hand, is on its own. Some lawyers even contend that New York police have no jurisdiction on Moses territory, such as the Triborough Bridge. It is a state within a state and, as Moses quickly noticed, "great for getting things done"—without anybody's noticing until it is too late. After the job is done, it is easy and even logical for the Authority chairman to hang on indefinitely. If he is smart, he can pledge the revenues to issue new bonds to finance new enterprises and Authorities which will produce new revenues to pay the interest on new bond issues for still more enterprises and authorities, and so on.

The arguments in favor of the Authority system never entirely escape the Fascist-Communist assumption that ordinary, democratic, political operations are unavoidably incompetent and wasteful. The authoritarian ring in the word Authority belongs there.

The legend that everything the Authority and Moses have done is good is as solidly established as homemade bread. No complete survey will be attempted here. But it will be instructive to notice some things he has wanted to do. He wanted to slap a bridge over the Narrows at the entrance to New York harbor. He wanted to throw a bridge from the Battery to Brooklyn because he "knew" that a tunnel was impossible and undesirable. (He finally had to build—and now takes credit for—the tunnel.) In general, Moses much prefers "improvements" that are highly visible; hence, tunnels are at a discount in his book. He still champions a preposterous plan to throw an elevated express highway right across the heart of Manhattan around 34th Street, presumably so that motorists from the West, headed for Long Island, can avoid the George Washington Bridge, which does not belong to Moses. The beauty of this plan is that it will get in the way of and be visible to more people more often than anything Moses has done yet. That makes it compulsive.

Moses has indeed got things done, and so have hundreds and thousands of other agencies in the United States. "Irresponsible mudslingers" criticize everything Moses has done. They say that his highways, compared to Connecticut's or New Jersey's, are not quite wide enough, are constantly under repair, and are not in the right places. They point out that the Henry Hudson Parkway, instead of taking an obvious route through the Kingsbridge shacktown which is still there, went out of its way to destroy the few remaining stately homes in Riverdale. (Perhaps Moses thought it would be more visible there.) They say the Coliseum will have no halls big enough to accommodate any convention much larger than a Moses family party. They say the Washington Square Southeast project will put out of business one thousand small businesses which will not be able to find comparable space. And so on. In all these matters I would guess that Moses could put up an equally impressive argument.

Something less debatable would be the character behind the Authority. When the Battery Tunnel was under debate in the New York Board of Estimate, Moses announced as fact that the old Aquarium, a famous New York landmark, would have to go for two reasons: first, the blasting for the tunnel would crumple the Aquarium; and second, a necessary tunnel under a corner of the Aquarium was impossible because of its weight. The tunnel was built; the Aquarium is still there (as a federal monument, but without fish) sitting on top of a tunnel. It was in no way involved in the construction of the Brooklyn-Battery Tunnel. Furthermore, the old Aquarium was ideally located and drew over two million visitors a year. Moses promised a new aquarium with fish at Coney Island, at no cost to the city; but if one is ever completed, it is now clear that it will cost the city several millions and the New York Zoological Society several more.

This fairly unimportant incident reveals several important things about the character behind the Authority. While getting one big thing done in the usual big way, he likes to put himself into position to accomplish a few other things—and he wanted the Aquarium at Coney Island. There may be a third point—that whenever Moses discovers that a thing is loved by people, he feels emotionally driven to move it or improve it. The Aquarium was popular; furthermore it was a favorite subject for the *New Yorker* magazine. Even though that magazine has given Moses unquestioning adulation (most recently by Lewis Mumford this year), its liking the Aquarium gave that institution an esoteric status that doomed it. A fourth point, often noted, is that Moses, who has a voice in all New York's museums and zoos, has never shown any interest in the exhibits. He doesn't care what people care about; he just wants to usher them into clean toilets.

There is no easy way of finding out whether his motives are good or bad toward the people of New York. But it may be helpful to observe how Moses treats what he himself, personally, as a land-owner and family man, loves.

In other words, what has he done with his own summer home in

Babylon? The answer is that he has let it alone. It is an unpretentious, shingled house in the village of Babylon. It backs on a little creek leading out of Great South Bay. It is not oversupplied with toilets and facilities. The grounds have not been torn up, earth-moved, concreted. It would seem as if this is the only land in his vast domain that Moses does not want to lay hands on.

Moses is described as generally behaving as if he felt out of things. His characteristic facial expressions have been listed as "Babylonian King at bay," "Babylonian King being sued for mercy," "Babylonian King graciously offering the poisoned cup." The reason for these impressions seems to be a fixed look of noble suffering, a little as if he smells something burning but didn't want to mention it. If one must pick a Babylonian King to rank on even terms with Moses, it would have to be Nebuchadnezzar II, who threw a grid of canals— the expressways of that time—across the country and built Babylon into a "wonder of the world." He also tore down Jerusalem. Soon after Nebuchadnezzar, Babylon's history ends.

Moses' present Power Authority fight reminds one of the New Deal days when he thanked Roosevelt and Ickes for the Triborough Bridge with torrents of invective. Now the United States Congress is the object of his attack, even as it considers whether to give the development of Niagara Falls to the Authority of Moses. His claim is that Congress is wrong in claiming, under the treaty with Canada, that it has the right to dispose of the job. Moses claims that the job is the Federal Power Commission's, with preference given to the Authority of Moses, and he has legal opinions to prove it.

Not unnaturally, Senator Herbert Lehman reproached Moses for this "unwise tactic." That was on January 2nd. Next day Moses, considered by the *New Yorker* a "glittering conversationalist," came back with this broadside: "Senator Lehman says . . . 'unwise tactic.' . . . We printed the [legal] opinion, as a matter of necessary public information. We did not procure it." (This sentence need not be taken literally.) "How can Senator Lehman say this is an unwise tactic? The Senator should consult his dictionary and book of synonyms. A tactic in this context is a little game or expedient." (But not in the Unabridged Webster's New International Dictionary.) "We are playing no game."

It almost sounds as if Moses were about to claim the right to negotiate treaties with foreign powers, levy war, and insure domestic tranquillity.

An indication that Moses may be slipping came late last year in his acceptance of helpless defeat on a wild plan to put a high fence around migrating birds' favorite Central Park hilltop so that old folks (who couldn't possibly have climbed the hill) could play checkers in peace. In the course of this small battle, the general fear of Moses' powers of persecution silenced every official in the following organizations, which were all opposed to the plan:

American Museum of Natural History
New York Zoological Society
Audubon Society
New York Park Association
Institute of Landscape Architects.

The bird watchers, Moses had discovered, loved the hilltop called The Ramble, but the protest against his plan was on much wider grounds, and finally included officials of the Garden Clubs and the Municipal Art Society. Faced with these minute slings, the Goliath retired from the field.

Another recent bell tolled in the New York State Assembly where a bill was introduced—*lèse-majesté!*—to supervise Moses on the Triborough Authority. A single skirmish of Moses threats and insults was enough to send the bill back to committee. A little public outcry should be enough to get it back on the floor of the assembly. Perhaps soon after, Governor Harriman and Mayor Wagner might consider lightening the load they have heaped on Robert Moses, unless they claim they can find no other single able man in this great Republic. If they can't, there is nothing else to do but make Moses dictator in name as well as fact.

I conclude that city civilization—the mingled lives of millions of people—offends him as a putrid enormity. He thinks of his public works as great cemeteries of death or great hospitals for the dying. He might have made a wonderful surgeon—or undertaker. He is especially happy with sick land, desolate dumps and sand spits, slums and wastes, as he points out in his new book. His highway system may be regarded as a calcified skeleton superseding the living tissue it was designed to support. If he were allowed to "complete" his work, we may imagine a magnificent, silent concrete mausoleum spreading from a monstrous bridge at the Narrows to the drowned St. Lawrence valley, saving only a little patch of life at Babylon.

Any such reading of the Moses character does not by any means disqualify him from building a road or bridge under public supervision. But it might say something about whether he is precisely the ideal man to plan the American way of life.

I will add my own personal intuition about Moses. I believe he is one of those numerous indefatigable workers who really hate their work.

The Mad Road Builders
(1956)

To some people the United States is not seen as people, but as a gigantic skeleton of hard-surface roads crawling with motor vehicles. Seen in this way, the mammoth web of concrete is a monstrosity. But the monstrosity is necessary, say the big thinkers, because seventy million American car owners are daily impelled to drive an average of twenty-five miles—a statistical total of 1,700,000,000 miles per day. Even if half or three-quarters of this traffic were utterly unnecessary and unprofitable to everybody, they say, it must be maintained and encouraged. The reason? American prosperity depends on perpetual boom in the automobile industry and the production and sale of eight million new cars every year.

It may be time these articles of faith were more closely examined. The crisis of a fatal illness attacking the country is adequately, though unintentionally, described in a new publicity book issued by Henry Ford II, *Freedom of the American Road*, plus the current news about toll roads. Mr. Ford's foreword justifies the fine title in a sentence that will be returned to later: "We Americans have always liked . . . freedom to come and go as we please in this big country of ours." However, the freedom he is discussing is only the "freedom" under license to drive a motor vehicle on a roadbed never paid for by the automobile industry. A licensed right is never an absolute, sovereign right. The use of the word "freedom" in this context is a play on words, perhaps a dangerous joke.

The book makes clear that America's present road-building boom began hardly ten (nearer five) years ago. In that interval little bands of patriots arose in such localities as California, New Jersey, Pennsylvania, North Carolina, Oregon, Washington, Maine, Boston, Portland (Oregon), San Francisco, Detroit, Albuquerque, Pittsburgh, Los Angeles, Dallas and Atlanta. Their communities were being strangled to death by traffic. Like modern Herculeses, they saved their world by epic labors and legislations. Henry Ford's writers raise them to the highest echelon of peacetime American heroes. One can hardly criticize anything they did; besides, now it is done.

Thus the total United States road picture is now as follows:

Roads	Miles
National Interstate	40,000
Federal-Aid Primary	195,000
Federal-Aid Secondary	483,000
Rural Feeder Roads	3,012,520
City Streets	353,670
TOTAL	4,084,190

Elsewhere in the Ford book another total, 3,366,000 miles, is given without a breakdown. For the present, I accept the larger total. The city streets are described as carrying half of all "traffic"—an undefined word, but one conveying the general fact that the cities are the crux of traffic.

Some of the expressways are over 400 feet wide. The New York Thruway is generally 200 feet wide; rural hard-surface roads run between thirty and fifty feet wide from margin to margin, including shoulders, ditches, and verges. If the average works out at only fifty feet, the total acreage taken over by United States roads is 40,000 square miles—a good deal more than the area of the five New England states, excluding Maine.

I do not resent this loss. For the sake of communication among all the forty-eight states, we can afford to liquidate five or six. The fact is given only to put a going value on this communication and pose the question of how much more calcified skeleton, how much more monstrosity, we can reasonably afford.

The Ford book for all its enthusiasm gives the unexpected effect of tracing a dreadful disease over the body of America. Pullulating bumper to bumper, unassimilable organisms were about to kill the victim; then the doctors stepped in and accelerated the flow. No wonder the treatments invariably conclude on an ominous diagnosis.

For California, the 1954–1955 highway budget was the highest in the nation and yet " 'All we can honestly say is that at the moment we are no longer losing ground.' . . . If anything has been learned, it's that it is almost impossible to overestimate modern highway needs. Yesterday's wildest dreams now seem quaintly reactionary. After completion, the common criticism of a highway that seemed fantastically expensive is, 'Why didn't they make it big enough in the first place?' "

For North Carolina: " 'The people of no other state by vote of their representatives or their own vote have committed so large a part of the wealth of their earnings to their roads.' Today the people of North Carolina need still another road program—just because of their foresightedness. Their once-splendid primary roads were built too early. Many are becoming less and less adequate for today's traffic."

This ominous note is fully justified. It is doubtful whether a continuously multiplying traffic load could be handled by doubling our 40,000 square miles of roads. Eighty thousand square miles? 200,000? 500,000? The United States has only three million square miles, many of them unsuitable for highways. But the crux is the cities. Adequate roads there obviously demand the flattening of at least half the buildings in our metropolises. End of joke.

The problem is not people. True, the cities are full of people, but a walking human being needs only three square feet of surface at any one moment, and the safety margin is important only for women with raised umbrellas. A slow-moving automobile needs a space eight by fifty feet for safety, or four hundred square feet. Hence, a city has a limit to the number of automobiles it can take. If all America's 75,000,000 motor vehicles were on the road at the same time, they would require over 5,000,000 miles of one-lane highway. The present roads could handle them if they would spread out evenly, moving slowly, over every existing road. But of course they don't, won't, and can't. Most of them are always going to the same places—fast. Too many want to get into the same four hundred square feet. Since each driver has been encouraged to believe that he is entitled to this "Freedom of the American Road," the organisms pile up monstrously at critical points. The classic California pile-up was at Bayshore's Boneyard Hill—seventy-four vehicles in one gigantic crash.

The old way of treating a bacterial infection was to slash at the pockets of pus. Men like Robert Moses of New York have grown famous for their bravura with this therapy. Their knives cut through the living tissue of our civilization and make way for artificial drains to carry off the strangling congestions. The destruction is epic; the drains are awe-inspiring; but there seems no end to the disease. Every day, every year, the great surgeon is called on for one more miracle of surgery.

And this sort of operation has really been quite easy to sell to government and people. The public need and willingness to pay are so obvious that toll roads have attracted the cupidity of private capital. Investors have liked the prospect of federal tax exemptions, sure earnings, and good yields on the investment. The only connection the private toll-road authorities have with government is usually that their boards are appointed by the governors. The bonds are specifically not state obligations.

The toll-road boom was opened with two bonanzas by the Pennsylvania and New Jersey turnpikes. The former at least proved an inspired road in eliminating murderous mountain driving at one of the lowest toll charges in the country—an average of 4.2 cents a mile for trucks. The New Jersey pike battened on luxury traffic along the seaboard, earning in 1955 on its $430 million in bonds nearly twenty million in net operating revenue (before interest). Its bonds are rated A by Moody.

Indiana and Ohio leaped onto this bandwagon to such purpose that by the end of this year a driver in a hell of a hurry can go from New York City to the outskirts of Chicago in sixteen hours at a toll cost of $11 and a speed up to seventy miles an hour.

But something has gone wrong. The Ohio Turnpike in its first five months of operation is well behind the rate of earnings required on its bonded interest. The chairman is indignantly optimistic but money men appear not to believe him. The trouble is that the Ohio Turnpike, crossing flatlands at an average truck toll of 7.2 cents a mile, parallels free roads that the turnpike has marvellously freed of the more nervous sort of traffic. Truckers are not fools. They have moved over to the free roads.

The flat failure of the West Virginia toll road, "the pike to nowhere" (Charleston to Princeton, West Virginia—eighty-eight miles), has apparently killed plans for connecting toll roads across Virginia and North Carolina. Altogether last year $3,600,000,000 worth of toll-road projects were "postponed."

The principle that toll roads cannot possibly solve the highway problem has already been laid down by the United States Bureau of Public Roads. It notes that virtually all the profitable ones parallel and duplicate the free-road system of the national interstate network. Congress has seemed to agree by knocking out of a pending road-aid appropriation for thirty-seven billion dollars in the next fifteen years (the Fallon bill) a provision calling for 90 per cent credit to toll roads begun after 1955.

In my opinion the chief indictment of the great skeleton of expressways derives from a discovery that the overwhelming mass of tolls on a road are for short hauls. The man or truck in a hell of a hurry all the way from New York to Chicago is, in fact, not a prime factor.

Neither the cross-country expressway nor private enterprise is going to solve the problem. In fact some bondholders have begun to wonder whether they will escape with their lives. They find themselves on the edge of a death struggle far too big for them—the Bureau of Public Roads is asking for $126 billion for roads over the next ten years. When a nation is fighting for its life, it is not easy to make a quiet buck. *Business Week* of February 11, 1956, thinks even the modest Fallon bill "could mean the end of toll-road financing."

The Province of Ontario last month gave the subject a dose of the usual magnificent Canadian common sense. No private companies, says Ontario, will be given toll-road concessions. All toll roads must be part of the over-all system. When the road is paid for, toll charges will cease. Since the people ultimately pay for all roads, there is no such thing as a "free road."

"Freedom of the road" recalls "the right of departure" lost by the Russian people after the Mongol conquest. This right has never been questioned for Americans. But should an American pedestrian claim "the right of departure" from New York City and try to go cross-country afoot, he would find himself confronted by highways as by a net of Chinese walls. Notably in the Bronx and Queens, he is stopped by a great embankment. If he can, he clambers up it, only to face the peril of his life in a stream of cars plunging past him. At a break in that one-way traffic, he darts to the median line and teeters there watching the other-way traffic. This next dash may cost him his life.

Most municipal magistrates would be astonished to be informed that that pedestrian has an absolute right to cross the expressway. Municipal "jaywalking" ordinances are all essentially unconstitutional. The driver contests the pedestrian's right with only a *licensed* right. If the sovereign citizen, the proprietor of the road, scuttles across it, he scuttles only as a practical matter of survival, not in fear of violating any ordinance forbidding him to leave his viscera "spread out like strawberry jam." The driver's right depends on his observance of his responsibilities and the rights of other drivers and pedestrians. Like a licensed pistol-wearer, he is given the power of life or death over his fellow citizen. Any sensible society naturally hedges such a right.

America's great problem is not even traffic but, as with every civilization that ever existed, to keep and curry the love of its citizens for the whole society and its arrangements. In an ancient Babylon, Egypt, and Rome some of that love drained out of a citizen confronted with mammoth public works comparable to the Queens highway that stops the cross-country pedestrian. It is not very metaphysical to say that when a civilization intimidates, excludes, and terrifies even one citizen, it is a little nearer its death.

These great highway structures cannot be loved, and are not. The East River Drive in Manhattan, for example, almost completely excludes pedestrian Manhattanites from the East River. Every expressway excludes a number of people from what they love on the other side of the road. Structural gigantism is a fairly sure way to kill the individual's love for his world.

This estrangement of the American family by gigantism may be the clue to the whole automobile problem. It may often be just this estrangement that gives the family head the compulsion to buy a car. His car identifies him with the gigantism. It is his car, with a bum carburetor, a few individual dents, and some interior litter. When he rides out into the maelstrom, he reestablishes his part in the huge thing rushing past his door. This compels the civilization to build yet more gigantic highways, and the citizen feels worse again.

The family drives out to visit Aunt Esther in Hempstead, whom they don't like, instead of dropping around the corner to see Aunt Myrtle, whom they do like; or to a restaurant twenty miles away that is worse than the one down two blocks. The real purpose of the trips is to get into the maelstrom, which they all pretend to hate.

The price they pay for their cars is ruinous. According to a crack car salesman, he will give a $4,000 car to a provably solvent customer for $3,600 nowadays. However, the price, including insurance and carrying charges, really comes to $4,200, if it is paid over three years. The car is worth about $2,500 practically as soon as it is driven out of the salesroom. At the end of one year, the customer will have paid $1,400, owe $2,800, and have a $2,000 car to show for it. A year's use costs him $2,200, excluding operating expenses.

We are told that Detroit must be kept happy, unless the United States is to go on the rocks. We have done our best with the subsidy of ten billions a year for the roadbed for Detroit's products. It is not enough.

But if we can allow Detroit to take care of itself, there is a solution to the highway and traffic problem: fewer cars on the roads. The details:

1. Because a single bus or train takes between twenty and 1,000 cars off the roads, we must certainly allocate subsidies to buses and, in particular, railroads. (The old antirailroad prejudice, inherited from the land-grant period, is obsolete; Eastern railroads never got land grants.) Intercity passenger traffic in 1953 was 86 per cent by car, 5.6 per cent by railroad and 5 per cent by bus. The railroads that year carried an average of about a million and a half passengers every day, pulling off the roads about a million cars. If the railroads were equipped to carry around twenty million passengers a day, the huge subsidies for highways could be cut down to size. The

saving in gasoline, rubber, and metal, as well as nervous system, would make America a rich and happy land.

The present auto mania is so appalling or ridiculous, depending on where your sense of humor lies, that even *urban* traffic is over 87 per cent by car and only 11 per cent by transit systems. Railroads won't solve this.

2. The privilege of driving a car must be made immensely more honorable and exclusive. License examinations must be rigorous.

3. Licenses must be suspended at the first violation of responsibility or first indication of incompetence. The suspension period ought to be in terms of years, not weeks.

4. Detroit must be required by law to build lower speeds into cars and trucks.

5. Ruinous terms of installment purchase must be outlawed.

6. Creation of central shopping districts cleared of motor vehicles and streets, except for underground service tunnels (as in the new Fort Worth plan). In Manhattan, for example, only people and subways would be admitted to an area at least from 34th to 59th Streets between Sixth and Lexington Avenues.

To these proposals I gladly add those submitted in the Henry Ford book by Robert Moses: movement of certain goods at night; staggered work hours; more parking meters; "adequate loading and unloading and off-street parking in all new buildings"; "public sub-surface, surface and upper-level public parking at reasonable rates"; "strategically located bus garages and truck terminals"; arcaded sidewalks to expand streets; "much more drastic zoning restrictions."

The Moses list might serve as interim measures while the railroads, bus lines, licensing bureaus, and police departments are getting into position for the all-out solution.

Whether or not the answer has been given here, some solution is inevitable—and fairly soon. America is not a sick body; the disease of the automobile is only a metaphor. Otherwise, with such a disease, the patient would surely die. But it can be predicted that any solution must stop the propagation of more and more cars and roads.

The automobile may have converted the descendants of American pioneers, the toughest, most energetic, and open-minded people in the civilized world, into lazy and fat-seated invalids in forty years. But it is yet to be proved that it has also made them fat-headed.

You, Too, Can Drive a Jukebox
(1956)

There were things going on in the United States this Christmas season that just could not be reconciled. On the one hand, at the National Automobile Show in New York—the first since 1940—grown men and women stared with the drunken eyes of children at the great tin gauds with "swept wings" (they fly?), "starflight styling" (oh, interplanetary), "tail fins" (no, they swim) and "anti-dive devices" (ah, submarines!).

On the other hand, elsewhere were symptoms of the seeing realism which gloriously comes to the top of the American character a little way short of disaster. Those who despair of the American destiny need to be reminded of Abraham Lincoln's data on fooling all the people some of the time, and so on.

Let us look at the fatuous part first—the $10,000,000 Automobile Show.

It's a fine show. A very noisy floor show goes on six times a day, loaded with several dozen dancers and singers. But these girls are not so elegant as those scattered around or inside the exhibits. These latter dolls are much too good for the common people unless of course one buys the car on display. The men customers kept speaking to them hopefully, and the smiles froze on the exquisite Gothic faces.

The cars are beautiful too. As objects to install in the parlor or back yard, there can be no cavil about their long, low, sneaky charm. I could understand a man who wanted to be buried in one. But as something to take down the street to get a coke, they are nearly as implausible as a four-horse Carthaginian chariot.

Consider that American cars are already eating up gasoline at an annual rate of a billion and a quarter forty-two-gallon-barrels, requiring something like three billion barrels of petroleum. And all new cars require high-octane gas. Proved United States oil reserves are currently only ten times the annual consumption, and have dropped as low as six times. And so the new cars boost power as high as 375 h.p. with greatly increased appetites for high-octane gas. Many go 140 miles an hour, but Buick supplies a buzzer to warn you when you exceed sixty. If you can't use that extra eighty miles an hour, what good is it? One answer is that your motor is always idling, even at sixty, and wasting more gas. Another answer is fast acceleration to get out of, and into, trouble on the road.

As for the increased car lengths, city parking is already a nightmare and the nation's road system already congested, even though the road surface is 40,000 square miles, equivalent to five New England states. The new cars will clog the streets with luxurious, empty luggage compartments.

Every American man is a car expert, like the small boys of 1914 who first began mouthing those lovely words, "horsepower," "carburetor," "ignition" and so on, around the first garages. Yet even horsepower is not yet clearly understood.

On a car with an advertised 375 h.p., the textbook's indicated horsepower would be something over 400 h.p. The 375 represents "brake horsepower" at maximum r.p.m. or speed, say, of 140 miles an hour. This is cut about 25 per cent by the time it gets past the differential to the rear wheels—or 300 h.p. The great torque of an American car is what produces the "thrust" that makes it dangerous. A racing driver would know enough to take the options (axle ratio, special springs, and so on) that gave him something he could handle. He would be afraid of the showroom car.

The tolerant British are very kind to the new American cars. *The Economist* writes, "The pattern of American design strategy depends, of course, on the general acceptance of one particular shape and size of automobile by the great majority of its customers— a roomy six-seater with a large trunk . . . automatic transmission; independent suspension in front and a beam axle behind; a structure in which most of the strength is concentrated in a frame below the body and comparatively little contributed by the body itself." Automatic transmissions "mass-produced in very high volume can nowadays be had for no great increase in price, and the 250 pounds they may add in weight are easily lost in the massive, powerful automobiles of Detroit. . . . In the United States, where freedom from noise and vibration is at a premium, and where most roads are so good that road-holding is at a discount . . . independent rear-springing has made no impact at all."

Detroit's conservatism has a reason; the industry has never forgotten Chrysler's almost fatal mistake in the thirties of offering the advanced Airflow to public apathy.

But the result is a car conceived as a featherbed on which the owner floats through life buoyed by feelings of enormous relaxed power. There would be no harm in selling these feelings to somebody in a seat at the movies, but selling them to him when he is in a two-ton vehicle moving at sixty m.p.h. is not nice. The driver's problem in reality is to maintain contact with the road and his vehicle, as if he were riding a horse. The American automobile's problem is to convince him that he is floating along one foot above the road. The two problems are in fatal conflict. The second sells the car; the first may kill the driver or somebody else. If the driver knowingly takes the chance, all right; but if he is surprised when it happens to him, as he usually is, his end is truly tragic.

The new cars make the driver feel as if he were at home in his favorite armchair, with the heat on, the radio playing, and the landscape as unobtrusive as a TV screen. This is all an escape from a volatile reality—a vehicle rolling along a curving road at sixty m.p.h. Thus, cold sober, in broad daylight, on a little-traveled thruway, he has the illusion of "flowing" around another car when his car is actually at seventy m.p.h., describing a self-made curve that his soft-sprung car cannot take without danger of rolling over or going out of control.

People do not necessarily buy a foreign car for the gasoline savings, the low upkeep, or the durable little engine. The foreign car also holds the road and handles like a well-broken horse. It has used the know-how of modern engineering—no mystery to Detroit—to produce the most efficient light engine possible, the most effective suspension, and the best road-holding qualities. On curving roads or city streets, I am told, a 375-h.p. showroom Chrysler could not catch an old, sixty h.p. Rolls-Royce. Within five minutes the Chrysler would be on its back, wheels spinning. Yet the Rolls-Royce would be three feet shorter and two feet higher than the Chrysler, and have only one sixth the horsepower.

As against such a performance, the American car's more famous faults are secondary. So it has too much power; so it uses too much gas; so the new engines are so arranged that you can hardly get at your own spark plugs; so the smallest dent in one of the idiotic fins means a $50 replacement (it can't be hammered out); so its length needs twice the road room to make a turn; so its chrome stripes merely fake new design; so it has ten motors that can get out of order (transmission, brakes, windows, seats, steering, and so on); so nothing can be repaired by the owner. Most of this has been described as "built-in obsolescence." All, all, are forgivable; but it is not forgivable that this gorgeous jukebox, with all its lights flashing, may be taking the driver to his death. At the moment when he feels safest and most powerful, he may die. A million and a quarter have already been killed at the moment of power (some of them pedestrians); an undetermined percentage of another fifty million have died later of their injuries.

Detroit expects to sell at least 6.3 million cars in 1957 against 1955's top 7.2. It had spent over a billion dollars over the past three years in tooling up. Probably the last great decisions were the new colors. These remind one of the colors in military service ribbons and are often properly metallic-looking. "Cutlass bronze, rose mist, artesian blue, desert glow, ice green" are some Oldsmobile samples. The Lincoln offers an ominous "Presidential black."

The dazed look did not blanket America. American realism was also on the job.

Preparatory to the Automobile Show, Dave Garroway and an audience of industrial designers were actually encouraged to badger the chief designers of these beautiful monstrosities. GM offered a ruddy, poker-playing Good Time Charlie, Ford a very talkative tennis-player, Chrysler a gray-faced, competent non-Ivy Leaguer, American a hoarse, straight-talking farmer, and Studebaker a balding Reserve Intelligence major.

I was informed privately that most Detroit designers would as soon be seen in a zoot suit as in the cars they design. But it was soon evident that the new cars were a joke.

All the designers seemed to resent the fact that Garroway had put a 1952 Jaguar XK-120 engine into his old 1934 SS Jaguar body, but a Big Three designer drives a 1934 racing Studebaker. At this gathering a tone of ridicule of the new cars seemed correct. Garroway asked, "I'm building a place in the country—how long should I make my garage? What's the future of the fin? What do you plan for the low car—how low can you get?" The audience's questions were in the same disenchanted vein. Raymond Loewy, asked to make a comment, rose gravely and pronounced, "I wish you all a very Merry Christmas."

The answers of the five designers charged with the idiocy of their designs, function-wise, boiled down to one answer: "The American public is to blame. If they want it, who are we not to let them have it?" The public, it seems, is not captive but captor; the automobile industry is not the creator, but the helpless creature, of its market. The stylists or designers had utterly accepted the sales department's thesis that every American car owner wants something orthodox but slightly different, wants to feel like a king for three months and will pay a high price for the feeling. He brings to a car purchase something of the emotion he brought downstairs on Christmas morning when he was six years old. The new car looks like a Christmas tree, not so much in his eyes (he will be inside it most of the time) as in the eyes (as he imagines) of his wife, children, and neighbors. The long slinky look, the unrepairable dozen motors, the chrome and the extras are childhood's miracles under the tree. Noel! Noel!

I do not believe in this cynical appraisal of the American citizen, which marches with the opinion of the slick magazine editor. Certainly American advertising and Communist propaganda are persuasive, but I do not believe that all the people are as foolish as Detroit and Moscow think. An annual turnover of seven million unpaid-for cars, swelling the citizen's present thirty billion dollar debt, is not really the foundation of American democracy.

The policeman at the Yale Bowl this year, faced with the worst traffic jam in his life, remembered that in the old days every car had held four or five people, but now the average car brought one or two. The larger, more powerful new cars transport only one-third the number of people as did the old cars. The car owners are growing less, not more, sociable; the traffic and the road system are alienating the people from their society. A man's pride in his car seems to be an antisocial emotion. On a mass-production level, it seems somehow related to the Egyptian Pharaoh's reasons for building a pyramid tomb.

At Forty-second Street and Madison Avenue, a hundred citizens are crossing the street, at the intersection, with the lights. One more unimportant citizen is added, going down the street for a beer, and the hundred fall back and let the 101st through, in sudden fear for their lives. Ridiculous? No, for the last man has a two-ton casing and even without glancing at you can kill you stone dead. The hundred know this well.

Before I finish with the new cars, I cannot resist quoting a little from a report on how to buy a used car. It seems that the cost of owning and operating a car is $1,316 the first year, $1,182 the second, $942 the third, $922 the fourth. The ideal buy is a three-year-old car that has been driven only 20,000 miles (but don't believe the speedometer).

Some of the recommended tests deserve to be described:

1. If the used car shows collision damage, abuse, or high mileage, go away. Worn floor mat or brake pedal may indicate high mileage. Try to poke pencil through paint over small bumps or pits.

2. Jump on each corner of bumpers. Shock absorbers are defective if car shakes both up and down to normal.

3. When you shake top of front tire, clanking shows worn suspension or loose wheel bearings.

4. Suspension is out of line if front wheels, sighted from thirty feet away, are not perfectly perpendicular.

5. Steering-gear linkage needs work if front wheels do not move before you have turned steering wheel two inches.

6. Clutch pedal needs work if resistance to your foot does not sharply increase after one inch.

7. The hydraulic brakes have a leak if foot brake sinks slowly after fifteen seconds of pressure.

8. If starter clanks, teeth may be missing in ring gear.

9. Big puff of blue smoke from exhaust after racing, idling, racing engine indicates very expensive job needed on valves or rings.

10. Trade your car before August, and get a car bonded by National Bonded Cars, Inc., at a cost of $35.

And so on.

Such sharp advice is particularly refreshing after one has been bemused by the dream boats at the Automobile Show. It is very Yankee, and the Automobile Show is certainly very un-Yankee.

One Woman's Family
(1957)

As the Queen of England was engulfed in the American woman's magazine myth of the perfect-mother-with-a-perfect-job, back home in England she was losing the argument. The English reassess their royalty every generation or so, sometimes with the musket and the ax, and had chosen this moment to go at it again, though only with the typewriter. The English were, as usual, ahead of us on their own specialties, in this case royalty.

It began in August when a Lord Altrincham, second of the name, wrote that Queen Elizabeth II gave him the public impression of a priggish schoolgirl, captain of the school field-hockey team. Lord Londonderry, of an older creation, concurred that the Queen's courtiers looked to him like "flunkeys and lackeys . . . [with] the social squalor of the upper classes." Other people chimed in about her devotion to the race tracks and Prince Philip's taking their son, Charles, sailing (risky). It was reported reproachfully that Charles was glum as he was dropped off at his father's old school, Cheam's, where he is liable to be caned. Instead, he caught the flu. Furthermore, two more of Princess Margaret's male companions—Nos. 16 and 17 in the series—engaged themselves to be married to other girls; and it was reported that she hasn't even a maid to pull on her stockings, and has vowed to die a spinster for love of Group Captain Townsend, divorced. The Queen's Consort, the Duke of Edinburgh, has a yen for a little more power, an explosive temper, and a pal who is about to have a messy divorce. All in all, good solid soap opera. Can a good woman be a dutiful queen and still hold a reckless young husband and rear her little ones?

The English chain reaction to Altrincham's modest remarks is interesting, perhaps less for itself than as a prototype test in an unusually volatile test tube of the modern total democracy's feelings toward any conspicuous symbol-figure, whether sovereign, politician, or merely entertainer. But England is not America, and a queen is not exactly a movie actress.

To understand the English version of the phenomenon, one more piece of data is needed. When Elizabeth gave birth to a second child, the British in Washington, D.C., gave a party to toast Anne's arrival. The Americans present were perplexed to see their English friends with tears in their eyes. What for? The tears didn't seem protocol.

The English are a vain, virile, and ambitious race and do not cry over nothing. They are taught that their greatness has been continuous since 1066 and must be guaranteed eternity, but most of the men at this party knew better. Still, they are determined to believe it, and if they believe it hard enough it may become true. They have one "proof" of this continuity: the House of England. The tears for a new baby of that House were not sentimental; they were for all Englishmen and the resolution to keep the great show on the road. The English, it is suggested, are not kidding; not even Noel Coward is kidding. They know their history and believe in it. For example, the imperial state crown has a great "ruby," which is actually a spinel, that Pedro the Cruel of Spain gave Edward the Black Prince in 1367 and Henry V wore at Agincourt "when it narrowly escaped destruction." To Englishmen, this is the most valuable ruby in the world, for Shakespeare gave an opinion on Agincourt, as follows:

> Henry V:
> ". . . And gentlemen in England now abed
> Shall think themselves accursed they were not here,
> And hold their manhoods cheap whiles any speaks
> That fought with us upon Saint Crispin's Day."

Englishmen of certain classes even today have a terror of being abed on another St. Crispin's Day. The honor of being *there* will, they believe, last a thousand years. The English diplomats who wept for Princess Anne really wept because somehow they missed out on Agincourt, but happily there may be other Agincourts. The passion of continuity may be fully as serious as the passion of revolution: a historical phenomenon now somewhat neglected.

However, such feelings have been restricted to a group consisting of the upper classes and the lower classes who believe in the upper classes. (Notice that it is always "upper classes," correctly, to embrace the very different genealogies of the Montagus, Bohuns, Herberts, Stanleys, Churchills, Ponsonbys, and Beaverbrooks.)

A mass-educated democracy, all of whom must fight for the realm, has enormously changed the problem of loyalty to either England or the House of England. This larger mass necessarily assays at the usual rate of cads, cowards, soreheads, screwballs, traitors, though the rate is probably higher in the Balkans, Egypt, and India. These people must now be sold, in terms of their new, sometimes ill-fitted education, on the royal family.

The trouble, of course, comes from the more highly educated rabble, stimulated by the daring of an Altrincham or Londonderry, who in fact would like the old personal monarchy and have been given instead a young president of the Federation of Women's Clubs. Altrincham was just the fuse.

The responsible press lords saw the danger clearly. The London *Times* declined even to mention Altrincham. *The Spectator* said tolerantly, "The Royal Family has to be both ordinary and royal, and at any given moment some people will think that they are being too royal and insufficiently ordinary, or too ordinary and insufficiently royal, while some, who are particularly hard to please, may even think that they are both too ordinary and too royal."

But Pandora's box was now open, and the weird beasties were loose. In the October *Encounter*, John Osborne, author of the plays *Look Back in Anger* and *The Entertainer*, wrote that royalty "is dead, it is the gold filling in a mouthful of decay . . . as nourishing and useful as wax fruit under a glass case." He expected no more from a nation that found "her most significant myths in the idiot heroes" [of the Battle of Britain and the Royal Navy]. Obviously a gentleman who is quite happy to be abed on St. Crispin's Day.

Behind this attitude are "the angry young men," the educated lower classes whose pride in their own brains and talent leads them to dismiss everything else in the English tradition: royalty, loyalty, courage, continuity, and calm. They feel themselves outside the Establishment, the corporate leadership of the *Times*' circulation, and they are determined to throw a voice right into the palace.

And who is in the palace? The conflict can be richly limned by giving the credentials of the four men who make up the Queen's official family.

Her private secretary is Lieutenant Colonel Sir Michael Edward Adeane of Babraham, Page of Honor to George V, Coldstream Guards, Brooks's and Guards clubs, married to Helen Chetwynd-Stapylton of Ladygrove Farm, Didcot, Berkshire. His father was killed in action in November, 1914. His nickname is "Tea and Sympathy."

The press secretary is Richard Colville of Culross, fifty, a younger branch of the Viscounts Colville, married to the daughter of General Halhed Brodrick Birdwood. His brother was killed at Dunkirk. The Colvilles, with the motto *Oublier ne puis* (I cannot forget), go back to the twelfth century.

The assistant secretary is the Honorable Martin Michael Charles Charteris, forty-four, brother of the twelfth Earl of Wemyss (the real family name), eighth Earl of March (strictly, this title is extinct in Scotland), and Baron Elcho, Viscount Peebles, Lord Elcho and Methil, and so on. His father was killed in 1916 and he married the daughter of Viscount Margesson. His mother was the daughter of the eighth Duke of Rutland. His family, whose motto is "This is our charter," also goes back to the twelfth century.

The Lord Chamberlain is Sir Lawrence Roger Lumley, sixty-one, eleventh Earl of Scarbrough, Viscount Lumley, and Baron Lumley of Lumley Castle, Viscount Lumley of Waterford. His motto is *Murus Aeneus Conscientia Sana* (brass wall clear conscience).* His brother was killed in action in October, 1914. His family also goes back to the twelfth century.

This is the crew that advises the Queen not to let Margaret marry

---

* The old guard's mottos are typically intransigeant. Lord Altrincham's family motto, in the new vein, is *servire et servare* (to serve and be independent). He is also Eton, Oxford, Grenadier Guards.

the divorced Townsend (the head of Adeane's house is divorced), to keep her husband in line, to retain her father's and grandfather's courtiers (themselves and their families), and that writes her speeches. These are the people that Altrincham and Londonderry can't stand and that are sitting ducks for the "angry young men." Their strength lies in the Queen's loyalty—not to them, but to her father and grandfather.

Yet the effects of their influence were probably the reason why public-opinion polls, starting anti-Altrincham, ended pro-Altrincham. The vote meant very little, but the royal family must be concerned if it meant anything at all.

Royalty without constitutional power can only be criticized for its appearance, manners, morals, and social talents, and no absolute judgment can be made on these; they are entirely a matter of taste and fashion.

In this connection, the recent genetic history of the House of England is interesting. Handsome mates were taken by Victoria, Edward VII, George V, and Elizabeth II, modifying the original grossness of the Hanoverian line. The result is a pleasant, dolichocephalic Nordic type with the typical flat-topped skull, lank, light-brown hair and big nose. For whatever reason, George V produced a family of neurotics who married a number of fairly plain people, the exception being the Duchess of Kent. At the end, he was adamant on one point: His reign must end respectably, no matter what a mess Edward VIII's reign should be. He had his wish.

George VI was a most affectionate, but very shy, parent. His elder daughter was also shy, but is said to have grown more truly regal, whatever that means. However, we shall soon be able to see for ourselves.

If there were a vote, as for Miss Rheingold, I should vote for the younger girl, Margaret, on looks, charm, and spirit. However, if women were voting, and considering that Elizabeth has Mama, the Duke, and the kids working for her, the Crown would stay where it is.

Margaret's quality is that, like Grace Kelly, she is neither ordinary nor royal; she is a distinguished human being in her effect.

The strength and weakness of Elizabeth's household lies in its validity as soap opera—and some English papers half-brushed the recognition. In fact, a soap opera using these elements faithfully could knock *One Man's Family* out of the ratings. There are so many elderly, middle-aged, and young problems in the family that you'd never run dry. It is soap opera that the wife in the palace gets the pay check, that the husband therefore drives cars and plays polo the more recklessly, that the sister gaily eats her heart out, and there in the alcove are Adeane, Colville, Charteris, and Lumley. It ceases to be soap opera when the characters start behaving unpredictably: in other words, as themselves. Prince Charles has already done this by turning out to be a pretty fair soccer player, even though glumly. Margaret is still a mystery to me, too.

The Queen of England does not have to be "ordinary"; she has the assets to be spectacular. I do not think she need be ashamed of a collection of jewelry whose value is usually quoted as $5,000,000, but is likely much greater. This is her own, not part of the Crown Jewels which include the great diamonds, Cullinan I and II. But Cullinans III to IX are personal property, as are the Russian "Fringe" tiara of solid diamonds, the Russian "Circles" tiara framing gigantic emeralds, her grandmother's diamond and emerald necklace, the Williamson pink diamond, and so on, and so on. The only rival collections are the one in the Kremlin and possibly those of the Nizam of Hyderabad, the Gaekwar of Baroda, and the Maharaja of Patiala. Elizabeth's view of her baubles was that "it would look a bit much" if she wore them. This is about as unregal and boring as you can get. Somebody has to own the great gems. So she does. So wear 'em.

The only fatal mistake the Queen is likely to make is to be a bore. A boring royalty is uneconomical, at these prices. There is no valid objection to being a little splendid now and then, if possible. And part of the Queen's job is to make England interesting enough to keep Englishmen in it.

Whether or not in boredom, Englishmen are emigrating out of England in increasing numbers. A Cambridge University survey this year showed that 39 per cent of male undergraduates polled in their second and third years were thinking seriously of emigrating. For women undergraduates, it was nearly 50 per cent. The poll was indicative, but not guaranteed; only a small proportion answered it, and three disqualified votes were for beachcomber in Bali, gigolo on the Riviera, and for joining "a glorious cousin in Venezuela." The serious plurality wanted to go to Canada, where they may be joined by the Queen Mother as the next Governor-General.

Before we leave this matter of royalty, perhaps forever, it should be noted that dynastic law is not the only way to pick kings and queens. Haakon of Norway was elected in 1905 by popular ballot. Monaco got a Princess née Grace Kelly because the Prince was smart and lucky; a popular vote could not possibly have done as well, and would not have had any standing with Grace, even if it had picked her. The American press outdid the British press in caddishness on the occasion of that wedding. Especially memorable were Dorothy Kilgallen's notes at the civil ceremony: "Grace sat like an image carved of ice. . . . Doe-like blue eyes which were heavily made up like a ballerina's . . . Only once did she move a muscle, and that was to adjust her skirt; she tucked it in, the way a fashion model would, to show the outline of her thigh. . . . The cords in her neck stood out . . . just an American girl striving to look truly regal." Later she had Grace's mother "strutting down the aisle with a gleam of triumph."

The Queen of England need not worry about Kilgallen's reception this time; it will be frightfully friendly. Who knows, the Queen might give her one of those emeralds. But Elizabeth should note that the American press does not play as clean as Altrincham.

V

America

The Variety of American Cities
(1957)

One of the prevalent myths about America is that it is losing its regional characteristics. We are being ironed smooth by mass communications, the myth runs, and we persuade ourselves that one American city is becoming essentially much like any other. In any event it is true that American cities are conscientious, even when they are blowing their own horns loudest, to avoid any opinion of the cultures of other cities.

I have recently indulged in a modest experiment which seems to me to demonstrate that the essential flavor of our cities is extremely varied. I conducted my experiment not by travel but by sitting still. My impressions are based on what people eat and what they are willing to pay for their food. I consulted the Thursday afternoon newspapers (December 13, 1956) of eleven cities, and two other cities two weeks later, and I include a table of what I discovered. The prices, I should like to point out firmly, are in real currency at an actual time and place; they are not "weighted," as official figures always are, or "indexed," or otherwise bewitched. If I read the cash prices correctly, which isn't difficult, there is a very considerable difference in the tastes and social structures of the cities from which they come.

My market list is short, comparable everywhere, and, I believe, significant, since most of the family food dollar goes for meat. One pound of beef is about as nourishing as another, but the price of the best steak tells as much about a city's standard of living as the price of the cheapest chuck roast, so I have included both (with bone). I have also included leg of lamb, canned peas, and corn, a "giant"

223

MARKET PRICES ACROSS THE U.S.A.

	Las Vegas, Nev.	Miami, Fla.	Houston, Tex.	Peoria, Ill.	Baltimore, Md.	St. Louis, Mo.	Portland, Me.	New York, N.Y.	Laredo, Tex.	Providence, R.I.	St. Paul, Minn.	New Orleans, La.	Charleston, S.C.
lb. chuck roast	**.52**	.39	.39	.39	.29	.33	.29	.33	.35	**.30**	.39	.39	.25
lb. best steak in town (porterhouse, Delmonico, T-bone)	1.59	.99	.99	.89	.85	.79	.75	.79	.65	.69	.79	.79	.65
lb. leg of lamb	.79	.53	.59	**.49**	.59	.59	.55	.49	**.47**	.49	.59	**.29**	**.45**
no. 303 can corn	.18	.15	.10	.15	**.17**	.16	.14	**.18**	.18	.18	.10	.15	**.19**
no. 303 can peas	.19	.20	.22	.18	.17	**.13**	.16	.17	.19	**.18**	.10	.23	**.18**
giant-size detergent (Tide, Duz, Dreft, etc.)	.78	.74	.73	.75	.77	.75	.82	.75	.83	.77	.61	.69	.74
qt. Mazola, Wesson oil	.79	.65	.55	.69	.69	.69	**.67**	.67	.69	.67	.59	.55	.39
Totals	$4.84	3.65	3.57	3.54	3.53	3.44	3.38	3.38	3.36	3.28	3.17	3.09	2.85

Figures in boldface are estimated or adjusted. Prices were taken December 13, 1956, except in Las Vegas and Laredo, where they were taken December 27, 1956.

224

box of detergent, and a quart of table oil because they are standard items and tell us something about the people who buy them.

Reading newspaper advertisements must seem a childishly direct way to collect food prices, since the United States Bureau of Labor Statistics has already done the work. At great trouble and expense it assembles first-of-week food prices every mid-month at chain stores and independent grocers in forty-six cities and towns. Unfortunately, what it issues annually are indexes, currently based on "1947–49 equals 100." An index, it should be noted, is not legal tender.

By writing to the Department of Labor one can indeed get a monthly list of apparent money prices for eighty-one different food items * but these too have been precooked in the statistical witches' caldron. They are "weighted" by a formula prescribed in the January, 1947, *Monthly Labor Review*. The "weighted" price for chuck roast in St. Louis was 49.1 cents while the price in real money last December ran from 33 to 43 cents. A weighted price is not legal tender either.

Conventional economic theory, which still fondly believes that economics is the cause of everything, would say that local prices are based on labor, rent, and transportation costs, and that the differences are quite unremarkable.

My table takes this pleasant theory, turns it upside down, and tears it into little pieces. Cities close to production areas do not *sometimes* pay high, they *usually* pay high (Houston and Peoria on meat, for example). Great ports simply do not follow any rule at all—Houston and Baltimore are high; Portland, Maine, and New York City around the middle; Providence and New Orleans low. New York, the city with by far the highest rent and labor costs, does not noticeably reflect them. St. Paul, which pays its only high prices for meat, is a meat-packing center. Distributing centers like New York, Providence, St. Louis, Baltimore, but not St. Paul, are just as likely to pay high for packaged goods. Entirely insane, on the economic plane, is the marked similarity between New York City and Laredo, Texas.

Yet there must be some answer.

* Too many, too variable, many too cheap or too exotic (pickles, frozen strawberries, and baby foods) to mean anything for the average family or any specific family that could be imagined. Of the eighty, thirty-two are fruits and vegetables, one is eggs.

I should like to suggest that it is a city's individual and provincial character that dominates its price levels and that people in one city are simply resigned to paying high prices, and people in another are not. A self-confident, orderly culture that has some tradition, status, and bounce is recognizable in what it pays for what kinds of food. The cities that obviously have a well-established tradition are Charleston, New Orleans, Providence, New York, St. Paul (and evidently Laredo); and these are indeed at the bottom of the price table.

If my theory is tenable, the expensive cities are equally understandable. Las Vegas and Miami are filled with crowds of people who have just arrived from somewhere else and are timidly showing off. Houston is a self-inflated city telling itself it is having a wonderful time. Baltimore, notorious in some ways, is still a genuine good-time city priding itself on a little extravagance. Peoria is a sad case of a certain kind that must be explained later.

There seems also to be an intermediate group of perfectly respectable cities with medium-high prices. Their characteristics are civic consciousness, the domination of big corporations, an atmosphere of discreet social climbing, and an insecure sense of superiority. Such would probably be, on our list, St. Louis and Portland, Maine; and off it, Rochester, New York; Knoxville, Tennessee; Portland, Oregon; and Wichita, Kansas, and so on. These latter cities are often used by the mass media as "the typical American city," perhaps because the mass media are most successful there. Yet even this rather similar group has distinct, and growing, differences. Their individual senses of superiority are leading them in very different directions.

Where prices are high I think we can properly look for civic corruption, extremes of wealth and poverty, and a red-light district. Where prices are low, we can expect to find a preponderantly middle-class city of some antiquity and self-assurance.

Even these generalized differences suggest, if they do not prove, that our cities are evolving toward a wider variety of more distinctly differentiated cultures. A Chicagoan, looking at his lake, is different from a Peorian, just a little way downstate, and still more different from a citizen of Cairo, which, unlike its Egyptian namesake, lives on two great rivers.

These differences rarely get mentioned and are never formulated, perhaps because they run counter to the fashionable belief that we are evolving instead into the uniform, undifferentiated mass state. It is a view that I believe exaggerates the influence of mass communications and minimizes the strength of provincial character, childhood influences, and states' rights. Look, for example, at the cheapest and most culturally distinct cities on this short table. They happen also to be the oldest. Compared to Charleston, for example, both Richmond and Atlanta are "new" cities. Baltimore, which is thought old, was the third site to receive the name and only became a county seat in 1767. Of the cheap cities, the youngest, St. Paul, was a temporary trading post before 1700.

Eating habits fluctuate, and often the food that is actually put on the table of a city is different from the city's mythical cuisine. Charleston's boast, for example, is that it dines on potted quail and she-crab soup. But the Negro servants long since decided to go home at three in the afternoon, and if the grocers believed in myths they would all go out of business. In Charleston, A & P sold five frozen chicken pies for 99 cents, saving a lot of quail and certainly earning a citation from the Audubon Society. In fact, Charleston lives on a starch base of rice and grits, plus raw fruit and nuts, pork but hardly any lamb, much canned meat and store pies. The shrimp of the street vendors and garden vegetables help to lower store prices.

New Orleans carries this diet further in every direction, adding fruit cakes, porterhouse steak, a lot of breaded shrimp and fish sticks, citron and fruit peel, and plenty of liquor.

In St. Paul lamb comes back strong with potatoes, plums, chile con carne, peanut butter, and kidney beans.

Providence is not very different but it puts more weight on local apples, French fried potatoes, tomatoes, haddock fillets. Wesson oil, which does well in the South, here gives way to Mazola.

Portland, Maine, does what you would expect on its cold northern bay, but with an unexpected variation. Of course, it depends on those fortifiers of the outer marches of the Yankee world, such as baked beans, doughnuts, piccalilli, oysters, chowders, squash and turnips, and mayonnaise. Oddly, it duplicates New Orleans taste in fish sticks, Italian sausage, fruit cake, marshmallows, Texas shrimp, and fruit peel.

Now go to the top of the list. Miami, like Las Vegas to a lesser degree, is an eclectic, characterless combination of all tastes: bananas and pears, grapefruit and pineapple juice, sauerkraut, chow mein, de luxe dog food, kosher corned beef, Long Island cauliflower, avocado, liverwurst, smelts, kingfish steak, and yams.

Houston is strong on hams, cakes, papaya, candies, beer, eggnog, kosher wines, oysters, soft drinks, chili, canned tuna, "Worcester sauce," both dog and cat food, and potatoes.

Baltimore, like New Orleans, gives the impression that it enjoys life and food. Oysters, ocean perch, flounder, and fried shrimp vie with frying chickens, sausage, "knockwurst," steaks, Brussels sprouts, sweet potatoes, baby lima beans, and apricot pie. The papers are filled with liquor advertisements; the food ads are in very big, black type, suggesting a hearty appetite.

St. Louis, on the contrary, uses advertising type that is fine and delicate; beef is surprisingly expensive; there are meats called braunschweiger and beer salami; spaghetti, macaroni, and noodles are in demand.

Laredo is poor, with a heavily Mexican diet.

Peoria, our sad case, seems to have no city pride, yet it has a brilliant, if abortive and forgotten, history. It has a red-light district, some very rich people, and a large proletariat. The fact that there is little or no lamb in the markets seems to be an indication of a feeble middle class. The Peoria diet has no distinction until one reaches the poor man's stores: catfish at 49 cents a pound, buffalo fish at 29, rabbit at 59, and live geese at 29 cents a pound. In Peoria, you'd better strangle your own goose.

This leaves on our list only New York City, where almost anything may be found at any price, if you look for it. New York's Peoria is Harlem, and New York Negroes try to shop elsewhere. On this particular Thursday, A & P featured rib beef, lamb shoulders, and tangerines; Bohack stores featured prime ribs, pot roast, and prefluffed rice; Safeway, chuck beef and fresh broccoli; and Daitch stores, leg of lamb and cheezlox. At the Grand Union it was McIntosh apples and hinds of beef.

This tea-leaf sort of reading of the culture of American cities, though it may seem superficial compared with the lofty surveys of the professional pollsters and of the statistical wizards, is surely not without its uses. We are all too submissive to the statistical rendering that levels the landscape of its delightful irregularities and eccentricities and reduces it to a great plain. When statistical myth begins to swallow human fact, which it can, of course, do, it is useful to look at the landscape from a man's-eye view.

The point is that the United States is a very big store offering a wide selection. It is incredible but true that the real variety of its charms has not begun to be fully appraised and defined. This country is not a promoter's or statistician's monolithic dream: it is filled with real and different cultures, people—and prices.

Truth About the Truth About Pearl Harbor
(1954)

According to the Fascist version of history, currently being revived by certain histories and in Pentagon debate, President Roosevelt and his advisers were traitors who frivolously plunged America into the Second World War either to increase their personal power and win a place in history or, since they were secret Communists, to preserve the Soviet Union. What is very significant, the Communists do not contradict this fantastic assertion. It suits their book as neatly as it does Senator McCarthy's. Unfortunately, many decent people more or less accept it. Its falsity, however, can be exposed by telling the long-suppressed truth about Pearl Harbor.

Fascists and Communists will probably always be with us. People of the posse mentality join the former; those of the secretive underdog mentality the latter. Both enjoy running in packs, in pursuit of the same prey, who turns out to be no other than you and I.

Today the menacing foreign power is labeled Communist, and the Fascist has nowhere to go except into the United States Government, dressed up as a sort of super-American. The American Fascist is today a tragic figure, and his torment began with Pearl Harbor. Because he had to help in the destruction of his foreign heroes, he needs a distorted picture of Pearl Harbor. But he should look farther back, to the Hitler-Stalin pact of August, 1939. This revealed to the rest of us that the apparent hostility of the Communist and the Fascist could not quite be depended on. Bullfighting has a term, "moment of truth." It applies to the nearly two years of that Communist-Fascist pact. It is dangerous, if gracious, to forget how some Americans responded to the headlines describing the collapse of parliamentary governments before dictatorship.

Until the fall of France one could argue honorably about Munich and appeasement and Neville Chamberlain's umbrella and the Treaty of Versailles and British imperialism and the Polish colonels' clique. But by the summer of 1940 it had all been turned into archaic rubbish by events. Anybody who still talked this nonsense was suspect. If he also ranted against the wicked Finns, the suspicion was a certainty.

The Fascist in that period could not conceal the inner, complacent smile. He could be very funny about the blunders of democracy. The idea that accused persons should be given the benefit of any doubt was hilarious to him, and he thought there was a kind of political "error" that was best corrected by hitting a man with a club. The smart ones were dismayed by Pearl Harbor, for reasons that will appear.

I knew only so-called "leader types," but I once saw the followers in the mass at a meeting of America First at Carnegie Hall. The faces with clenched jaws, with popping and wandering eyes, with dangling locks or shaven pates, male and female, the younger the more obviously deviant, such were the dedicated people, but not yet quite dedicated enough for the asylum. After Pearl Harbor, these people mysteriously vanished from public view. They were not seen again until, I am told, McCarthy charmed them out of the woodwork.

In contrast to the Fascist and the Communist, the mass of the American people were simply dismayed and frightened by the destruction of democracy in most of the homelands of Americans, save only England, Ireland, Sweden, and Switzerland. Real Americans did not take the implied Communist-Fascist advice: how better can it be expressed than in the expletive "Drop dead"? Democracy did not drop dead.

How else should Americans have reacted, when Hitler invaded Russia in June, 1941, than to be delighted? Americans saw that their advantage lay in Russia's not losing, especially in not losing quickly and bloodlessly. But this attitude had elements of inhumanity that forbade its too open expression.

The following five months can be characterized as a "moment of untruth." The Fascists slowly stopped smiling. The Communists began admiring Churchill and Roosevelt.

The hour of Pearl Harbor approached, the ultimate "moment of truth," the single moment that will fill most of the page or so given to the Second World War in the history books a hundred years from now. And most of that unwritten page would astonish any living American, for so far as I know, the factors that produced Pearl Harbor have not yet been reported. Churchill in his *The Second World War* misses the point; he writes all around the point, but I feel confident that he avoided it deliberately.

Pearl Harbor exploded out of a misunderstanding. History does not generally favor tricky plots such as any hack writer can contrive to confuse the reader. But Pearl Harbor was the climax of as grimly pretty a piece of farce as ever saw a stage. Its elements were these: In Europe, Hitler had uttered the big boast that in a few minutes he would have Moscow, assuming that the German armies had overrun or destroyed the mobilization centers, the reserves, and the Russian tank armies. The Japanese believed him, and for them the degree of the German victory was terrible news. It meant that in 1942 the German armies would probably overrun the Middle East and South Asia and destroy the British and Dutch empires. The Japanese were enclosed by competitive fears—of Russia, of Hitler, and of the United States—but the greatest of these was the fear of doing nothing, and at once. In Japan, in December, 1941, the nettle, danger, and the flower, safety, seemed both very close.

The German attack on Moscow was launched from twenty miles away on December 4th. The Japanese struck on December 8th (their time). Between those two dates the fog of war before Moscow drifted aside and disclosed a huge Russian tank army, unmauled, unterrified, and fresh as a daisy. The Germans took one look at it and canceled the winter campaign, on December 8th. But it was then too late for the Japanese to retract Pearl Harbor. They were inextricably committed to fighting alone in the Pacific against a power with an annual steel production of nearly a hundred million tons, a good deal of which presently began coming their way in a variety of disquieting shapes and sizes.

The key to the farce was that tank army. The key to the tank army was the arrival at Murmansk and Archangel in October and November, 1941, of the first cargoes of American and British armaments. Unimportant in themselves, they had enabled the Russians to throw everything they had into the defense of Moscow, in the assurance of replacements all winter and spring. The timing of the democracies had been impeccable. The timing of the Axis had been disastrously competitive and uncoordinated.

The reason is moral and philosophical. Churchill and Roosevelt had put aside their distrust of Soviet Russia, which they either knew or suspected was already trying to make peace with Hitler. But the Germans and Japanese were operating on the morality of rival hyenas eyeing the same toothsome carcass. Japan had a sense of desperation, like a hyena that has come late to the feast and sees its favorite parts being gobbled. Germany, bloated and cynical, saw no reason to tell its fellow hyena that the carcass was not quite dead. The climate of murderous greed and jealousy is not conducive to good timing.

The dates are worth noticing.

In October–November the first British-American supplies reached Russia.

On November 25th the Japanese carrier fleet sailed for Pearl Harbor, subject to recall at the last moment.

On November 30th we knew, because we had broken the Japanese code, that Tokyo had radioed Berlin that Japan might attack "quicker than anyone dreams."

On December 1st the Imperial Conference in Tokyo decided for war.

On December 4th the Germans attacked Moscow.

On December 5th the Russian tank army counterattacked.

On December 8th Pearl Harbor.

On December 8th a military spokesman in Berlin announced that the capture of Moscow was no longer to be expected in 1941.

Japan had brought America into the Axis war, on a misunderstanding. The consequences of this ill-timed act are well known.

However, the prosecution of a war presented peculiar problems to Roosevelt, who was not a native-born democrat but an aristocrat who could never feel any real identity with the mixed rabble of the

Congress. He believed in the people, but he was not one of them. In this case his solution was to play it safe. For the duration of the war I waited for Roosevelt to say what we were fighting for, but he never said it. I supposed that his reason was that any platform for war would have antagonized some section of that people which he did not understand.

Because I loved him, I cannot say that he was wrong. In the event, the Communists and Fascists among us, the Germans, Italians, and Nisei, helped wage the war. One parlor Fascist whose boast was that he had marched into Madrid with Franco became a rear admiral in the United States Navy. On the other hand, we need no reminder of how keen the Communists were for the American war effort, even as they slipped Moscow items of special interest.

For solid political reasons, the truth about Pearl Harbor was shuffled out of sight. The "moment of truth" slipped away; the long moment of untruth covered the alliance with Soviet Russia.

The meaning of Pearl Harbor, which was so quickly suppressed, can most easily be read by imagining the Second World War without a Pearl Harbor. The course of history without Pearl Harbor is less cloudy than most such speculations. The German armed forces of 1941–1942 were probably the most formidable offensive weapon of modern times. Had Russia not received all-out American and British aid, it is likely that it would have been pushed into a disgraceful peace and possible Fascist revolution in 1942. (The peace feelers between Stalin and Hitler continued for several years, primarily at Stockholm.) Delightful as the collapse of Communism may seem by itself, its replacement by German Fascism over the whole land mass of Eurasia and Africa would hardly be an improvement. Indeed, the possibility frightens me far more than the present state of the world.

America's ultimate chances in a war against the whole Eastern Hemisphere under German domination baffle me still. At the most sanguine, one must suppose it would have lasted as long as twenty years. But when one remembers that during most of those years the Germans would have had an atom bomb and a great strategic air force, the nature, duration, and outcome of that war assume a face one does not care to contemplate. And its most appalling feature is high-lighted by the reflection that America developed its own atom bomb only under the actual stimulus of war.

Without that stimulus? Perhaps.

It is only human to shirk the obvious conclusion, which is that democracy, the American way of life, would probably have been destroyed, to await the goodwill of some German government of the future for its grudged rebirth.

This disaster was averted by Pearl Harbor. Because it was averted, it is now easy to claim that it was never a possibility. Anticipating such a day, I began saving the copies of the New York *Times* from Pearl Harbor on, so that I would have a reminder if I were ever tempted to "such boastings as the Gentiles use." Those terrible headlines still have the power to teach a sense of history.

It was in the light of those headlines and an averted possibility, that Roosevelt put out of sight such truths about Pearl Harbor as the following: (1) A Japanese attack was expected, and even hoped for. (2) The Japanese move was directed primarily against Hitler, on a misreading of the battle of Moscow. (3) American and British aid won the battle of Moscow. (4) The strategic value of the Japanese attack changed overnight from an easy sneak grab of some loose empires, on the eve of Axis victory, to a nuisance holding operation. (5) Pearl Harbor could not be excused as a "day in infamy." It was simply the worst naval disaster of a great power in modern history, and grows more inexcusable as our perspective improves. Its anniversary should be observed as a humbling day of national mourning.

This last fact had to be kept secret as long as possible, for overbearing reasons of the very security of the nation. Such legitimate censorship spread naturally to the other truths, for Pearl Harbor presented America as the huge, arrogant talker at a bar who is knocked to the floor by the first blow of the serious little maniac who is inwardly scared out of his wits. We were brought into the war, not by the big bully in Europe, but by the little one in Asia, on a misunderstanding. Fortunately the Second World War was not a one-punch bar brawl. After our line-of-battle ships had been raised, towed to the West Coast, and repaired, Pearl Harbor began to look like what it really was—the absolutely fatal mistake of the Axis.

The double-talk about Pearl Harbor gets into Churchill's great book when he notes the hope of a good many American congressmen that the Japanese, if they attacked, would by-pass the Philippines and "only" attack the British and Dutch empires. Churchill writes:

All the great Americans round the President and in his confidence felt, as acutely as I did, the awful danger that Japan would attack British and Dutch possessions in the Far East and would carefully avoid the United States, and that in consequence Congress would not sanction an American declaration of war. The American leaders understood that this might mean vast Japanese conquests, which if combined with a German victory over Russia and thereafter an invasion of Great Britain, would leave America alone to face an overwhelming combination of triumphant aggressors.

The peril that was averted is the key to this paragraph. If one has a good memory, one accepts it as history and truth. Most of the American people, I feel sure, so accept it. But a minority, whom one may call Fascist or merely short-memoried, now say that "the great Americans round the President" must have been Communist traitors for having regarded the "awful danger" that faced them as *no Pearl Harbor*. What terrified them was the possibility that Japan might *not* attack the United States. They were afraid that America might *not* go to war.

In the long run, it does not pay to suppress so huge and crucial a truth as this. So long as Americans evade it, men of bad faith will go on proclaiming that we could have had our cake and eaten it too, that we could have made our bed like Sweden, Switzerland, and Ireland and made history too. A half-witted child could make good easy politics of telling the people, "If we had not been betrayed, no Pearl Harbor and no more Communism; lots of dead Russians, Germans, Japanese, Englishmen, Australians, and Dutchmen and no dead Americans; no Vishinsky and no Stalin. What more do you want?"

Nor is it necessary for them to add the corollary: "Only Hitler. From the Atlantic to the Pacific, only Hitler." For Hitler is dead. The quiet, sane body of the American people, who do not talk very much, saw to that.

There seems to be a clear continuity in this history, and much honor. With our eyes open we destroyed the more efficient and dangerous of two sets of dictators, in alliance with the other. In consequence, the democracies hold today the better half of Europe, Africa, South Asia, the Pacific and have no fear for the Western Hemisphere. They have nearly all the fleets, all the commerce, and nearly all the natural resources. On this showing, it is evident that the American majority, headed by President Eisenhower, not only accepts our past but is proud of it.

That past has certainly not produced a present paradise on earth. The second set of dictators still remains to be accounted for. Our past has taught us one lesson, and we are infinitely better prepared for the second set than we were for the first set. Our past can teach us the other lesson, which is not to trust either Communists or Fascists. But we should look with some sympathy on those Fascists who, under the American flag, were obliged to fight formally against Fascism for four years and have now returned full circle to the point where they started.

Certainly there are poor devils living under the mercy of democracy who profoundly dislike democracy, though they will accept its benefits. One such senator has declared that he could make a good American out of a rival politician if he had a club, and that it is ridiculous to give an accused person the benefit of the doubt. When the cry of the Fascist is heard again, some may say sadly, "This is where I came in."

It is not necessary to say that we must forgive the Fascist, for he has some bitter memories and wounds; the American people are all too tolerant of him. But if we accept the Fascist version of our history, our past, present, and future will never have any honor or continuity. It will not even make any sense.

The St. Lawrence: Seaway to the Midwest
(1958)

North America, alone among continents, was designed by the last Ice Age with a great inland deep-water seaway, half-bisecting the continent at right angles to the normal drainage systems. This is of course the Great Lakes–St. Lawrence system. All that mankind was asked to do was to dig around several rapids and waterfalls.

And so for the whole 170 years of its existence under the Constitution, the United States has turned its back on the St. Lawrence River. It built the Erie Canal to bypass it. Its Congress repudiated a 1932 treaty with Canada to build a deep waterway and refused to approve a 1941 Executive agreement to the same end. When Canada decided in 1952 to do it alone, the United States Congress at last embraced the inevitable. This perfect tribute to the impossibility of two national sovereignties' working together on a joint asset will be obsolete on July 1, 1958, when deep water will be let into the Barnhart Island Power Project at Massena, New York. By next spring, ocean-going ships will be able to go as far as Lake Erie. In the following years, the twenty-seven-foot channel will be completed to Lake Superior.

The enormous future can only be defined by looking at the past effects of the peculiar paths taken in man's "conquest" of North America. In the United States, the Erie and the Chesapeake and Ohio canals led the way for the railway network; in Canada, the rail systems left western Ontario undeveloped, tied the crowded Old Ontario peninsula to Detroit and Buffalo, and rushed on West. Closed in behind these two swinging doors to the West, the St. Lawrence, from the Montreal rapids to the lake, has lain in a waking sleep since the War of 1812. These shores, along which a dozen great cities might by now have risen, seem, after the summer visitors have left, as if it were still the noble redskin who had just vanished.

Any serious student of the civilization of the upper St. Lawrence must have sensed something peculiar and unique—the feeling of a cultural dead water, of a potential greatness that destiny had inexplicably withheld. This feeling, unlike that of Bruges and Ghent, Baghdad and Samarkand, Novgorod and Kiev, is based on no memory of greatness, but only on a long-unfulfilled abstraction.

The men who have passed through have indeed left footprints: Cartier, Champlain, La Salle, Cadillac, Frontenac, Duluth, Jolliet, Marquette. But of history there is only the rather ignoble story of "The Thousand Islands Pirate" and the Patriots' War of 1837–1838, the most utterly and happily forgotten episode in our history.

The power of the river was never an abstraction. When one looks out from Clayton across two miles of massively moving water, the islands conceal six more miles of river. Under the November winds, the river is in a fury; in the winter it may freeze three-feet thick; as the ice flows out, tearing docks with it, the rains come; and then toward the end of May the river turns into Paradise. The air is suddenly sparkling clear, the prevailing winds coming in north of Lake Ontario. The thunderstorms are only jocular; the river has regained its great composure. However, even then most of the river is not suitable for the average American vacationer, who must have his pleasures packaged, policed, and mass dispensed. It requires some personal trouble to maintain life on an island, nor would I wish to encourage anybody to live on the islands of the St. Lawrence River.

For the historical record, an attempt has been made to describe this long-thwarted area just before its long-deferred destiny descends on it. The study, *The St. Lawrence Seaway*, by Sidney C. Sufrin and Edward E. Palmer (Syracuse University Press, ninety-eight pages), does not touch on the Canadian towns, which are much older and more mature, but only on the shore country of New York's counties of Jefferson, St. Lawrence, and Franklin.

The most suggestive point made in this scholarly work is the authors' sudden discovery that for some pages they have not mentioned the St. Lawrence River: ". . . a most significant fact: the St. Lawrence River is relatively unimportant to the area. . . . Thus it becomes clear that such a development as the St. Lawrence Seaway may radically change the economic and social nature of the whole area." (How careful can you get?)

As of 1950, however, the authors give scholastic definition to a world not unlike that of Gray's *Elegy in a Country Churchyard*. The communities they describe are relatively unrelated and self-sufficient. The persons in agriculture (18.4 per cent) are compared to New York State's (6.3 per cent, with New York City excluded from the calculation), and those of the whole United States (12.2 per cent). The manufacturing labor force, which has declined since 1930 (!), is 50 per cent concentrated in three firms—Alcoa at Massena, New York Airbrake at Watertown, and St. Regis Paper at

Carthage. The other firms are small, and the skills involved are not highly specialized.

At the same time, the old craft skills have died. The beautiful St. Lawrence sailing skiffs have not been made for some fifty years. The old boatmen, who could do everything to a boat including upholster it, have died off. There are no sailors, except for summer people. Good boat mechanics are extremely rare. In 1946 there was only one taxidermist on the coast between Clayton and Alexandria Bay, and he would not even pickle a small fish.

The authors can identify in this whole 130-mile zone only twelve communities that could meet the definition of "primary communities" (that is, having a general range of service stores): Watertown, Ogdensburg, Massena, Malone, Potsdam, Gouverneur, Carthage, Canton, Clayton, Adams, Alexandria Bay, and Chateaugay; of these, the last four had under two thousand population. Secondary communities: twenty-eight; tertiary communities (virtually nothing except a grocer): ninety-seven.

Out of such apparent nonsense we see the recognizable, breathing, living viscera of an area immobilized by the failure of its destiny. The symptoms are various. Nearly every family needs a car, but the roads are poor. The railroad service is worse. Passenger service to Clayton was discontinued by the New York Central a good many years ago. This was bad enough, but now the buses which are supposed to meet the trains at Watertown leave just too soon, so that people have to hire a taxi. Clayton refused to maintain a marine fire department and let all the old wooden hotels on the islands burn to the ground, until that source of prosperity was extinct. The counties always overassess and overtax the property of the summer people who, in consequence, dwindle away. The local politics never admits to its councils, as in most other resorts, an occasional summer immigrant. For indeed there is a real gulf between the summer people and the river people, though it is not at all snobbish.

It is obvious and unbelievable: the river people do not like the river. Few adults swim; few are good with boats; few even know the main shoals and rocks. The stories told gloatingly are of whom the river has last killed, who drowned, who vanished through the ice, who smashed up on a shoal, whose boat exploded. These stories are told, not as correctives but as inevitabilities, and are in that sense shocking to summer people who spend a good deal of their time on the river, with no intention of dying of it. This dislike of the river can perhaps be explained. To a society that had finally realized it was not going anywhere, it may have been annoying to stare at a river that was indubitably, remorselessly, majestically, indifferently going somewhere.

Of course, this attitude has to change now, but it has been changing for thirty years. The rather sulky and self-righteous obstructionism of the past generation has gone into the shadows. The important people are an unusually high type of American, who would be important anywhere—in Clayton, for example, Ellis, Mrs. Cerow, Hungerford, Farrell; on Grindstone, Emmett Dodge and Bob Garnsey; and so on. Still, the old antisocial, piratical spirit survives, as in the chief machine shop in Clayton, which consistently enrages its customers. Though the booty for a local robber baron is always small, there is a certain small percentage of river people who regard anybody as a Spanish galleon. These few who could not resign themselves to a frustrated environment either emigrated or developed this dream of becoming a great pirate. It is a favorite local dream, even among modest, hardheaded, courteous realists.

Now for the river people, the long frustration is over. Their new problem is to turn toward the river.

The opportunity for this area is completed by the Barnhart Island Power Project which will generate at least 1,880,000 kilowatts, making it the second biggest hydroelectric plant in the world, after Grand Coulee Dam. Since electricity can economically be transported about two hundred miles, the project will energize an area that could cover the Adirondacks, Vermont and New Hampshire, all upper New York, and all southern Quebec.

By the spring of 1959, ocean-going ships drawing up to twenty-seven feet will be able to pass through the river and into lakes Ontario and Erie. But there, unless somebody moves awfully fast, they will find only ports capable of handling ships of fourteen-foot draught. In succeeding years, Army engineers will deepen the Detroit, St. Clair, and St. Marys Rivers and the Straits of Mackinac, at a cost of $150,000,000, to extend the deep channel into Lake Superior.

The cities of the lakes will become, serially, true oceanic ports, with immense social, economic, and political consequences. But as of this moment, the cities are far from ready. The shores of the Great Lakes do not provide many natural harbors; and these are not sited at the large cities. There will certainly be a great battle between chambers of commerce and geography.

The battle is already on. Chicago is building a large deep-water port at Lake Calumet and widening the Cal-Sag Channel which connects it with the Mississippi. Chicago is seriously planning to become "the world's largest port." Milwaukee, with the slogan "The World Is Coming to Milwaukee," is spending $5,500,000 on new cargo terminals. It already handles the exports of fifteen states through fourteen foreign lines using the old shallow-draught ships. Duluth, already a great grain and ore port, is spending $10,000,000, and has the support of the governors of Wyoming, Montana, Colorado, North and South Dakota and Iowa to attract seaway traffic. Detroit proposed a $9,500,000 bond issue to improve the port, but the voters turned it down. It will try again.

All these cities beyond Lake Erie have at least two more years to get ready; the same cannot be said for the cities of lakes Erie and Ontario. The latter will be receiving the big ships—750 feet long, eighty-foot beam, twenty-seven-foot draught—this year; the former by next spring. Cleveland and Toledo in particular hope to use the year's advantage over the Lake Michigan cities to get the flow of Midwest exports and imports coming their way. But their ports aren't yet adequate.

A small city nearby, Ashtabula, has named itself "The Seaway City of Progress" and is spending $8,000,000 on its harbor. It expects to handle Labrador iron ore, locally produced chemicals, automobiles, machine tools and raw rubber, copra and manganese ore.

A number of natural harbors, though small and shallow, occur where Lake Ontario empties into the river—Sacketts Harbor, Kingston, Gananoque, Chaumont, and Clayton. They should attract some industry. Their future, however, is overshadowed by two great existing powers. To the southeast is great and growing Toronto, with a fair harbor. To the south is Syracuse, a bursting industrial center seated where the Barge Canal branches west to Buffalo and north to Oswego. If this latter thirty-mile stretch were widened and deepened, Syracuse would be a seaway port, and another North-South connection would have been made between the two East-West axes of the Canadian and American industrial worlds.

The concept of suction and vacuums forces itself into this whole subject. For over a century, two great westward suctions pulled trade along two lines, leaving the St. Lawrence vacuum. Now new cross-suctions may become dominant, set up by cities like Syracuse, Toronto, Cleveland, and so on, that have existing industries and populous hinterlands.

But not necessarily so. Canadian industry, in particular, may well elect to move over to the American side of the river to save tariff tolls (and thus build up the small St. Lawrence villages). This is more probable than American development, for the good reason that on the American side the best transport system does not lie behind the river towns; it lies now right in front of them.

The future of all these many cities now rests on the solid, age-old fact of the economy of water transport. The savings involved in shipping by sea from Duluth or Cleveland to Europe, as against adding a train or truck haul to the seaboard, are so huge as to be unbelievable. The rates from Cleveland to London will probably be the same as from New York to London. Estimates of the savings in shipping costs run from 25 to 50 per cent but, unless seaway tolls are exorbitant, actual savings in some instances will be even higher.

As against this dazzling advantage of the seaway, the skeptics are still making much of certain flaws in the whole picture:

First, although 96 per cent of all the world's ships draw less than 26.5 feet, 70 per cent of the American mercantile fleet draws between 26.5 and 28.5 feet, and might thus be excluded from the seaway. However, they might carry high-value, low-density cargo such as automobiles. Or they might go light on fuel and stores while in the seaway. In fact, most ships anywhere are loaded to a depth of twenty-five feet or less.

Second, the upper St. Lawrence River generally freezes solid for four months, from December to April. This would mean that any ship not out of the lakes by mid-December would lie idle until mid-April. And this fact in turn would put the shipping lines in the power of any union, such as pilots, that threatened to go on strike and tie up shipping around November of any year.

Any legislation permitting such a situation (a bill requiring ships to use local pilots has already been reported by the House Merchant Marine Committee) would seem to be foolish. As for the river's part, some recent winters have been so mild that the river might easily have been kept open all winter. Finally, any ship caught in the lakes by a freeze could be diverted to the considerable Erie-Ontario intra-lake traffic.

Third, it is suggested that the Midwest, while delighted to export, will be much less interested in increasing imports. Yet the ships will not be allowed to make the four-to-five-day run in empty. The Midwest will have to import to bring in the ships to carry out its own exports.

It is inconceivable that the Midwest will find this process too painful. Indeed, the whole area will find itself growing much more world-minded and the effects should be interesting—culturally, economically, and even politically. Chicago, as a world port, may reclaim the cultural pride and ambition of 1910 which, so far as one can see from here, came to nothing. Nor was this good for America. A Chicago revival would have the virtue of keeping alive the memory of Sherwood Anderson, and many other virtues. Indeed, the impact of foreign trade, foreign ships, and foreign seamen on the homeland of McCarthy, Taft, and isolationism is an event very easy to think on. There will be shooting pains in various members, but eventually the whole national health will certainly benefit.

The current news, of course, has not yet reached the lakes; it is still in the river, the bottleneck that must first be opened. The luck of the river people was to get as overlord of the Authority on the American side that veteran master of concrete and invective, New York's Robert Moses. *The New St. Lawrence Frontier* reports the inevitable result. A Massena supervisor, watching the local and probably necessary chaos, called Moses' operations "asinine . . . destructive . . . dangerous." In good voice, Moses replied: "Not the slightest interest. . . . File your tongue. . . . Your letter is just cheap local politics." Even the millennium may arrive in a snarl of bicker.

Now on July 1st, which is Dominion Day in Canada, at 8:00 A.M., thirty tons of dynamite will blow the last earth keeping the water out of the thirty-mile lake basin behind the Barnhart Island Dam. Great dikes will hold in the water; and forty feet beneath the lake level lie the town of Massena and three Alcoa plants, on the other side of Moses' dike.

The Canadian authorities have renamed the day "Inundation Day." Don't they trust Moses?

Arms and the Man
(1959)

In any human society that combines guns with passion, greed, heartbreak, family fights, children, and hard liquor, somebody is going to get shot now and then, and maybe killed. Every third household in America owns a gun, and 15,000,000 Americans go hunting every year. Gunfire homicides, criminal, personal, and accidental, come each year in the United States to about 5,000. (This does not include police killings of criminals.) Murders and non-negligent manslaughter with weapons other than guns are much more common than gun murders. In addition, automobiles kill nearly 40,000 each year.

The elementary attitude toward the United States Constitution's "right to bear arms" seems to depend on which end of the gun the individual sees himself at. The Second Amendment would not reassure a duck.

The typical sociologist's attitude toward guns is that they are totally a bad thing—he evidently expects to be at the bad end.

Probably every state legislature in the country now has some bill before it to restrict further the ownership of firearms. Rhode Island is considering one that would provide that "no person shall possess firearms of any kind in his home unless a permit has been obtained from the police chief in a city or from the next top police authority in a town."

With every respect for the legislators' honorable intentions, it must be noted that similar regulations were decreed by Hitler, Mussolini, Franco and, of course, the Communists everywhere. Dictators have to know who has the guns. The Nazis' war against the underground was greatly facilitated by the lists of licensed gun owners in the town halls of conquered western Europe. They made fascinating reading for the *Gauleiters*. England's licensing system had so disarmed the English people before the Battle of Britain that what Churchill wanted most and first from the United States was the shipment of a half-million .300 rifles for the Home Guard. That ship was very carefully convoyed, because Churchill believed it carried the survival of England.

These terrible lessons are not so obsolete as is supposed in the atomic age. In an atomic war, intelligently conducted to conquer something worth having afterward, small units of enemy troops would appear suddenly in key areas of the United States. An American citizenry with guns at the right time at the right place would then be useful. In an atomic war insanely conducted to commit world suicide, the survivors with guns would be a few criminals (who always have them) who would not scruple to loot and spoil the last remnants of civilization, and make brief holiday. Why not let the honest heads of family have guns, too? Some people think that if civilization dies, they would want to die with it, but others would expect to make some effort to survive even that great death.

The Founding Fathers thought this matter of guns so crucial that they made it the concern of the *Second* Amendment to the Constitution: . . . "the right of the people to keep and bear arms shall not be infringed." They put this right ahead of the amendments guaranteeing the sanctity of the home and person and the citizen's trial rights. They believed in the sovereign citizen; they were not afraid of him with a gun; if they were afraid of anything, it was of the State. Guns were a very important part of the system of "checks and balances" conceived by the writers of the Constitution. It takes an extraordinary, lunatic faith in the modern official to believe that they were wrong.

Many state and local laws would seem to infringe the sovereign right to keep and bear arms. The reason the Supreme Court has held them constitutional revolves around two points: (1) whether the right is individual, or collective (as of "the people," who may be held as identical with "the State"); and (2) whether and how far this sovereign individual, or collective, right limits the powers of the separate states.

The Founding Fathers believed, and I believe today, that an honest, responsible man with a gun is a support of the free society.

The state and local laws respecting guns are generally conflicting, badly worded, ineffective and, in a country where everybody is constantly crossing state lines, ignored by peripatetic criminals. The criminal acquisition of weapons is explained by the hundreds of thefts from armories and military piers which go to outfit the underworld.

There are two relevant federal laws—the Firearms Acts of 1934 and 1938. The first taxes heavily the making or transfer of any fully automatic weapon, rifle, or shotgun with a barrel less than eighteen inches long (sixteen inches in the case of .22 caliber or smaller) or other concealable weapons except a pistol or revolver. The second controls the movement in interstate or foreign commerce of all firearms and all handgun ammunition. These laws are specifically aimed at stolen weapons and convicts, indicted persons and fugitives from justice.

New York's Sullivan Law objects to any unlicensed person's even owning a concealable weapon. California objects only to its being carried (barrel less than twelve inches) without a license. Los Angeles imposes a three-day waiting period before a weapon sale is concluded, permitting a check on the purchaser, and urges the whole state to adopt these procedures. Vermont, a very law-abiding state, has no law whatever about guns, except as in the commission of a crime.

If there is to be any further law restricting ownership of guns, it should probably be a well-publicized federal law specifically aimed at criminals and stolen weapons. We could easily do without most local ordinances and concentrate on enforcing one uniform law. Hunting rifles and shotguns should never require a license or registration.

Personally, I am not keen on having a gun around the house. Too many people, including children, sometimes pass through a mood where they would like to terminate a situation forever. A gun offers an unhappily irrevocable way to carry such a whim into fact. In homes where such moments are conceivable, a suggestion would be to keep the ammunition in the house of a neighbor who, in turn, has no gun it would fit. Still, the total of such homicides is amazingly small. Their importance is swollen by the fact that newspapers love them. Such headlines must have inspired the recent amazing statement of New York City Supreme Court Justice Samuel H. Hofstadter: "The Police Commissioner is valiantly striving against desperate odds to protect an *already lawless community*. . . ."

What? For one lovely moment one could almost believe that modern New York City is undistinguishable from Tombstone or Dodge City in the glorious age of handguns, as small boys would like to believe. For American thinking about guns is blanketed by an influence much more powerful than even police ordinances.

At every nightfall, twenty to thirty million American homes rock with the sound of sudden gunfire, preceded by an ominous uproar and followed by deadly silence. For all this suburban gunfire, the police are never interested. The gunmen are merely TV actors acting as if, in their scriptwriters' conception, they were living west of the Mississippi in a brief period following the year 1870.

The Western art form brings us to still another popular opinion about guns: that they represent virility. And so the population divides for and against guns about as it divides for and against virility.

It is surely safe to say that the strutters of virility tend to be deficient in virility, but not absolutely invariably. Most men look askance at men who must continually prove that they are men, unless they are obviously boys. This applies to the great hunters, muscle benders, wife beaters, muggers, saloon fighters, and so on. A strange note of effeminacy creeps into some of the avowedly manly magazines (while a note of manliness creeps into the so-called women's magazines). Virility, it may be recalled, was once the secret ingredient of the Hearst press empire, but has been abandoned.

It is evidently heady stuff for an actor to be allowed to call another actor's bluff of virility, whip out the six gun and blast away with the blanks. Bang, bang! Bang! Bluff called.

You won't believe this, but these actors have sincerely convinced themselves, even if a few small boys remain skeptical. One TV gunfighter, Hugh O'Brian (*Wyatt Earp*), recently announced that he is the fastest gun in Hollywood. Well, on reexamination, it seemed that several obscure stunt men are faster. O'Brian redefined his brag by saying that he was still the fastest gun among Hollywood stars of TV Western series. A star who has actually been shot at, Audie Murphy, thereupon challenged O'Brian to a duel with live ammunition. Mr. O'Brian politely explained that all he had ever meant in the first place was that he was the fastest gun merely in the sense of getting the gun out of the holster quick. He had not, he said, ever meant to imply that he knew what to do with the gun after he had got it out of the holster.

No sooner had this colossal gunfight died down than Steve McQueen (*Wanted: Dead or Alive*) made himself wanted by deposing that he is the only real he-man on TV among a crowd of sissies. Jock Mahoney (*Yancey Derringer*) responded: "I've got a hunch that if you were to stack Steve McQueen against a big boy like Chuck Connors (*Rifleman*), Clint Walker (*Cheyenne*), or Rory Calhoun (*The Texan*), Mr. McQueen would really be the weak sister of the group." Mr. Mahoney then challenged Mr. McQueen to an ordinary paratrooper survival test to determine which was the more man. These fellows are evidently feeling their glands in an important way, yet several of the TV heroes are middle-aged millionaires.

Another middle-aged millionaire, *Life*, has now got into the virility gunfight (succeeding Hearst) with a series on the winning of the West, with color pictures. Here were "the Earps and Doc Holliday, marching to have it out with the Clanton gang at thirty paces," the grim gamblers of Tombstone, a lynching reenacted for tourists (there's a harness under the victim's shirt), and so on, and so on. The grinning camera-pointing tourists make these reenactment pictures a savage and subtle satire.

In one of those fraternal ambushes peculiar to Time Inc., *Time* (March 30) cuts the ground from under *Life* with a cover story on TV Westerns. This proved that *Time* is more virile than *Life*. It was written in the new, arduously awful *Time* style that would have made the old managing editors throw up:

"The networks have saddled up no fewer than 35 of the bangtail brigade. . . . Every wring-tailed old oat snorter they could rustle.

. . . Perseus of the purple sage. . . . Smokewagon Siegfried. . . . Cactus-happy. . . . Chaparral clichés. . . . Hasty passel of horse operators. . . . Jump like a bronc with a bellyful of bedsprings. . . ." and so on. Not a word of this can be checked. It is also very fatiguing to read, and must be agony to write.

Life's thing about the gun fight "at thirty paces" collides heavily with *Time*'s statement that the Colt pistol of the time was not accurate beyond twenty feet. *Time* is right: the handgun couldn't hit a horse at twenty-five feet, except by accident, and in that famous fight Doc Holliday carried a shotgun.

The original function of the six-shooter in the clumsy holster was to shoot wolves and coyotes from horseback. It was of no use at a poker table where it required two fatal seconds to get out, up, and level. Meanwhile the gambler took a split second to pick his derringer, carrying a big bullet, out of his sleeve or shirtfront and blow a hole in the bold cowboy. Most of these murders were transacted on gambler's terrain. But the holstered gun, as a visible insigne of virility, infatuated the cowboys and the cruder gunmen, as it has the TV audience.

The "walk-down" in the West was simply bad-tempered bluff calling, like a crude duel. A man at a hundred feet could draw his gun and start firing. The other man had the choice of running away or walking up, returning the fire. The noise was splendid. Everybody was scared. At about twenty feet, somebody got hit. The custom did not contribute much to the winning of the West.

Possibly the two greatest gun fighters of that decade and a half were Doc Holliday, the gambler, and Wyatt Earp, neither ostentatiously virile. (*Time*'s nominee is a Texan, Wes Hardin, who was.) Both died in bed, Earp of sheer old age and decrepitude, Doc at thirty-five of tuberculosis, drinking and laughing to the end. Their secret was that they knew the limitations of handguns, were incredibly suspicious and mean-minded men, had lightning reflexes, couldn't get drunk, and stayed cold even in a rage. Holliday's cursing seemed to improve his shooting. But most of his killing was at eight feet across a poker table against helpless virilities like the TV actors with the holstered hardware. Doc was six feet tall but weighed only about 115 pounds. He dressed very neatly in black and was a qualified dentist.

A handgun, then and now, is an inefficient weapon except at very short range. A good pitcher can throw a baseball more accurately and effectively at middle range than a fair pistoleer can fire quickly. (This might be an idea for a TV duel.) But even at close-work gun fighting, a holstered handgun is poor. According to experts like Brooks Mendell, a man drawing such a gun can be disabled by a good commando. (At least, Mendell demonstrated it to me.) Possibly policemen should wear a small gun in the shirtfront or sleeve as Doc Holliday did and, I gather, Paladin does on TV. The holstered gun may make a man feel important but it is of no use against a man who is either too close or too far away.

It should be evident that in any conceivable struggle against tyranny, native or foreign, the citizenry need not rely on handguns. The Western on TV in the thirty million homes gives us a very bum steer as to either virility or guns. It is not especially virile to kill a man; it is merely a skilled operation based on the proved ballistic characteristics of the weapon. And the less virile weapon may very well be the more effective gun.

VI

The Higher Communication

Death of Tragedy
(1959)

At first, a twentieth century man must be bewildered by the question whether modern America is capable of producing true high tragedy. Who wants to be tragic? Today one pays a psychoanalyst precisely to get rid of one's possibly tragic potentials. Everyone wants to be like Bing Crosby or Bernard Baruch; nobody wants to be like Oedipus or Joan of Arc or even Abraham Lincoln.

Yet the question has a singular, if unexpected, force. Would the destruction of the United States today seem tragic to historians five hundred years from now? Or of Communist Russia? Or of England or France or Ireland or Switzerland? Which would be more, or less, tragic? Does the reader believe his own destruction would be, or in fact, will be tragic? More tragic or less than, say, that of Mr. Jones next door?

Certainly we must exclude from consideration neurotics bent on self-destruction, and the togetherness fans living a continuous soap opera, bathetic and nontragic.

Modern, sane America confronted the tragic potential most characteristically in the supremely hazardous trip of the atomic submarine *Nautilus* under the Arctic ice pack. The mind can hardly conceive of a more intolerable human tragedy than if the *Nautilus* had stalled under the ice. But this tragedy would have been played out, at least for some weeks, to the strains of a jukebox, regular nightly movies, air-conditioned temperature of 72 degrees (46 per cent humidity), cribbage, and acey-deucy tournaments, fresh-water shower baths, and of course in this environment, young men going slowly or suddenly insane. In fact, the jukebox tunes and words, the movie stories, and the acey-deucey games would probably hasten the looming of sheer horror. Yet the drama would not be tragedy, unless we had a hero who rejected the jukebox and the movies and the acey-deucy, and in that case he would not be a proper member of the crew of the *Nautilus*. We would have only a mistake in personnel screening. This is not the stuff of tragedy.

The tragedy of Christ's crucifixion can indeed be told as in Anatole France's "Procurator of Judea," but if the New Testament were abolished there would be no tragedy and no point to the story. The procurator, Pontius Pilate, like the crew of the *Nautilus*, disapproved of tragedy.

This sort of disapproval is one of the key passwords of American civilization, and one that the hot-blooded races find it difficult to learn, even after they have their naturalization papers. Since the first requirement of the tragic hero is that he be conspicuous, Americans take pains not to be conspicuous. By some mysterious agreement, the men all dress very much alike. Away from the job, the truck drivers, scientists, gangsters, professors, millionaires, and bankrupts are almost indistinguishable, the most distinguished being the most conformist, the least distinguished daring a little dash of eccentricity. In this way, the tragic hero avoids attention and escapes his tragedy.

The fashion for cremation after death can be interpreted only as a removal of the last trace of overt tragedy from the funeral proceedings. Only the old-fashioned wear mourning or go to visit the grave now and then.

When anybody loses a job or a lover, it is the custom either to avoid him entirely or to advise him to get another quickly. Society's regular failure to take care of the potentially tragic figure throws the whole burden of sympathy on bored bartenders or psychiatrists. A more discreditable version of this pattern is the universal horror, especially in big cities, of being a witness to a crime or an accident.

People in certain situations cannot avoid some degree of conspicuousness, and these naturally furnish the plots of most serious American plays. Homosexuals are a prime example, but even they have taken on the protective coloration of apparent normality. Decadent Southerners often want to be conspicuous. Anybody accused of any crime is inevitably conspicuous. Accusations of Communist sympathies, murder, mutiny, or homosexuality seem to offer America's last hope of producing tragedy.

Yet in real life, the ruin by Nixon and McCarthy of innocent scientists, by mere irresponsible accusation, curiously failed to take on the colors of tragedy. The villain's act was too transparently merely for political advantage, and soon forgotten by him. The victims came in too large carload lots for the purposes of tragedy; and McCarthy and Nixon well understood the purposes of indiscriminate persecution, borrowing this unassailable and unanswerable technique from the *Führer* of them all. They remained above the fight, having hurriedly passed on to new great affairs of state, shuffling their papers distractedly, while the victims were left behind asking, "How did it happen?" Nixon and McCarthy were determined not to qualify these men as tragic heroes, and the individuals involved did not want the role either. The Fifth Amendment greatly reduces the stature of tragedy. Alger Hiss seems especially averse to being a tragic hero while his accuser, Whittaker Chambers, wraps himself in every form of bathos, including a heart condition, which he suddenly discovered after a colleague, whom he had overworked, died of a heart attack.

Nor is it a tragedy when a child or a distinguished citizen is killed stone dead by a motorist, busily turning a corner on two wheels in the fulfillment of his important business. The motorist stops, he weeps sincerely; as if to say, "I didn't mean it." And after all, every year sees nearly forty thousand of these traffic victims. There goes the tragedy.

If tragedy is numerically doubled, it is dramatically halved, as has often been said. As the numbers increase, the drama very rapidly approaches zero. Recent war books have demonstrated that the massive slaughters on the German-Russian front in World War II soon reduced potential heroes to subhuman apes. Perhaps tragedy is no longer possible in a world of 2,500,000,000 heroes.

Worse yet, according to Malcolm Muggeridge in the *New Statesman*, on September 13, 1958:

Everywhere is becoming noticeably like everywhere else, and . . . everyone tends to want what everyone else wants. . . . Very few Russians, Chinese, and satellite peoples really want communism; very few

Americans really want freedom; very few Western Europeans really care much about Christian or any other civilization; very few Indians really want welfare and parliamentary democracy. What they all want, and what practically everyone else really wants, is what the Americans have got. . . .

This pessimistic view assumes that they are going to get what the Americans have got (unlikely), that the Americans are going to keep forever what they have got (unlikely), and that all human desires except the materialistic are permanently dead (inconceivable).

The worst enemy of tragedy is the sacrifice of individuality to the greater effectiveness of the whole team, or what is now called "social adjustment." In such a world the superior person is not at home. The sergeant in Norman Mailer's *The Naked and the Dead* would have been a hero to Homer; to Mailer he is a scoundrel. The heroes of present fiction would all have been assigned to K.P. by the Greeks in front of Troy. And those same Greeks, if found in the United States Army, would mostly have received fast medical discharges.

What made the ancient heroes tragic was that a hero was stuck with being a hero, a king was stuck with kingship, a duke with his dukedom, and none of them could walk away from the situation. The tragedy would vanish from the famous tragedies if the characters just left town for a while. Since Romeo and Juliet didn't, the indications are that they were motivated by an extraneous love for their home place or local status, or didn't want the neighbors to think they were yellow, or just didn't think of it, or didn't have the carfare. Where honor is postulated, the character cannot walk away from his honor. The tragedy then becomes very much like a scheduled baseball game, just waiting for the other team to show up.

Having written the appalling paragraph above, I am obviously unfit for tragedy.

One who has thought more and better about tragedy is the playwright Arthur Miller, whose *Collected Plays* (Viking) has just been published with a long, thoughtful introduction on tragedy by Mr. Miller himself. Between the introduction and the five plays, we can make some headway into modern tragedy.

We quickly see that there is another situation one cannot walk away from and where an individual is locally conspicuous—the family. Three of the plays are about families; the other two about tight communities. A son is disgusted by a father's cheating on war material (*All My Sons*); a father realizes the consequences of the rah-rah college-coach technique of raising sons (*Death of a Salesman*); the young girls in a close, hot Puritan community produce a hysteria convenient to the fanatics to get rid of the remaining sane citizens (*The Crucible*); a boy is rather feebly disappointed by his shopmates' indifference to his leaving (*A Memory of Two Mondays*); two illegal Italian immigrants bring to a fatal head the dilemma of their relative's unconscious infatuation with his wife's niece (*A View from the Bridge*).

There is a good deal of not unforgivable unreality here. Rich men's sons simply do not bring their tough fathers to jail or suicide. The belated confrontation of the failure of oneself and one's children is not necessarily fatal. The memories of a failed examination, an old adultery, are cured by a very little walking away. *The Crucible*, a play that certainly helped to purify the American climate, is still about as tragic as a panic when somebody yells "Fire!" in a theater. Skipping the *Monday* play, the hero of *A View from the Bridge* is real mixed up. He seems so expendable that the play might have been written with the immigrants as the heroes. Miller's expressed idea in the introduction is that this man had really lived because he had fully expressed himself, that is, conveyed just how he was real

If this is taken as advice, in the twentieth century, on how to live mixed up.
a good life, one must reject it as very bad advice. People who take it are likely to commit that unforgivable sin—to get into a headline.

Yet Mr. Miller is far more aware than anyone of the difficulty of tragedy in the twentieth century.

He writes:

It is necessary, if one is to reflect reality, not only to depict why a man does what he does, or why he nearly didn't do it, but why he cannot simply walk away and say to hell with it. To ask this last question of a play is a cruel thing. . . . The less capable a man is of walking away from the central conflict of the play, the closer he approaches a tragic existence . . . what in life we call fanaticism.

He also expresses his basic dramatic interest: to show that people become "less alone" and "more human" as they identify their secrets with the secrets of all their fellow citizens, and see themselves as part of a truly social process.

And yet, Mr. Miller actually makes the heroes of four of the five plays end in an utter, eccentric solitude and quickly, then, in death. (The *Monday* hero simply realizes that he is alone.) What Mr. Miller really did in *Death of a Salesman* is given in some beautiful thinking on pages 20 ff. of the introduction, too long to quote here. But as one thinks on Willy Loman, he acquires some of the quality of a great happy porpoise strangling to death on a shoal. He has no idea of the social process; and his family have no grasp of him. He dies alone. Mr. Miller, to justify himself, rejects the Aristotelian definition of tragedy. He is, after all, the dedicated man trying to pluck tragedy out of the untragic modern world, and we must allow him any redefinition he likes and pray that it will suit him. But the dilemma is that (1) Mr. Miller has a need to write tragic plays, and (2) he actually likes the modern world; like any other sensible man, that is, he is instinctively opposed to living a tragic life. Practically, this may well mean that a totally new concept of tragedy may be born, and that these notes may become obsolete.

(It will be noted that, as of *Death of a Salesman*, I have entirely ignored the existence of any "law which says that a failure in society and in business has no right to live." Since this means nothing at all to me, I must be defective.)

But in this introduction, Mr. Miller says a wonderfully true thing, among others: "For myself, it has never been possible to generate the energy to write and complete a play if I know in advance everything it signifies and all it will contain. The very impulse to write, I think, springs from an inner chaos crying for order. . . ." He concludes that to describe a work of art as propaganda is, therefore, "an almost biological kind of nonsense."

About *The Crucible*, he says: "I believe now . . . that there are people dedicated to evil in the world. . . . A dedication to evil, not mistaking it for good, but knowing it as evil and loving it as evil, is possible in human beings who appear agreeable and normal." I do not believe this, any more than that the New York Yankees love evil when they wish to defeat the Milwaukee Braves. As long as Mr. Miller believes that evil is a worshiped god, he cuts himself off from the hope of inventing the modern tragedy.

Mankind, it must be said again, is not really looking for happiness and goodness. And this truth is what justifies Mr. Miller's explorations of tragedy. People are simply trying to use up their energy. Silly as a "tragic existence" appears to a twentieth century person, it is not at all silly to wish to impose on one's world the nature of one's crystallized being, opinions, talents, charms, and so on, and in trying to do this, one is immediately "evil" to other, competitive beings and systems. If the individual, even in modern America, *really* tries to express himself, with every safeguard, he is tending toward that area where tragedy is, to some degree, possible. Of course he hates his "enemies"; of course he resorts to ruthless stratagems; but he does not "know it as evil and love it as evil"; on the contrary, should he begin to have misgivings about his tactics, he will have abdicated the role of splendid tragic hero, and be lost to Mr. Miller's later plays.

The secret of the tragic hero is that he acknowledges and deeply commits himself to a Rôle. Such rôle-players are the young mugger who is "crying inside," the stern paterfamilias, the difficult mother-in-law. The most famous rôle player of our era was Hitler, and indeed he played his to the end. A milder case is Paul Robeson, who found his rôle while playing O'Neill's Emperor Jones. Actors might be thought susceptible to this kind of thing, but most of them, at least in public, are scrupulously humorous about themselves.

The typical twentieth century American never commits himself completely to the Rôle; indeed, he may act a cover rôle. The commuter trains are filled with these antitragic actors who believe they have taken every precaution against being the tragic hero of anything. The modern American tries to be fluid and adaptable, never to be caught in a "corner" or "bind."

Should he be in fact caught in some sort of "corner" and required to make his fight once for all, he does not seem especially tragic, for all Mr. Miller can do with him. Perhaps because the American misses this sense of tragedy, we have the popularity of "Western" fiction ennobling a brief and trivial gun-fighting phase in the 1870's west of the Mississippi.

Very suggestively, a picture in the papers of Robeson and Khrushchev the other day exhibited that expression so much admired in TV "Westerns"—brutal and reckless and delicately thoughtful, as it might be Wyatt Earp or Doc Holliday. Look at the eyes: the meaner, the more harmless; Robeson's looked the meaner. But Khrushchev, Earp, and Holliday knew better. The latter two at least had no intention of becoming tragic heroes; both died in their beds, in reasonably good humor.

Renaissance for Sale
(1958)

The twentieth century Renaissance, so impatiently awaited, has at last been officially announced in book-review advertisements, in glossy direct-mail announcements and, for all I know, on billboards. The subject is a new magazine called *Horizon*, six issues a year, $3.95 a copy.

Normally, anything announced in advance as a work of art is entitled to a review *after* its first appearance. So meticulous a courtesy would be wasted in this case. It is too easy to foresee the event complete. What this new Renaissance will actually be is controlled by personalities, drives, gimmicks, and cost accountings far too rigid and familiar to permit any random element to explode the show into any sort of art.

It is asserted here that what you will see in the middle of September can be absolutely predicted right now. It will not be art, it will not open the Renaissance, it will not even be nice.

First, let us look at the claim made by *Horizon:* "America today exhibits all the elements which, in ages past, produced great cultures: wealth, leisure, education, energy, the great challenge of a warring world. On all sides we see signs of a cultural explosion" (What! Where?) "and perhaps the dawn of our Golden Age. Such a significant popular" (key word) "movement needs a voice concerned with nothing else." The voice will be this here new magazine, *Horizon*, $3.95, a quarter of its 144 pages in two, three, and four colors.

The prospectus promises you "excitement and surprise . . . love in its infinite variety, laughter, revelation, strong opinions from strong minds. . . ."

These are priceless experiences. So are Christmas hymns and

"Auld Lang Syne." But when these really important treasures of the human spirit are exploited for cold profit, with no prospect of fulfillment, it is time to intervene.

The proprietors of *Horizon* are an unobtrusive trio named Thorndike, Jensen, and Parton. They already run the similar magazine *American Heritage.* Taking them in order, the first is cold, the second is lovable, the third is sharp; taken together, they spell out something like Bennett Cerf. They are products of Harvard in the thirties and of Time Inc., for which they were a little too unhumble. Madison Avenue must have beckoned to them, but they resisted. They were looking for a magical gimmick of their own. They have invented children's games, formats for *This Week*, and anything that looked like the Golden Fleece.

For long the magic gimmick eluded them, possibly because they were still ex-Time Incers. But part of the Time Inc. formula is a superficial patriotism in terms of a swollen, imaginary America.

And so in 1954 the boys started the Magazine of Patriotism, *American Heritage.*

Moving to a circulation of about 350,000, this has proved that history, that unsalable fossil, can be put to use to reassure specific presold audiences. Frustrated Republican thieves want to read about old robber barons who were All-Man. D.A.R.'s, or people who feel like D.A.R.'s, fatten on a particular history. People who feel aristocratic because they live in Charleston, S.C., or Memphis or Peoria want to be told they're right. The cowboys-and-Indians group must add a few solvent subscribers. And then there are the Civil War buffs who will read anything on their subject.

American Heritage is terribly unexciting, and this with material that is often inherently dramatic. It is cold, lovable, and sharp. Nor can it be blamed on the editor, Bruce Catton, who is boxed in by his editor in chief, Thorndike, his assistant managing editor, Jensen, and his publisher, Parton.

The invention of *Horizon* must have grown out of the boys' discovery of all that free, classy history outside the United States, all going to waste. It aroused their cupidity, but they did not lose their caution. None of those American gimmicks—frustrated robber barons, Civil War buffs, D.A.R.'s, provincial aristocrats—would be running for them here. And it must have come to them, as it has to me, that Americans are less interested than usual, in this decade, in foreign history.

Applying the earlier technique, they had to look for some presold audiences. Among those whom they found, there are some who believe that culture is classy, dictatorships are bad, republics are good, beautiful women are fascinating, foreigners are crazy, and the Bible story is literally true. There is nothing here as good as the gimmicks of *American Heritage*, but together they might prove good enough if one added the magic ingredient, color pictures. The boys' use of pictures, as seen in *American Heritage*, is peculiarly niggardly, decorative rather than pictorial, and must reflect some internal conflict and compromise. The classiness is there, but it is Yankee, stingy, and hick.

The boys hope to raise the level of *Horizon* by getting better writers—André Malraux, Robert Graves, Louis Kronenberger, Cleveland Amory, Julian Huxley. This could lead to trouble. One of them, Louis Kronenberger, may have given the boys the idea for *Horizon* while showing why it couldn't succeed in America. In a passage in his book *Company Manners*, he wrote:

Art's kind of magic again—art's refusal to be achieved through laboratory methods, through getting up charts or symposiums or sales conferences, through looking at smears under the microscope—its magic seems behind the times, almost downright retarded, to a people with a genius for the synthetic. Art's kind of uselessness, finally—its non-vitamin-giving health, its non-pep-you-up modes of pleasure, its non-materialistic enrichment—quite genuinely confuses a people who have been educated to have something to show for their efforts, if only a title or a medal or a diploma.

A pretense of art will be practically impossible for *Horizon;* instead, it will fall back on a pretense of scholarship. Every writer, says the prospectus, "must really *know* his subject." This conveys merely that *Horizon* will run those leisurely, much-too-long pieces which *The Reporter* has imitated from *The New Yorker*, which borrowed them from Mencken's *American Mercury*, which was largely unreadable. (All right. Go back and look at it.)

To old-fashioned people who thought a book was a two-dollar

hard-cover object and a magazine a cheap paperback, a $3.95 magazine in hard covers (while books are cheap paperbacks) must be confusing. Still, *Horizon* will be a magazine. The test is whether all the issues are alike. They will be. That makes it a magazine. But one must ask how such a magazine is worth the equivalent of a four-pound pot roast, five dozen eggs, or a quart of gin, when you can have the contents of the next hundred issues by buying a second-hand *Encyclopaedia Britannica*.

The prospectus statement that great cultures are produced by "the great challenge of a warring world" deserves a look. The present moment may be compared to England's mood in the Napoleonic era. In literature this was, for England, a relative doldrums between two great periods. By straining a little, one can place in the period Jane Austen, Byron, Coleridge, Hazlitt, Lamb, Landor, Scott, Southey, Shelley, and Wordsworth, but most of them did their best work after the military challenge was removed. Actually, one would hesitate to make any connection between great cultures and military challenges. The sort of thinking that must make the connection is essentially characteristic of the boys. They demand that every syllogism feather their nest, every sum add up to their benefit, every sun be rising on their fortunes, and no tide wet their feet. In fact, hordes of these little Canutes daily command the sun to shine on Madison Avenue.

But how grotesque they seem when they order up the Renaissance! *Horizon* has the further impudence to append its rules for the Renaissance: "*Horizon* will be kept free of esthetic snobbery, the obscure reference, the pedant's footnote." Translated, the owners are trying to promise that they will be neither cold, lovable, nor sharp.

The Book Clubs: Culture Once a Month
(1957)

A book club, as here referred to, is a mass-distribution cooperative which offers to save a potential reader the chore of reading all the reviews and making up his own mind. Thus it combines the separate functions of disinterested judgment and profitable promotion. In one act it claims to be a better judge than the reviewers and a better promoter than the publisher. Yet a judge who profits from his judgments is not a judge. Part of this claim is therefore likely to be false.

There can be no doubt that in the past twenty years, coinciding with the book-club careers, the writer in America has suffered a diminution. If he cannot or will not submit to the canons of hungry publishers and book clubs, he may presently stop selling at all. The rich writer, chosen by a book club, is also eminent; the much more eminent poor writer is also contemptible. In America, the area left for honest, unambitious talent grows constantly smaller.

Must the book clubs share the blame for these developments? They have certainly promoted a lot of pleasure and instruction for the American reader. But have they also helped to corrupt the reader and to separate him from his only true friend, the writer? In lieu of that old unpredictable meeting of individual minds, the mass editor flirts massively with the mass reader. But as the mass society grows a little bored by the mass literature, one must begin to suppose that it is not quite exactly a mass society.

Book clubs fall into two kinds. One is the mass distributor averaging 500,000 members (the Book-of-the-Month Club figure). The Literary Guild has hit 800,000; Dollar, 400,000, and the new Reader's Digest Condensed Club has 2,200,000 (distributed four times a year).

The second kind is the small, specialized club that limits itself to the arcane mysteries of a single clique, such as yachtsmen, horsemen, farmers, art collectors, or religious denominations. These are what bring the total of adult book clubs to ninety, besides twelve juvenile. Most have from three to ten thousand subscribers and have trouble keeping up office appearances. They tend to be absorbed by regular publishers: Doubleday has half a dozen, in addition to the Dollar and the Guild. In essence, they consist of a list of names of people who are probably interested in one special subject. Anybody who owns such a list can invent a new club tonight.

The only crime charged against the book clubs is that they have distributed 500,000,000 books in the thirty years since Harry Scherman started the Book-of-the-Month Club. This works out, allowing for some population turnover, at two and one-third books per living head.

The profits will only be applauded here. The motives, and the effects, are more interesting. As for the former, the purest idealism to be heard anywhere on earth issues from book-club proprietors; it reminded me of my childhood when I was given the beauty of universal education with breakfast. Harry Scherman, for example, sees a connection between his BOMC and the fact that "I doubt whether anywhere else in the world, or in any other era, has there been a society more open and wide-ranging in its curiosities . . ." That opinion does not march with my impressions.

The publishing fortunes that began in the twenties nearly always grew out of the astonished discovery that classics were not copyrighted (or else out of crossword puzzles). Harry Scherman was among the first with his Little Leather Library of Classics (forty million copies); Bennett Cerf, George Macy, and others rushed through the breach. Several presently realized that royalties to living writers were not really very dear and led to a more lively social career than the works of Tennyson. Applying the classic aura to a chosen current book, the Book-of-the-Month Club's first venture was the distribution of *Lolly Willowes*, by Sylvia Townsend Warner, in April, 1926.

The BOMC will serve as the prototype for the old-line book clubs. In thirty years it has grossed $240 million cash and given away another $192 million in retail values (call it $50 million cash). Yet nearly half its 500,000 subscribers pass up the books offered in any given month.

The month's No. 1 selection is made by five judges who cerebrate at the summit of a reading apparatus of five full-time literates and thirty-five part-time (some paid $5 a reading) and a grading bureaucracy who stamp A, B, and C on the month's crop. The judges pick only the first selection. The numerous alternates are chosen by Mr. Scherman and his executives after listening to the judges argue.

These No. 1 selections have come to just under five hundred books since 1926. They seem to include nearly everything written by Margery Sharp, Esther Forbes, T. H. White, Pearl Buck, C. S. Forester, and Nevil Shute: not exactly the giants of our age. For the thirty years, the selections work out at nearly 75 per cent in favor of male authors against female and about 56 per cent in favor of Americans over non-Americans and fiction over nonfiction. The war raised the percentage on nonfiction, men, and Americans. These seem to be still gaining.

The character of the judges has changed. They used to include such individualistic eccentrics as Heywood Broun, Christopher Morley, Dorothy Canfield, and William Allen White. This type has long since been scrapped. The present judges, all estimable citizens, represent a neurotic mass type frequently presented in the works of John Marquand: the brisk, slightly stammering egghead who hides a wry self-consciousness, the Master of Arts who has learned to humor the Philistines. A delightful fellow—who so surly as to carp? In simple gratitude for inventing the type, the BOMC has made Mr. Marquand the last of the judges. Yet in passing we should note the importance of Mr. Marquand's invention in the current American culture. This is actually Big Brother.

The BOMC publicity makes much of the premise that they pick only what they like. In ordinary decency, let us dismiss this premise at once. The people they are picking for have expressed themselves; indeed, do it every month. An educated mass taste in books is much too difficult to analyze; but the BOMC audience has registered its taste in another area which is more easily assessed. It has voted on "the greatest artists of all time," and I list them in order, with the selections that seem out of their class in italics: Michelangelo, Rembrandt, Da Vinci, *Raphael, Gainsborough, Van Gogh, Whistler,* Titian, *Rubens, Picasso,* Botticelli, El Greco, Renoir, Cézanne, and *Millet.* These wonderful people came up with another grading: "The Most Interesting Artists of All Time." The same names were rearranged in an uninteresting way, except for the fact that *Grant Wood* was added!

But how are we to judge books? Published current criticism is simply of no use. There are in fact three true, absolute, and final tests of a book.

By far the best test is to wait three hundred years. The BOMC cannot afford to do this; indeed it would throw Mr. Scherman back into his Little Leather Classics (which were, however, first published at the time they were written). Furthermore, if all books had to be held for three hundred years before reading, literature would die a sudden death, and there would be nothing to read for three hundred years. Thus, we have to do the best we can at the moment with what is written at the moment.

The second best test is to ask oneself after a lapse of time whether the book has remained in the mind. And a third—or perhaps it should have been the second—is to reread a book after twenty or thirty years.

There is a fourth, though somewhat ephemeral test: did the book influence your life and behavior? Reviewing the BOMC list, some claim could be made for *Bambi* by Felix Salten, *Grischa* by Arnold Zweig, *Henry VIII* by Francis Hackett, *All Quiet* by Remarque, *Robber Barons* by Josephson, *The Road to War* by Walter Millis, *Ordeal* by Nevil Shute, *Verdun* by Jules Romains, *For Whom the Bell Tolls* by Hemingway, *Darkness at Noon* by Koestler, *The Road to Survival* by Vogt, *The Disenchanted* by Schulberg, *Catcher in the Rye* by Salinger, *Witness* by Whittaker Chambers, and some Churchill. How any particular one of these influenced my life and behavior is a longer story.

Working backward to the third proposed test (rereading), books that may have influenced me, though they were not BOMC choices: Aldous Huxley's *Antic Hay* (I can name and describe every character); Hemingway's *The Sun Also Rises* (I was a little vaguer here); and Evelyn Waugh's *Decline and Fall* (pretty cloudy). The first and last of these three, on rereading a little while ago, merely embarrassed me for my youth; they were a bore. Hemingway's novel climbed back into my mind like the rising sun in the title; I had even forgotten the best parts, such as the fishing expedition. Demonstrably and unpredictably, this is a great book.

Still working back I applied my second proposed test (recollection) on ten literate people's memories of six BOMC selections. In practice, the test ran into a fact of the American culture which quickly dominates and rephrases the question. The question becomes instead: "Do you remember the book or the movie?" The answers to the revised question destroy a good many of the sincere pretensions of the Book-of-the-Month Club. Their most famous books—and these are the only ones I am bothering with—were also famous movies. The question arises whether the judges did not pick them for the same reasons that one would pick a movie script.

The answers to the questions opened a locked room that explains a great deal about what the printed page can do, and usually doesn't do, and the nature of the inimitable vision of the first-class creator. Of inadequately created books, the ten people remembered the movie; they could see the actors in their mind's eye; the movie had usually displaced the vision, if any, created by the book. I submit that whenever this happens, it is a ruthless indictment of the writer's original work (with the possible qualification that a marvelous job of acting can sometimes assume a life of its own quite equal to the original vision, though sometimes different from it.) For example, nearly everybody has a picture in his mind, that no movie could ever entirely displace, of faces and scenes in *Treasure Island*, *The Prisoner of Zenda*, *Dracula*, *The Three Musketeers*, *Alice Adams*, *An American Tragedy*, and so on, and so on. The fact makes these good books, no matter what their style.

Let us apply the test to six of BOMC's proudest boasts: Remarque's *All Quiet on the Western Front*, Buck's *The Good Earth*, Allen's *Anthony Adverse*, Mitchell's *Gone with the Wind*, Hemingway's *For Whom the Bell Tolls* and Koestler's *Darkness at Noon* (never a movie). My friends reviewed the books as follows—

All Quiet: Lew Ayres. Sometimes also Wolheim and Slim Summerville. More on this will be given later.

The Good Earth: Luise Rainer and Claude Rains.

Anthony Adverse: Fredric March and Olivia De Haviland.

Gone with the Wind: Clark Gable and Vivien Leigh.

Koestler, not competing with a movie, is still clear as day to his readers; and Hemingway's characters entirely transcended and even successfully conflicted with the actors, Gary Cooper and Ingrid Bergman, who did not seem appropriate to a number of readers (they saw the girl clearly as dark and frail). *For Whom the Bell Tolls* is therefore to be defined as a good book, though not as good as *The Sun Also Rises*. The others have a heavy count against them.

Gone with the Wind gets a stay on appeal. It seems to have held the minds of a number of readers. Some have a picture of Rhett Butler that is quite different from Clark Gable; and this is a strong count for Miss Mitchell's creation. A very discerning reader pointed out that Hergesheimer did the spadework much better in *Balisand*. Yet *Gone with the Wind* remains a truly created work.

The one BOMC selection I reread was *All Quiet*. Some of the readers "remembered" the powerful love story: there is no love story. The clearest recollection was in the mind of a man who had read the book in the original German, unexpurgated. The appeal of *All Quiet* in 1929 was primarily journalistic and must have influenced a great many lives. It said emotionally two (then) surprising things: (1) war is bad; (2) Germans are not bad. What good these two lessons have done Americans in the intervening twenty-seven years I would not dare to say; but they certainly helped Hitler.

The book is an utterly honest series of vignettes about nineteen-year-olds plunged into war; the connective tissue is of group self-pity, comradeship, soldierly pride, and revenge on the adults. "We are not beaten," says the hero. A clever man in 1920 could have created Adolf Hitler out of these elements. Indeed, even Mr. Remarque is not as antiwar as Hitler was, verbally; and Hitler may have learned this tactic from Remarque's book. Mr. Scherman certainly cannot be blamed for these results; nor can Remarque, a notable anti-Nazi. The book, then very readable though rather a chore today, would have been popular without the BOMC stamp, because the Americans were ready for it, having overlooked Geoffrey Moss's development of the same theme in the early 1920s.

The really memorable books do not usually get published by BOMC. It did not pick the most original book of the past two years, Nigel Dennis' *Cards of Identity*, which I too neglected for a year because I had read that the author was a *Time*-writer. The BOMC will never pick such a book; indeed its apparatus is designed to eliminate such a monstrosity.

The major book clubs, not unlike the mass magazines, may be said to fatten on the garbage in the American public's mind. They profit by confirming what everybody already thinks he knows. But lately the old-line clubs have been threatened by the Reader's Digest Condensed Book Club which condenses five books in a single average-size volume. The great, dead-serious new club is far hungrier for that garbage than the sleek black rats that have heretofore had it so cozy. One cannot help remembering the brown, short-tailed rats that invaded Europe in the early eighteenth century and wiped out the black (or Alexandrian) rats that until then had fed underneath Europe's table. The hungriest competitor will have the field; and the Reader's Digest Condensed Book Club simplifies the battle for the reader's mind to its essence, or travesty.

The Digest pretense is that of "condensation," as if a body of thought or fantasy were the same as milk or eggs. It removes the surplus water; the reader need only add water and it will be the whole thing again. The Digest books are not advertised as cut, expurgated, castrated or sophisticated; they are "condensed." DeWitt Wallace has the dream or delusion that life itself can be condensed. So it can. The truth when it is found a thousand years from now will be very simple, and five minutes later, very dull. The continuing entertainment in life, which keeps people sane, is that different things are all different, not that they are all the same.

Mr. Wallace is genuinely more interested in their sameness. It is estimated that his magazine keeps publishing the same hundred articles over and over again. It can safely be predicted that he will publish the same hundred—or perhaps only twenty—books over and over again. (This suggestion is worth a million dollars to Mr. Wallace, if he hasn't yet realized it. The check can be mailed in care of the publisher.)

The honor of opening Mr. Wallace's eyes to the possibilities in evaporating books goes to a gifted book condenser on the magazine, M. T. Ragsdale. The technique has now been mastered by half a dozen people on the Condensed Book Club.

I read both the whole and evaporated versions of *Harry Black* in the summer of 1956: the first ran 110,000 words, the second under 50,000. The book revealed that the new club is already finding its base formulas. This one is the formula of the tired falcon, crying inside, who has sudden misgivings as he stoops to his last kill. Hemingway invented the formula with his soldiers and matadors, but he generally broadens a story out of the formula. The author of *Harry Black* tried to do as much, but the evaporation reduced his book back to pure, stark formula, still quite enjoyable.

To read the condensation, especially comparing it line for line with the original, is to watch an autopsy. In the condensation, the whole quality of the first jungle part has been lost; a whole polo game has disappeared; developed characters are reduced to names; the techniques of prison escapes are dropped; and also there is an elimination of some embarrassing non-love-making and stiff upper lip. But all this was what the author had to offer. And the author was not kidding; his name is (David) Harry Walker. One could show that two pages of effective writing come out as one paragraph of pasted-up bits. One quick example is that of evaporating "more real and sordidly simple and beautifully nightmarish" into just "more real." Wherever the author assumes any intelligence on the reader's part, the editors paint signposts all over the place. The elliptical is turned into the all-too obvious. Long brush strokes are reduced to little pinpoints of color, as in a Seurat painting.

The Reader's Digest has a defense. It is that its evaporated books reach a completely untouched market. Since nobody I know even knows anyone who subscribes to this new club, the claim seems to stand up. These new readers must be the same amiable people who think they are sailors because they have taken an airliner across the Atlantic Ocean, or think they know the Thousand Islands because they drove their Chevrolet across the International Bridge. If only life were that simple! But for Mr. Wallace that is just how simple it is.

The Exclusive Label
(1959)

The human desire to be a special sort of person or belong to a special group has not been destroyed by the mass society. Now and then somebody offers a new system for separating the U's from the Non-U's (upper and non-upper class), and even the Socialists give it anguished attention, sly smiles, and sulky disbelief. Some examples of the label marked "Exclusive" are currently on view.

An unpredictable one is surely the country-wide, but highly selective, fashion of growing a beard. The exhibitors' efforts to rationalize these ornaments are as incomprehensible as a new religion, but the devotees are self-confident; they seem to know they are on to something good.

The wearers seem to be the "new men," as in Tudor England. They have a sort of bravado or bravura or seriousness, which seems essential. A beard is not trivial. No matter what they say, their motives must be: (1) to assert that they are men, (2) to make a dead-pan protest against the women's magazine propaganda, (3) to express a kind of personality symbolized by the kind of beard, and (4) to hide. All four could be condensed in the statement, "I always told you I was Monsieur Beaucaire," or Henry VIII or Karl Marx or Shaw or Jeremiah.

Complementary to the men's beards is a strange self-diminishment on the part of American women. The appearance on the street of housewives as well as young girls in tight pants and ballet slippers, or heavy ribbed sweaters and long black socks, may be taken as encouragement to the male to show off a little. Men with beards are often seen with these recessive mice. The beard thus becomes a secondary sexual characteristic, like the long hair the women have meanwhile cut off.

It is agreed that the beard thing began in New York, among artists, actors, and writers, and spread to college campuses everywhere, among both undergraduates and young faculty. It got a helpful boost from several TV musicians, and the boxer Archie Moore. It is said to be doing well in San Francisco, Los Angeles, St. Louis, New Orleans. (Lives there a city with soul so dead it has not one single beard?)

The social value of a beard is surprising. A man in St. Louis said, "A bearded man's social chart goes up considerably." Headwaiters are definitely impressed by men with beards; nobody knows why, but headwaiters are never wrong. On the other hand, another St. Louis man reported, "In certain types of joints, a beard is just an invitation to trouble. . . . You're surrounded by a bunch of guys with an aggregate weight of several tons, all of whom seem to take your beard as a personal affront." These are obviously joints without a headwaiter. A beard, it is agreed, is a fine conversation piece, in this case perhaps excessively so, but at parties with young ladies just about right.

Beards will probably remain fairly exclusive, since most offices will doubtless forbid them and in many factories a beard could be near-fatal. The beard is not quite in harmony with industrialization. It suggests leisure, meditation, and craftsmanship. It cannot properly give a snap decision. It seems wrong on nervous, high-pitched personalities like Mitch Miller and Skitch Henderson. A beard really ought to do a lot of listening, like a bird in a bush.

Since bearded men verbally object to shaving, a word may be added for shaving. It is not much of a nuisance; on the contrary a good shave is as refreshing as a shower and starts the day with a new chapter heading. Looking at his face, a man says, "So that's what I have to work with," and feels stripped for action.

Why men in some periods shave their faces is a baffling matter, if one may tiptoe into that field of anthropology which Margaret Mead bestrides, blowing on her hands.

From around 1700 until the American Civil War, the men of the West were preponderantly clean-shaven, except for a few eccentrics. This was a period of vast colonial expansion. The West felt good; it could afford to appear candid, kindly, tolerant, and clean-shaven, as it conquered. The beginnings of breakdown in the old systems, or perhaps of overconfidence, were masked in the late nineteenth century behind beards—certainly a kind of bluff. All the bluffs were called between 1914 and today, until now the Russians, the greatest bluffers on earth, have entered the big poker game. And now they too are clean-shaven. The candid pretensions of a shaven face give rise to the expression "bare-faced liar," somehow worse than a bearded liar. But bearded men are not usually liars or bluffers, and sometimes heroes, as among the R.A.F., the Spanish Loyalists, and Castro's men in Cuba.

Another élite growing so fast it may have lost exclusiveness is now serving wine with dinner. Since 1948 the American production of beer has wavered from 91 million barrels down to 89 million in 1957. Meanwhile imports of wines have been steadily rising (at a rate of about 600,000 gallons a year), and American production of wines is rapidly expanding. Since imports are still under eight million gallons, the cult is still fairly restricted.

One might suspect that the women were responsible for the shift to wine except that one hears the connoisseur mumbo jumbo primarily from men. "Knowing" wines is the easiest way to be U, though the American and English experts sound unmistakably Non-U. Their pseudo-eighteenth century works regularly appear in *Holiday* and *Esquire*. They write as if they took the full twenty-four hours to trickle an ounce of wine down their gullets, and bliss all the way. This is not quite so bad as an adult's (except oneself) describing his ingestion of food; still, it is pretty carnal.

This nonsense carries on the elaborate French pretense that the point of an alcoholic beverage is everything except the alcohol. The experts appear sincere, since they generally despise the wines whose alcoholic content has been "fortified," such as the ports, sherries, and even champagnes. But they write as if the alcohol were smothered in vitamins, Beethoven, hummingbird tongues, and incense.

This matter of the exclusive label recently inspired a serious lawsuit in England. The Champagne Association was suing to enjoin the Costa Brava Wine Company from using the label "Spanish Champagne," on the grounds that "Champagne" is a definite district of France, and any wine not originating there cannot be champagne. It was brought out that there are things called champagne produced in both the United States and Soviet Russia, as well as Spain, Germany, and Italy. Some experts called the Spanish champagne "a very pleasant sparkling white wine . . . like champagne." Raymond Postgate testified that unless he had been given a bad bottle, it was a nasty sour drink.

Not part of the evidence but distinctly relevant was an illustrated syndicated feature in American newspapers on December 14, 1958, saying as editorial matter, "Vineyards in New York State . . . have been yielding some of the most superlative wines and champagnes in the world . . . comparable in quality with the best from Europe . . . Particularly delectable . . . The finest grapes on earth . . ."

This is bare-faced lying, going far beyond Costa Brava's mere use of the word "champagne." American champagne is generally inferior to German champagne, which is inferior to Spanish champagne, which is abysmally inferior to French champagne of good quality. (As for my experience, I drank nothing but champagne for some years.)

But the Champagne Association was trying to refight a war that was already in the history books. "Champagne" is a word in the dictionary as, secondly, any wine of the type of champagne or, loosely, "any effervescent wine." It is too tough to take words back out of the dictionary, once they get in. The word "champagne" is a common noun, and so the jury decided in thirty-five minutes.

"French champagne" remains an exclusive label, but champagne is not, by jury verdict. It is still a travesty to take a glass of American champagne and follow it with a good French one. One little area sloping up from the river Marne near Rheims still produces the true beverage.

Transported by a similar opinion, the French replied to the English jury's verdict by closing for a week seventeen Paris bars that specialized in Scotch whisky. The head of the champagne syndicate said, "There is only one champagne in the world, just as there is only one Scotch whisky. Apparently some countries do not know this. . . . If diplomatic action should prove inadequate, we might very well subsidize a French whisky company to sell whisky abroad cheaply."

The Frenchman's threat was, by implausible coincidence, already much more than that; indeed, the Scotch Whisky Association was already suing a French importer for selling Dutch alcohol under the label "Williams Scotch Whisky, Glasgow." The thrifty French court awarded the Scots one franc, awarded the French Government a fine against the importer for a million francs (about $1,500), and awarded the National Confederation of Wine Sellers of France 100,000 francs ($150) because people drink less wine when they drink cheap whisky.

Indignant at this ruling that Scotland has more validity than the old province of Champagne, the French again sued the Costa Brava Company, this time in a civil action.

There begin to peep at us the symptoms of a split personality inherent in a mass capitalistic civilization. The society does positively want to encourage and protect the superior workman who has created a superior product and attached his "exclusive label." But on the other hand it wants to adulterate the prestige product down to mass-producible elements and sell a reasonable facsimile to a hundred million people. The distinguished, lone inventor is figuratively caught up in a lynch mob which has a lot of law and a lot of money. The people get their almost-champagne, and the exclusive label is destroyed.

We have hordes of people whose full-time business is to discover, steal, and exploit new "exclusive labels." The young lady editors of the women's magazines are sleeplessly on the prowl for new habits, fashions, affectations, and gimmicks. Within two months, from two million to fifteen million readers discover that they can be as chic as Mrs. X merely by painting one ear blue. Even an ephemeral fashion whim on a single college campus is almost instantly communicated to all the readers of all the magazines aimed at young men and young women.

Theoretically, as democrats, we approve of this sharing of the idea-wealth, and disapprove of the "exclusive label." But this kindly, theoretical benevolence ignores the fact that when a thing is multiplied a hundred million times and given to a hundred million people, it changes in nature, in the kind of experience it stimulates. A thing becomes something of what its user is; it is enlarged or diminished by the relative intensity of its user's use of it. Formerly, a way of complimenting a fine dinner was to say, "Too good for the common people." Far from being undemocratic, this was a way of assuring the hostess, perhaps hypocritically, that you had brought to her dinner an intensity worthy of it. But how much intensity can one bring to anything that one must think of as shared with a hundred million people? (That is, anything except the sunlight, oxygen, photosynthesis, the whole natural world, and the Constitution of the United States?)

The benevolence also ignores the fact that everybody, even the humblest, knows somebody else he looks down on. If he sees the other in a Cadillac, he will no longer take pleasure in his own Cadillac. His idea of an "exclusive label" is one that excludes that other.

In other words, nearly everybody in a democracy wants "exclusive labels." They merely want them to be just exclusive enough, including them but excluding certain others.

The invisible "exclusive label" has of course the best chance of remaining exclusive. If nobody but a certain élite even notices that you never button one button on a shirt with a button-down collar, and nobody tells a magazine editor about it, your club will stay exclusive. The customs, fashions, and recipes within the walls of great houses ought properly to remain exclusive for some time; but this is not so. The great houses seem all too anxious to share their secrets with the journalists. The ladies are photographed in their negligees and call in their cooks to confide the secret recipes on which they have earned their position in society. There is even a new book of "celebrities'" recipes which have been syndicated.

For the purposes of this essay, I tried out one: Clare Boothe Luce's Risotto Milanese alla Pucci. Ingredients cost three dollars. It is very generous with butter, saffron ($1.29 per handful), chicken broth, Parmesan cheese, and mushrooms, and stingy on white wine. I ate four forkfuls and threw the rest out. The taste was antiseptic.

On the food thing, it is interesting and natural that the fashionable thing to eat in the Midwest is what is hard to get and probably bad—lobster.

In Northern white gatherings, it is very smart to have a Negro or Asiatic friend. Some fortunate groups hold their own jam sessions and, though not at the same time, life classes in drawing. It is permissible to be dilettante in these matters, but much better to be in dead earnest.

A man lined with exclusive labels gave me a scoop of what he requires from life, as follows: (1) breakfast in bed immediately on awaking, (2) a long razor and hook to hang the strop on—rare in modern hotels, (3) shoes from Maxwell in London, made to last fifteen years, (4) no cocktail at lunch and a guest who does not say, "You can put this on your expense account," (5) iced sweet butter and a silver knife which shreds the butter, (6) the Oriental custom of steaming hot washcloths to wipe the face before and after meals, (7) a nap after lunch, (8) a second hot bath at 6:00 P.M., possibly with an ice-cold Martini, and (9) dinner at eight with a well-spoken wife. Since he is not going to tell *Woman's Day* about his plan, it will probably remain exclusive.

On this subject, there is no use looking to monied society in America. It has virtually gone underground and comes aboveground only for taxi drivers, waiters, politics, and picnics. Nelson Rockefeller, for example, wouldn't know an exclusive label when he saw one, nor would Jack Kennedy. Adlai Stevenson might, but he would run in the opposite direction. Society men are fleeing into politics.

And nobody in his right mind ever claimed that society men had to have any taste. Madame de Sévigné had that ideal, but Proust knew better.

In this society the only labels that can possibly stay exclusive for any useful period of time are simply those that clearly demand more trouble, risk, knowledge, and talent than they seem, to outsiders, to be worth. Mere expense is not enough to balk anybody today. But the immense trouble and polish that Proust's Swann and Odette gave to what would seem little or nothing will keep their commodities forever out of the supermarket; and I believe that even without servants Swann would have gone to all that trouble himself, personally.

The exclusive label is not of itself wicked; it is harmless and human and even inspirational. But it is a fact that when its harmless forms are denied, it degenerates into wickedness and perversion, as in the eighteenth century English clubs that celebrated the Black Mass at midnight and in the nineteenth century religious sects of Russian self-mutilators. The present cult of juvenile delinquency is obviously based on the affectation of great wickedness, in youths who have no idea of what wickedness is, except to violate the Ten Commandments. In my opinion, the cult of much jazz must be based on the sadism of the musicians and the masochism of the listeners, for the sounds are extremely painful to a baby or a dog. The cult of homosexuality, thoroughly explained by Freud, seems to have outgrown its sense of great wickedness and developed a sense of its own great cleverness. The cult of Fascism, no longer necessarily anti-Semitic, seems to me to be testing its muscles in respectable quarters again; I regard Westbrook Pegler as respectable, and his idea of the best government in the Western Hemisphere is Trujillo's, in the Dominican Republic. The man who long ago got me interested in Babe Herman and the Brooklyn Dodgers and then in the possibility that labor leaders were not all beatified, has now degraded my gratitude, beyond slavering on the great Roosevelt family, by fouling my Constitution and its first Ten Amendments.

You see where we can get on this subject. The little clique can be vicious, and then, as in Nazi Germany, it is not so little. Mr. Pegler, forgetting the old days in the Stork Club where his views were softened by Heywood Broun but perhaps stimulated by Hanfstaengl who escaped over the back fence, is not so safe as he sounds. The beetles in the woodwork creep out and speak sometimes. I will forgive Pegler nearly anything, but not outspoken treason.

Still, Fascism is now an exclusive label.

The best club of all, in a country where nearly everybody has a nine-to-five job, is that of the unemployed. Consider the unemployed who have no boss to answer to and are always ready for a fight, a frolic, or a new assignment: Eleanor Roosevelt, the Rockefeller boys, Adlai Stevenson, Harriman, Baruch, Carmine de Sapio, Hemingway, Rodgers and Hammerstein, Howard Hughes, Hoover, Truman, Moses, Callas, Mr. and Mrs. Luce, Buckminster Fuller, Lippmann, Pegler, Winchell, Frank Costello, O'Malley, Bob Hope, Bing Crosby, Elsa Maxwell, Orson Welles, King Edward VIII, Elizabeth Taylor, and Dwight Eisenhower. Why, those people practically run the country, and not one punches a time clock. That's what U and Non-U really stand for—Unemployed and Non-Unemployed.

Proust and the Cool Cats
(1958)

On any bright beautiful day, the current writings of the generation of despair in the United States, England, and France seem especially irrelevant to life, or at best related to the sulks and tantrums of very small children in a sandpile.

In America there are the "cool cats," the "beat generation," who have given to Bohemian life a predominantly Negro accent and who thrive in the dark, like homeless cats, on the judgment "Life is an insult." Society has betrayed them, not by its terms but by theirs; the rewards and conditions of democratic abundance seem to them merely insulting.

In England, the so-called "angry young men," now well fed, have a more intelligible complaint. As the social scientists would say, democracy has failed to give them, along with abundance, the status and self-confidence it had promised, in return for gifted effort and true-blue virtue. In essence they say, "Life is a swindle."

The world of the existentialists, in France particularly, is more difficult to define. They do not exactly say, "Life is an outrage." They may say, "Life is . . ." But one cannot prove that they say any more than, "Life . . ." Books on Camus coalesce his intent as "Everything is absurd, except those who believe so." In short, the existentialists create, like the others, an upside-down élite.

But for all three groups the drama is very real. The Negro hipster's exclusion from some areas of American life is not merely a bad dream. The frustrated, angry English careerist is dealing with a reality. The Europeans have real memories of inscrutable bureaucracy and the insane Nazi terror, and a present civilization that is at once overelaborated and oversimplified. But this does not explain the fellow travelers: the white boys who want to share the Negroes' code jargon, the solid bourgeois who feels that the "angry young men" speak for him too, the existentialist who never saw a concentration camp. One can admire some of the feelings that impel them to identify themselves with the originals, yet they remain dilettantes of despair.

Their problem is not our subject here. Instead, it is proposed to find a predecessor of the "beat generation," "the angry young men," and the existentialists, one who outdid them all, who found his material in "high life" instead of "low life," who did not need to make a special or esoteric case but took a representative world, who began with a discriminating love of life in its most minute details and still gives us the assurance that, when he talked about life, he knew what he was talking about. Yet his single, reiterated message was far more terrible than that of these new voices. It was "Life is a joke."

His name may surprise some people, especially since a spokesman for the "beat generation" has written that Marcel Proust had a "humorless mind." To me, this seems something like calling Shakespeare inarticulate.

Proust lovers, among whom I count myself, will at first be shocked by the end conclusion that he wanted primarily to say that he found life a joke or infinite series of jokes. I propose therefore to take them through the experience by which I made this shaking discovery. Let me synopsize pages 160–310 of the Random House edition of *Within a Budding Grove*.

Swann and his wife, Odette, the former courtesan, take the hero to the park and are greeted by a growling old lady who turns out to be Her Imperial Highness, the Princess Mathilde, niece of Napoleon I. She tells of Musset's coming to dine, dead drunk, and of having refused the Government's invitation to the Invalides to receive the Czar Nicholas ("If the government desires my presence there, it will not be on the platform, it will be in our vault, where the Emperor's tomb is.") She speaks of a "soldier in the family"—this would be Napoleon. Swann mutters that his feet are hurting.

Next, Swann is enraged because, on the anniversary of his father's death, his daughter, Gilberte, insists on going to the theater.

Next, the "I" is invited to meet a famous writer, Bergotte, whose works "I" humbly admires, and finds him to be, not a frail wise old man, but a "young common little thick-set peering person." The books' "gentle and godlike wisdom" is at odds with the writer's "alert and self-satisfied" air. "I" is mystified by a carnation by his plate (he puts it in his buttonhole) and by a plate of caviar (which he firmly determines not to put in his mouth.) Listening to Bergotte's oral mannerisms, he is led to twenty pages relating these to his genius, his upbringing, family, harmony, and austerity of taste, as opposed to his social ambitions.

Next, when Swann says, "Nervous men ought always to love 'beneath' them," the "I" senses that Swann momentarily hates him, thinking that "I" has thought of Swann's own marriage. Now Gilberte appears, showing her mother's nose and sly expression, her father's red hair, golden skin, and open gaze.

"I" leaves with Bergotte who says of Swann, "He's typical of the man who had married a whore." A moment later, "I" is home, hearing his father say ironically, "Swann introduced you to Bergotte? It only wanted that . . . a set that will finish you off altogether." But when the parents learn that Bergotte found "I" extremely intelligent, they allow that he may have his points.

An aside tells us that "I" dares not invite Gilberte to tea because (1) his mother also serves chocolate, which is unfashionable, and (2) she refuses to ask Gilberte, "How is your mother?"

Next, the intellectual bounder Bloch introduces "I" to a whore-house where "I" rejects a girl he nicknames "Rachel when from the Lord" but enjoys talking to the naked girls as they mix drinks. He presents the madame with some of his inherited furniture and then cannot visit the place again because of the outrage to the furniture's memories, among them his own first dalliance with a cousin.

Meanwhile, "I" puts off getting to work at writing and is vaguely dissatisfied with his relationship with Gilberte. Essentially the next seventy pages are given to the values of *not* seeing Gilberte while continually the guest of her parents. The suffering for the daughter is shattered in the delight of the mother.

Thus, it is observed that a great courtesan like Odette has the most "housewifely" of virtues, that is, she lives for her home, where the crucial act is not dressing herself for the world to see, but undressing for one man to see, and the perfect, private illusion is the most essential, the more often it is invaded. Now we find Mme. Swann serving tartlets for her teatime guests, now mostly female, gabbling of their servant problems, the dullness of their husbands' colleagues' wives. Swann puts his head through the curtains to call that the Prince d'Agrigente wants to pay his respects.

Odette has developed a plumper, healthier, cooler beauty, much less satisfactory to Swann than her former Botticelli grace, visible in an old photograph he keeps in his room.

And so we end in May with the Sunday noonday strolls in the Avenue du Bois, Odette backed by Swann and a troop of gentlemen from the Club, Odette "unhurrying cool luxuriant" in a toilet typically mauve, under a matching wide parasol, in public as secret as on the paths of her own garden. The picture convinces the "shabbygenteel" of their own hopeless unworthiness far more effectively than would the sight of a real duchess. Odette says to "I," "So it's all over between you and Gilberte, but don't drop me straight away." "Odette," Swann calls, "Sagan is trying to speak to you." And there on horseback is the Prince, wheeling the horse and sweeping his hat in a flourish. This scene the "I" will always remember, when he has long forgotten his sorrow for the daughter.

Next comes the summer at Balbec where—with the first meetings with Mme. de Villeparisis, Saint-Loup, Charlus, Elstir, Albertine, and "the little band"—"nothing happens" and the ironic juxtapositions become still more savage.

There is no end of jokes in the material given, so different in subject and treatment from the "hipsters," the "angry young men," and the existentialists.

The old Second Empire niece of Napoleon makes a joke of the Emperor by her familiar respect, and of Musset by her anecdote. On the other hand, Swann makes a joke of her because his feet hurt.

Gilberte makes a joke of her father by going to the theater. The physical presence of Bergotte makes a joke of his own work but Proust dismisses this as a poor joke. Swann makes a joke of himself by imagining that his hearer thinks that Swann married beneath himself, and his good qualities are travestied by their appearance in Gilberte commingled with Odette's bad ones.

Bergotte makes a joke of himself and his hostess by calling her a whore. Proust's family makes a joke of Swann's set, including Bergotte, then of themselves by accepting Bergotte's compliments to their son.

The mother makes a joke of herself, on two trifling points of manners that keep her son from asking Gilberte to tea. Proust's visits to the whorehouse make a joke of his parents, Gilberte, Swann's set and, finally, even of his own furniture and his childish amours.

A protracted joke is Proust's rather unconvincing agony over the renounced daughter while he goes on enjoying the parents. The joke on love, as evasion from reality, here becomes quite abstract. And so the joke goes on until the final scene in the park, such a superb period piece that no joke should be permitted but even here, just as Odette is telling Proust that she knows about his tragic feelings, the comic interjection has to break it off, "Sagan is trying to speak to you," and there is the triumph of period, turned comic, the wheeling horse and the prince sweeping his tall hat, the immense trouble and polish over little or nothing. And this, not Gilberte, is what Proust will always remember, he says, and is to be believed. And so they are all jokes on one another.

This précis by no means ends the jokes in this action but must have conveyed that Proust regarded this little part of life as a joke. And as will have been seen, the part is not so very little. I do not go on to the Balbec section which tells chiefly of first acquaintance, because the jokes become, where there has been no time for emotional development, extreme and even brutal. I chanced on a section which tells of the developed decaying ends of old relationships, where the mood is "idyllic," the jokes relatively mild, and this best makes the point.

I think some kinship is proved between Proust and the "hipsters," "the angry young men," and the existentialists, but I think it is evident that Proust is on a far higher level of art and life. In nearly every case the act of the protagonist is not an absolute but merely a point on an exquisitely drawn curve. Thus, in the park, Swann raises his hat to strangers, no longer with the indifference of the clubman, but now with some irritation if the stranger were ill-dressed, and also pleasure at his wife's knowing "so many people" and a blend in his comment to his fellow clubmen of the old splendid snobbery and the new husbandly satisfaction.

Indeed, in every one of these admirable jokes, every element is a point on a curve, a quantity to be stated in voltage, resistance, capacitance, and the like, not digitally, not a sum but a differential equation. Perhaps that is why Proust is more relevant to today (given the utter death of his world) than he was to 1920; and why former critics felt obliged to describe his work as a symphony with themes. Proust knew the difference between music and verbal ideas, and between ideas and actual human deportment. He was not writing music. He was writing a joke book, put to music.

Perhaps Proust's superiority to the "hipsters," "the angry young men," and existentialists is that his characters are never conscious of being jokers, as in fact in life people are not. As in life, his people are deadly serious about their own lives, *and for that reason* cannot understand the deadly seriousness of the one who is talking to them. The self-consciousness of the modern characters, their self-pity, their pitiable crusher, "I didn't ask to be born," make them poor company and poor art, and take them at least through the front gate of the park leading to the madhouse or prison.

What has thrown off Proust's critics is that he has never, never revealed by the smallest sign that he was making jokes. There would seem to be an obvious reason for such perfect taciturnity. To a man of so much discretion, it must have been clear that the theme, "Life is a joke," would be the most terrible message imaginable. Proust stopped at presenting and proving it; he did not confide it.

Proust's stoic self-discipline is of course a reproach to modern writers. But this is not the lesson I want to find in him. It may be that he points the way, instead, toward a higher plateau for current literature.

This may be sensed if we recognize that Proust's attitude toward his jokes was precisely what the hipsters mean by "cool," that is, secret, uncommitted, in cipher. In other words, "cool" is a respectable and even distinguished point of view. If the moderns would outgrow their self-pity, a true "cool" literature is quite conceivable. It may already, as in the later works of Camus, have begun to appear.

VII

A Final Word of Reassurance

The First Nightmare

The nightmare futures described in Aldous Huxley's *Brave New World* and George Orwell's *1984* have come, to a remarkable degree, to be accepted as valid and objective predictions. Even the intelligent individual today accepts a growing conviction that he cannot do anything important, while the state can do everything. This cynicism would seem a by-product of the Marxist premise that all problems in a complex world must be solved in one package, by one plan, from the top down.

The nightmare is redrawn by Huxley in *Brave New World Revisited*, in which he measures the progress the modern world has made in fact toward the society forecast twenty-seven years ago. The whole dreadful deadfall, he concludes, is not so very far off.

The "inevitable" progress, briefly, travels from overpopulation (over five billion by A.D. 2000) to overorganization for man's own good to the "inevitable" rise of the dictator and the melting down of the proud individual into the antlike components of the servile mob, chiefly by means of applied science.

It all sounds rational; and yet it is wholly irrational, unhistoric, sentimental, and inoperable. The reply can be given quickly or slowly. First, quickly.

The free peoples largely invented modern industrialization and technology and then shared them with Germany and Russia, which had scant experience of freedom. When these two were faced with disaster, they plunged into the tyrannies of the Nazis and the Communists, under special circumstances, with much internal dissent.

Huxley and Orwell, however, confer tyranny on societies with both a history of freedom and a high technology. Since such creations have as yet no historical precedent, they are enormities—a fact that heightens their horror.

Tyranny of course is never uncommon, and operates today in more or less backward countries all over the world. Nazi Germany was not "backward"—but it endured only twelve years, not an impressive performance. Russia is now making a transit from semi-backwardness to reliance on modern industry, science, and mass education. Such a state must relax its controls on at least its educated élite, now appallingly numerous. The Kremlin's problem remains how to get the maximum energy out of its people; and some degree of freedom (not necessarily America's kind of freedom) has historically proved the most efficient. If the leaders refuse to surrender tyranny, its technology cannot long remain competitive with a free world.

Let us look calmly at overpopulation. (The five-billion figure is ridiculous.) Actually there is room for a lot more people in the Western Hemisphere, south and central Africa, Asiatic U.S.S.R. and Australia, though certainly not in western Europe, India, China, or Japan. Improved hygiene has lowered the high death rates in many backward (and usually underpopulated) nations where they had always canceled out high birth rates. The penalty for this population spree is that in the last fifty years the standard of living in most underdeveloped countries has not risen; it has, instead, sharply declined.

Neither individuals nor societies are wholly crazy forever; and if they carry it on too long, they are destroyed. The population increases in Japan and Germany, once given as requiring *Lebensraum*, have leveled off.

Kindly liberals have deluded backward countries into believing that anybody, if only America's heart is in the right place, can ascend quickly to a high standard of living, even if they do not have mineral fuels, water power, or anything of value with which to pay for imported energy or commodities. This is a cruel idealism. These people will be the easiest sort of prey for dictators, national adventures, and the Communist solution.

Many Western idealists, demanding a 3,000-calories-a-day diet for the whole world, live on under 2,000 calories a day themselves. The

American diet has dropped in calorie count since 1900, the emphasis having shifted to proteins and vitamins. An overfed person is often as listless as an underfed one; one in the middle is irritable, combative, and ready for revolution.

Huxley then argues, now on a thinning thread, that the great powers will placidly watch *all* these adventures (as they have watched Egypt) until their industrial machines are stalled and they must themselves embrace tyranny.

A good mind has rarely produced a neater package of nonsense. Present American foreign policy gives it some countenance, but that cannot be counted on to remain forever foolish, in the style but without the dignity of Pontius Pilate.

Huxley now makes interchangeable the free democratic technological society and the backward slave society. What a sleight of hand! The real world fades away; a chessboard appears in its place; and now the dialectician opens his play.

However, he has misgivings, and so he adds, before he starts play, the generalization that a corrupt propaganda, skillfully applied, must always and everywhere be omnipotent.

Let us whittle this down to reality. A corrupt propaganda, even in a free society, has often had a quick success with a working minority and kept the majority inert long enough to accomplish the short-term ends of its manipulators. Democratic history is a succession of these affairs, and somebody usually gets hurt. The society always has a number of unsolved problems, or failures. The adventurer says: "Politicians are bad. Rely on a Man. Me." For a while people are excited or puzzled. Then the more violent counter-propaganda comes rolling in. And worse yet, the original propaganda exhausts itself; it is a bore.

Perhaps propaganda has had its great day in the West; I would wonder whether it has not seen its sunset. The sun of course has moved eastward.

As Huxley moves on to the more innocuous matter of advertising, he gets still deeper into the boredom of propaganda. He gives the sentence, "The cosmetics manufacturers are not selling lanolin, they are selling hope." Hope unfulfilled becomes worse than boring. He quotes somebody as saying, "Think of what it can mean to your firm in profits if you can condition a million or ten million children, who will grow up into adults trained to buy your product, as soldiers are trained in advance when they hear the trigger words, Forward March!" This glib transposition of a childish experience into an adult reflex is at odds with every observation on how completely childish stimuli are forgotten, so that it is even a priceless rediscovery to be able to dredge up the old memory.

An advertisement can rarely remain the same long enough to become any sort of mass neurosis. It makes its brief claim as best it can: that is its right. It is usually vulgar, but not dangerous.

Now Huxley moves on to red meat: brainwashing. For here we come to the central matter, the human brain. No matter how disgraced, this great organ can always answer truly that it has not yet begun to fight.

Brainwashing, Huxley reminds us, was invented by Ivan Pavlov who gave dogs nervous breakdowns. In the course of this kindly work, he discovered that a dog just short of a final breakdown was highly suggestible. In this state it could be taught a whole new set of tricks and reflexes, to which it would forever after fanatically adhere.

But as Huxley points out, brainwashing has been going on since the world began. Nagging wives, brutal husbands, army sergeants, hazing fraternities, hell-fire pastors, inspirational athletic coaches all try to brainwash their victims, and often succeed. For the victims would rather like to repudiate their past lives and embrace a new, purifying faith; and there is no use getting pompous about the desire to enjoy two or more lives instead of just one.

What is especially horrible about a process that half a billion people are continually applying, and another half a billion accepting? Huxley's awe of it is reflected in his figure that the average man can stand only thirty days of continuous stress under battle combat conditions, the exceptional man up to fifty days. Not so. In World War II, a good many men remained effective, though not normal, under a solid year of combat. They were still under fire during the brief and rare so-called "rest" periods. Huxley's figures are an insult to the modern man.

The peculiar fact is that a brainwashed person, though dangerous, is not effective. One has known such people, and in a sane world they are impotent. They miss all the tiny social signals; they cannot identify themselves with the others; they make the most inconspicuous and ruinous social mistakes; they seem to invite their own destruction.

Still fooling with the human brain, Huxley moves on to the use a dictator might make of tranquillizer drugs (reserpine, chlorpromazine, and meprobamate or Miltown) and the stimulants and the new vision-producing drug (LSD-25). The dictator would make the first highly available and cheap during normal times, the second in crisis, and the third in depression and catastrophe. The masses, says Huxley with the voice of Hitler, would gobble them up.

Wait a minute. It is true that anybody, thinking that he was looking for happiness, might try a tranquillizer, and in fact billions of them have already been consumed. But the idea that people seriously want to be happy and stay happy is the worst fallacy ever palmed off by philosophers. Almost anybody would sell happiness for some interesting and suitable trouble. The only valid historical test of a good life or a good society is how much energy it generated, not how happy it was.

Any society using tranquillizer drugs on a mass scale would soon be overthrown by a competitive, untranquillized society. And what of the dictator: wouldn't he be taking tranquillizers himself?

Continuing with this much-abused human brain, Huxley brings up what is called subliminal advertising. The fact behind this is that a human being sees and hears far more than he consciously notes; and that this apparently "lost" material tends to appear in his dreams more often than the consciously noted and censored material. Thus, it is thought just now that the best part of a human being to address is his subconscious, preferably with a sound, picture, or word flashed on the TV or movie screen or radio so quickly that it is not noted.

Again, I think that this is to make light of the human brain. Possibly you could sell heroin to my subconscious once by associating it with a picture of Santa Claus, Lincoln, or a pretty girl; but when I had to suffer the aftereffects, I would tend to conclude that Santa Claus, Lincoln, and pretty girls were bad news. To say it another way, the superego may not be able to evaluate the stimulus but it certainly evaluates the consequent experience. And all this is to assume that the subliminal message is effective. This is far from proved.

Should it be proved, it becomes as easy to subject the dictator as the masses to subliminal messages. The main difficulty with the subliminal message is that it is faceless, irresponsible, unaccountable, and unpaid for. Yet this is morally impossible. I suspect that there are catches in it I haven't even thought of.

Huxley now gives the dictator another dubious tool, "hyp-nopaedia," or teaching during light sleep, much as under light hypnosis. The mere concept of such a tool assumes an already developed dictatorship. In a free or transitional society, I cannot imagine how you, the dictator, are going to manage to talk to me in my sleep. Huxley answers this by saying that I will be caught in hypnopaedia (a word not in my big dictionary) when I am in a hospital, prison, military barracks, labor camp (I have never been in any of these) or ship, train, airplane, bus terminal or railway station (I don't get much sleep in these).

Huxley gives the figures for hypnotic suggestibility: 20 per cent cannot be hypnotized at all; 60 per cent can be hypnotized with moderate difficulty; and the last 20 per cent fall into hypnosis with glad little cries. Suppose at 4:00 A.M. a railway loudspeaker began intoning, "All redheaded people are enemies of the state," and one nonhypnotizable redhead awaked. Even the 20 per cent of happily hypnotized jerks would have to weigh the ensuing goings-on.

Huxley parses suggestibility with helpless passivity. But think about "suggestible" people—those who quickly get the point, who readily enjoy a wide range of experiences, who give themselves to books, plays, and relationships. Aren't they in fact the most independent and difficult to influence? Aren't they skilled at distinguishing and choosing among a number of offered experiences? They also tend to influence the rest of the population.

It is shocking to read Huxley's thoughtless line: "The ideals of democracy and freedom confront the brute fact of human sug-gestibility." Huxley's own value as a human being resides largely in his suggestibility, that is, his quick and subtle responsiveness to varied stimuli. (But on this subject, he may have let his suggestibility go too far.) Responsiveness is one of the chief requisites for charm, talent, wealth, and power. The hope of youth is that it is responsive; the despair of age is that it may not be.

Huxley's fear of suggestibility is a treason against his own nature and talent. This does not make him necessarily either wrong or wicked, since one of man's noblest instincts is to doubt himself. But that is no reason to doubt all of us.

Having said so much, I shall now agree that modern forces are indeed undermining the old virile concept of freedom, which was close to individualistic anarchy. I would define the most important of these as the corporation, scientists, and women.

What women want has fully as much right to be represented in the Government as what men want. However, as was said in an earlier section, it is not primarily freedom.

The modern corporation is essentially feminine. Like a jealous wife, it demands absolute fidelity, and like a female praying mantis, it eats the males that fertilize it. It promotes to the top its best housekeepers. It might surprise most board chairmen to be told that they owed their success to their female traits, but again it might not surprise them at all.

Thirdly, scientists are as practical as women and businessmen. The only freedom a scientist really cares about is the freedom to prove out something like: "A carbon-dioxide-basic barium hydro-carbon sulfonate reaction product is used as a lubricating oil additive and is produced from a compound of the formula: $HO-Ba-SO_3-R-R'N$, in which R is an aryl radical, and R' is a C_8 or higher aryl radical. Preferably R' in the formula is a wax radical and N is 2." On this one, I like "Preferably . . . N is 2."

The systematic pursuit of scientific truth is a hard discipline and tends to purify scientists of the last trace of free hoodlum, such as the rest of us have.

It is up to the rest of us to preserve freedom for the sake of the women, the scientists, and even the corporations, but books about freedom issued by any of them sometimes make one wonder what they are really talking about.

The final fallacy of Huxley's Brave New World derives from a fact that few people are fully conscious of but Huxley knows well. Every year millions of reports on new research issue from the world's government agencies, learned societies, universities and colleges, technical journals, foundations and industrial research centers. In American chemistry alone, 100,000 new chemical abstracts, such as that quoted above, are published every year. And every year the number increases. The life of science and technology depends on this vast, free, antimonopolistic flow and exchange of knowledge.

Freedom is an indispensable associate and by-product of this life. No tyrant would dare tamper with this freedom if he thought he would kill off any part of the scientific product. Huxley's tyrant may have temperamental objections to freedom, but if he cannot find out whether "preferably . . . N is 2," he has no future.

The Second Nightmare
(1959)

A terrible vision of total annihilation by incineration and radiation can certainly be said to obsess the modern world, especially the United States and Russia. For these two, says a reputable magazine, "war is obsolete as a means of any policy save that of mutual annihilation, yet in both, virtually all policies and actions fall within the perspective of a third world war."

The hysteria in this sentence is pitched so high that it is almost inaudible, and it is the key of all contemporary thinking. Before we set about lowering the pitch to something within reach of the human ear, it may be noted that the hysteria is useful, politically, morally, and financially, to the ruling groups in both the United States and Russia. Their half-conscious satisfaction with the situation sits horribly beside the fact that the hysteria must be responsible for the universal decay of morality. The small, human, decent fears are obliterated by the great fear. And in this nightmare, what can possibly evolve but a kind of man suitable for mass extermination and capable of effecting it?

It is profoundly shocking that all these active little brains have not given five minutes' thought to what a third world war would probably be like, if we except the commercial hysterics of novelists like Philip Wylie and Nevil Shute. But the people themselves should have begun to suspect that all the lovely terror, like the thrills at a horror movie, cannot be taken at exactly face value.

They should have shown some interest, less in the propaganda utility of the truth than in the simple face of probability.

The present propaganda is based on three principles of xenophobia so ancient that they are inherited intact from primitive man: (1) something awful is going to happen, (2) the enemy is crazy, and (3) the weapons are irresistible, both his and ours. To a man with a wooden club who saw a stranger peeking around a tree, all subsequent action was based on these three beliefs, so contemporary today, which required also the invention of religion. Mankind has always, it is safe to say, feared himself, his own kind, more than any natural phenomenon except the open sea.

The first and third principles can be allowed for the moment to stand. In some sense they are, always have been, and always will be more or less valid. But let us dismiss completely the second, that the enemy is crazy. If that is too difficult to do quickly, then let us just assume that he is not crazy, and see where we get.

Since the subject is Communist Russia, we know that the Communists are obsessed, to the point of idolatry, by faith in The Plan, in imitation of the Germans and Americans. Thus we know they have a Plan for the third war. We know their best and sanest brains have worked on this Plan. We know they are still arguing over it.

We also know that all military men "know" that the third war will not last more than a week or month. In the Russian case, this immediately brought into question the World War II policy of trying to destroy the enemy's industrial establishment. The point of such bombing was to keep the actual product from going into shooting action several months or years later. Whether or not the World War II bombing was a relative waste of power, there can be no doubt that the atom bomb could really do the job that the old bombs notably failed to do. However, it is obvious that in a short war that particular job would not be worth doing at all. On the contrary, it would be crazy.

The Russians making The Plan are not crazy. They know that the United States is run by groups of civilians, not by generals who may be individually crazy, and that the American civilians are not going to start the war. The war is going to be started by the Russians, and only on the supersafe assumption that Russians are going to win it. Therefore, The Plan assumes that at the end of the war Russians will have control of the United States and, indeed, of the world.

The Russian Plan therefore describes a war from which the Russians will get the maximum profit, after it is finished. And what are these sugar plums? They are of course electrical power, critical natural resources, and heavy industry establishments, at the very minimum. But as the makers of The Plan continue to think, they would wish to recover the United States intact, complete with personnel, at the end of the war.

Taking the minimum, what The Plan will not bomb would therefore include all the great dams, all the great power plants, all the oil, gas, and coal fields, all the oil refineries and a calculated selection of such cities as Philadelphia, Pittsburgh, Johnstown, Trenton, Wilmington, Birmingham, Syracuse, Schenectady, Buffalo, Endicott, N.Y., Cleveland, Akron, Youngstown, Dayton, Sandusky, Toledo, Fort Wayne, Gary, Detroit, and a good many more.

Still, the Russian Plan cannot neglect the advantage of *Schrechlichkeit* to nuclear war, which has been so helpfully prepared by the American press. The important day in this sort of war is the first day, and the American press in its first editions will certainly respond the way the Russians plan. The big headlines would be provided by putting a bomb on Washington, D.C. Where else? New York? Chicago? Los Angeles?

New York, as the world's greatest port, can probably be crossed off the list, since any Russian Plan would require a considerable sea traffic after and, perhaps, during the war. There are heavy arguments both for and against New York.

The primary Russian targets would be military targets, as in every other exercise of the art of war. Strategic Air Force bases. Known missile-launching sites. Submarine and other naval bases. Missile-launching submarines and other ships, as discovered.

The present Russian mastery of electronics is not such as to convince one that the Russian ICBM's could hit exactly what they were aimed at. Short-range missiles from submarines are of course another matter. In other words, the present ICBM aimed at New York would probably be very bad news for Westport or Newburgh

or Newark or some oceanic fish, but the terror achieved by wiping
Westport off the map would not be what the Russian planners
have in mind, unless Sid Perelman has worked his way into the
Russian Operations Room.

Atomic war still keeps the necessity to invade, and therefore
calls for either coordination or alternation of invasion areas and
bombed areas. One can imagine Russian paratroopers taking over
the three great airfields in the New York area to receive the following troop carriers. One can imagine fleets of transports trying to
sneak up to ports on both coasts by unfrequented northern routes.
If the Russians moved into a bombed port, we would of course have
no hesitation about bombing it again, but if they managed to secure
an unbombed port our problem would be agonizing.

At this stage we would wake up from the nightmare of annihilation that was after all only a dream; but in fact we would be
slaves, and that would be no dream. Of such are the uses of propaganda in the hands of fools and hysterics.

Let us suppose that at about this same time American paratroopers are sitting down on Leningrad, Archangel, Odessa,
Vladivostok, and so on.

It might be that the victory would go to that people which
recovered its sane composure the sooner, or had never lost it.
Russian communications are not so good as American, and so the
war of "mutual annihilation" has not been sold so completely to
the Russian country people as it has been sold to the Americans by
the indefatigable American press whose political writers are now
all writing horror-movie scenarios and are regarded with dreadful
awe at their favorite bars.

Our civil defense should be organized on the possibility that
after the week of war we are alive and confronted with live human
beings of the hostile power. For this sort of operation I think the
Americans have always had great talent and courage and team
spirit.

That is as far as I can go into the third world war. Obviously,
Plans are one thing; and wars tend to get out of control as the
people running them get out of control; and nobody can predict the
incredible blunders or the incredible luck.

Now, what is the serious probability of any Russian government launching an all-out, everything-or-nothing gamble for the rule of the world?

First, I must say that the journalists and politicians who keep up the most continuous and highest-pitched keening that the Russians are about to attack are, by an unpeculiar coincidence, those who know least about Russia or Russian history or warfare and evidently have made no effort in all these years to repair the hiatus in their education. The gradations in lack of knowledge seem to correspond almost exactly with the gradations in the pitch of the keening.

I do not know much. Still, I am pitched fairly low.

One lesson of Russian history for the past five hundred years is that Russia has never won a major offensive war, and it has taken enormous gains from a number of major defensive wars. Even Peter the Great could not win offensively, but he could not lose defensively. The Russians could conquer Asiatic tribesmen, but in several cases only after a number of humiliating defeats. Their failures against the decadent Ottoman Empire are still unbelievable. The rise of modern Japan is largely based on its overthrow, not only of the Russian Navy, but, at Mukden, of the Russian Army, in a decisive battle on a front of forty miles.

In such matters, the atavistic Muscovite pattern, the race memory of what has never worked, ought to be a hundred times more important to Muscovites than the views of the intellectual German Karl Marx who was not a military man though he took an intense interest in military matters. The reason for the Russian failure to advance successfully into enemy country has been given as incompetence at communications, which become progressively more important as one advances. The lack of communications in Russia is also one reason for the defeat of the invaders. An atomic war would be the greatest challenge to communications ever presented by a war. Even an ICBM is a problem in communications.

For such reasons, I believe that the masters of the Kremlin positively cringe from taking the gamble on a great offensive war which, if the coin fell heads instead of tails, in their opinion, might wipe the whole Russian race and its civilization forever off the earth and out of history, as if it had never been.

Nobody would want his people to come to this end, but in the Russian case the emotion is more profound than it might be in many societies. The fact is that Russians love Russia; they are crazy about Russia; it is an incurable infatuation. For example, not unlike the Anglo-Saxon colonizers of America, they rarely interbred with the conquered races, and do not to this day; they always long to get home to the forest-steppe. A Russian does not greatly mind the death of tens of millions of other Russians; the death of Russia is quite another matter. So long as a third world war is to any degree a gamble on the death of Russia, it is, to say the least, unlikely that a Russian government would initiate it.

I wish Russia didn't have the atom bomb; but it would be still more alarming if it were acquired by any other countries, such as Egypt, the Dominican Republic, China, Yugoslavia, Spain, Morocco, Rumania, Liberia, Ghana, Ethiopia, and others. The psychological effect on the dictator of a small country of being able to wipe another capital or country off the map is an actual psychological horror. It is only comparable to the social disaster of an atom bomb in the possession of a criminal mob. In this matter, there is no room for courtesy to the small nations which have a majority in the United Nations Assembly. Indeed, the United Nations would be well advised to declare war on any small nation that manages to acquire the means of making atom bombs.

The present uproar about the awful imminence of the third world war makes an interesting contrast to the lethargy about the imminence of the Second World War in most of the American press.

Furthermore, the contrast between Hitler's menace and the present Russian menace is well worth exploring for a few lines. Hitler concealed his weapons until he had a battle opportunity to use them for surprise; the Russians actually boast about their achievements, as in showing us the Sputniks. Hitler claimed that he wanted only one little thing at a time: the Saar, Austria, the Sudeten, Danzig; the Russians boast that they want and will have the whole world. Hitler would have answered any little defeat by throwing in everything he had; the Russians accepted the failure of the Korean War, the Berlin airlift, and the rise of China. The Russians are, as they have historically been for five hundred years, bluffers, in a sense that the Germans are not. When the Germans have great power, it is time to be alarmed. When the Russians make atrocious faces—I do not know, but I know it is different.

A study of the journalistic record before World War II shows that some qualified journalists did accurately predict every move that the enemy made. I recently went through the New York *Times* for 1938. The correct predictions were there; but beside them were the incorrect predictions. And the more correct were made by the better informed journalists, who had obviously done their homework. The shape of things to come is usually visible to somebody. It is important to realize that it is actually possible to predict what the enemy will do, *unless he is crazy*—and we have agreed to exclude that possibility. If one assumes he is perfectly sane, cunning, dead serious, and sometimes desperate and ambitious, it is amazing how often one is right. The enemy, marvelous to say, has only the mind of man; still more marvelous, one has this same instrument oneself.

What outraged us most about the Nazis was that they were Westerners, whereas our outrage about the Russians is really quite shallow, for they are historically the barbarians and we expect them to be outrageous. Thus, it is not terribly revelatory that the masters of the Kremlin do not behave exactly as Hitler did. Each race and culture has its own way of approaching an assassination. The Russian pattern may be to threaten and boast and then actually throw the big punch. They may begin by bluffing, scare themselves into seriousness and then, since they are Russians, try a dirty blow, as if nobody were looking, and then cry. This sequence, in fact, recurs in Russian history, and of course also Russian literature.

The mass of Russians are likable people; the Russians we have to think about, however, are the leaders whom the Russians monotonously put into command. There has never been an American President as disgraceful in one way or another as the last ten Autocrats of All the Russias, Communist and Czarist. They have all been very much of a type, but the Communist ones do it better, with no conscience whatever. The dictator in the Kremlin refrains from taking the name of Czar only out of proletarian prejudice. To restore it to him would be a nice courtesy on the part of foreign governments and the United Nations.

Whatever their faults, however, the Russians have become the second greatest industrial power in the world, a useful addition to the human establishment. The performance has been so astonishing it must leave them as incredulous as us.

So much for whether "the enemy is crazy." Let us return to the third proposition, "The weapons are irresistible."

Since Hitler's V-2 first came in over London, military men have envisaged the anti-missile missile. Why is this not by now long since perfected, in production and operation? Electronics are our specialty; in this field at least we are far ahead of the Russians.

Instead, I recently read a learned exposition of the futility of trying to shoot down an ICBM. This view is so wrong as to amount to suicidal treason. The ICBM is necessarily detectable for thousands of miles before it reaches its target. It sets out on an absolute, undeviating trajectory. If it is equipped to change course when an anti-missile missile approaches, it will not hit what it was aimed at. If it does not change course, it can be hit, and on the first shot, no matter what its speed.

I do not know or want to know any secrets. Maybe we have the anti-missile missile. But the delay in getting it may have a psychological basis, in the immense unearned prestige with which the Second World War left airmen. Their courage is incontestable, but their contribution to the victory has been overrated. The numerous semiyouthful airmen in the Pentagon are not emotionally sympathetic to anything, such as an anti-missile missile, that could shoot down aircraft. They think of their friends flying the big bombers in over Russia and they flinch from the thought of antiaircraft weapons, their personal nightmare.

Another poison may have infected the American military mind, for it is a heady draught to have won two great wars. Our victories and the atom bomb seem to have inflated the Pentagon's sense of brute might, as against intellect. Yet both the victories and the bomb came out of pure intellect. What the Pentagon needs most now is a great big dose of humility, if necessary administered forcibly. Kipling's "Recessional" ought to be recited daily, by all hands.

This brings us at last to our first proposition, "Something awful is going to happen."

When men are so busy everywhere about their mischiefs, who would dare to dismiss this prediction? To do so would be a grave and unmerited insult to the great cleverness of mankind. Still, the best and the worst that is going to happen is that the generations will die away, to be replaced by new generations. And each generation will die in its own way.